Walking in Zen /

/ Sitting in Zen

Published by
Rajneesh Foundation International
Rajneeshpuram, Oregon 97741 U.S.A.

BHAGWAN SHREE RAJNEESH

Responses to disciples' and
visitors' questions and Zen stories

These sixteen discourses were given by
Bhagwan Shree Rajneesh in response to
questions from disciples and visitors
from March 5-10 and May 1-10, 1980
at the Shree Rajneesh Ashram, Poona, India.

CONTENTS

INTRODUCTION

"Zen does not talk about God at all, but only of godliness: a certain quality, a fragrance which is everywhere. Only when you have the capacity to learn will you be able to see it. All that is needed on your part is the capacity to be silent, receptive, welcoming, open."

Bhagwan Shree Rajneesh

I rarely admit it — for it does rather give away my age: I am a remnant of the Beat Generation.

In the late '50's, I grew a beard, wore boots, a black leather jacket and sunglasses, dug jazz and was "into Zen." My little collection of books, strewn around a Village pad, included — alongside Kerouac, Blake and Whitman — slim copies of Zen koans and anecdotes, the works of D. T. Suzuki, and the obligatory *Zen in the Art of Archery.* My friends and I were the Dharma Bums, cool zennists.

Except, deep inside — though we couldn't admit it then — nothing had changed: our Zen was even shallower than the Catholicism, Judaism, Methodism or atheism of our earlier years. For all our ecstatic rambling talk about *satoris*, we approached Zen the way we did history, literature, philosophy or whatever else we were studying at Columbia or NYU. We were professed anti-intellectuals, using our minds to learn about No-mind, secret rebels in the Houses of Intellect but all the while earning graduate degrees — just to be on the safe side.

Twenty years later, an older and, if not wiser at least luckier man, I had my first taste of Zen: one summer morning, in the late '70's, in the meditation hall of an ashram in India, I sat in the presence of Bhagwan Shree Rajneesh, who, when he walks, walks in Zen, when he sits, sits in Zen, and when he talks, appeals to every level of my being — from that persistent one which hankers to *know about* Zen to that one which, in those rare and lovely moments, *knows*!

Swami Das Anudas

1

The first question

Bhagwan,
Why have you called this series of discourses:
"Walking in Zen, Sitting in Zen"?

I AM NOT TO BLAME. The whole blame goes to this old guy Yoka. Yoka is one of the rarest enlightened people; his sayings are tremendously beautiful. Very few sayings are available, but each saying is a diamond unique in itself.

Reading his sayings, I came across this statement:

A man of Zen walks in Zen and sits in Zen.
Whether he speaks or acts, whether he is
silent or inactive, his body is always peaceful.
He smiles, looking straight at the sword which
takes his life. He keeps his balance even at the
moment of death.

I love the statement that the "man of Zen walks in Zen and sits in Zen" for the simple reason that meditation cannot be just a part of your life. You cannot make a fragment of your life meditative; it is not possible to be meditative for one hour and then non-meditative for twenty-three hours. It is absolutely impossible. If you are doing that, that means your meditation is false.

Meditation can either be a twenty-four-hour affair or it cannot be at all. It is like breathing: you cannot breathe for one hour and then put it aside for twenty-three hours, otherwise you will be dead. You have to go on breathing. Even while you are asleep you have to go on breathing. Even in a deep coma you have to go on breathing.

Meditation is the breath of your soul. Just as breathing is the life of the body, meditation is the life of the soul.

The people who are not aware of meditation are spiritually dead.

George Gurdjieff used to say that very few people have souls — and he is right. One is born not with a soul but only with a seed which can grow into a soul — which may not grow. It will depend on you. You will have to create the right soil, the right climate for it to grow, to bloom. You will have to provoke the spring into coming to you so that your soul can flower, otherwise you are just a body-mind. The soul is only an empty word. Meditation makes it a reality. Meditation is the climate in which the soul happens.

Zen is another name for meditation. The word *zen* comes from the Sanskrit root *dhyan* — it has traveled far. *Dhyan* means a state of absolute silence, of thoughtless silence, but full of awareness. Even the thought that "I am aware" is enough to distract you from your meditation. Even to know that "I am in meditation" is enough to destroy it.

A state of meditation is an innocent, silent state. You are blissfully unaware of your awareness. You *are*, but you are utterly relaxed. You are not in a state of sleep; you are fully alert, more alert than ever. You are alertness, rather.

Dhyan is the greatest contribution of the East to the evolution of humanity.

Buddha himself never used Sanskrit; he used a language that was used by the masses of those days, he used Pali. In Pali, *dhyan* becomes *jhan*. When Buddha's message reached China, *jhan* became *chan*. And when it traveled from China to Japan, it became *zen*. But it originates from *dhyan*. *Dhyan* means meditation, but the English word "meditation" does not have that flavor, it has a long association with contemplation. The English word "meditation" means meditation upon something; there is an object of meditation.

And in Zen there is no object at all, only pure subjectivity. You are aware, but not aware of something. There is nothing to be aware of; everything has disappeared. You are not even aware of nothingness, because then nothingness becomes your object, then nothingness becomes your thought. You are not aware of emptiness either. You are simply aware; there is no object to your awareness. The mirror is empty, reflecting nothing, because there is nothing to reflect.

You have to remember it, otherwise "meditation" can give you a wrong impression. Whenever the word "meditation" is used, immediately the question arises, "On what?" That question is irrelevant. If you are asking, "On what?" then you are asking what to think about, contemplate about, concentrate on — and that is not meditation.

Concentration is not meditation, concentration is an effort of the mind to focus itself. It has certain purposes of its own. It is a method in science — useful, but it is not meditation.

Contemplation is a little vague, more abstract. In concentration, the object is more visible; in contemplation, the object is abstract. You concentrate on a flame of light; you contemplate on love. And in Christianity, contemplation and meditation have become synonymous.

3

Meditation should be given a new meaning, a new fragrance — the fragrance of Zen. Concentration is of the mind, meditation is not of the mind at all, and contemplation is just in between, in a limbo. It is something of the mind and something of the no-mind, a mixture; a state where mind and no-mind meet, the boundary.

One has to reach to the absolute state of awareness: that is Zen. You cannot do it every morning for a few minutes or for half an hour and then forget all about it. It has to become like your heartbeat. You have to sit in it, you have to walk in it. Yes, you have even to sleep in it.

Ananda, one of Gautam Buddha's chief disciples, asked Buddha, "One thing always puzzles me and I cannot contain my curiosity anymore although my question is irrelevant. The question is that when you go to sleep you remain the whole night in the same posture. Wherever you put your hands, your feet, whatsoever side you lie on, you remain exactly the same, like a statue. You don't move, you don't change your side, you don't move your hands, your feet — nothing changes. You wake up in the morning in exactly the same posture that you had gone to sleep in. One night, just out of curiosity, I looked at you the whole night — not a single movement. Are you controlling yourself even in your sleep?"

Buddha said, "There is no question of control. I am awake, I am in meditation. I sleep in meditation. Just as I wake up early in the morning in meditation, every night I go to sleep in meditation. My day is my meditation, my night too. I remain absolutely calm and quiet because deep down I am perfectly aware. The flame of meditation goes on burning smokeless. That's why there is no need to move."

Yoka says:

A man of Zen walks in Zen and sits in Zen.

This is of great significance for you all. Meditation has to become something so deep in you that wherever you go it remains, abides with you; whatsoever you do it is always there. Only then can your life be transformed. Then not only will you be meditative in your life, you will be meditative in your death too. You will die in deep meditation.

That's how Buddha died. That's how all the Buddhas have always died: their death is something exquisitely beautiful. Their life is beautiful, their death too. There is no gap between their life and death. Their death is a crescendo of their life, the ultimate peak, the absolute expression.

When Buddha died he was eighty-two years old. He called his disciples together — just as he used to when he talked to them every morning. They all gathered. Nobody was thinking at all about his death.

And then Buddha said, "This is my last sermon to you. Whatsoever I had to say to you I have said. Forty-two years I have been telling you, saying to you . . . I have poured out my whole heart. Now, if somebody has any question left he can ask, because this is the last day of my life. Today I leave for the other shore. My boat has arrived."

They were shocked! They had come just to listen to the daily discourse. They were not thinking that he was going to die — and without making any fuss about death! It was just a simple phenomenon, a simple declaration that "My boat has come and I have to leave. If you have any question left you can ask me, because if you don't ask me today, I will never again be available. Then the question will remain with you. So please, be kind and don't be shy," he told his disciples.

They started crying. And Buddha said, "Stop all this nonsense! This is no time to waste on crying and weeping! Ask if you have something to ask, otherwise let me go. The time has come. I cannot linger any longer."

They said, "We have nothing to ask. You have given more than we would have ever asked. You have answered all the questions that we have asked, that we could have asked. You have answered questions which for centuries will be fulfilling for all kinds of inquirers."

Then Buddha said, "So I can take leave of you. Good-bye."

And he closed his eyes, sat in a lotus posture, and started moving towards the other shore.

It is said: the first step was that he left his body, the second step was that he left his mind, the third step was that he left his heart, the fourth step was that he left his soul. He disappeared into the universal so peacefully, so silently, so joyously. The birds were chirping; it was early morning — the sun was still on the horizon. And ten thousand sannyasins were sitting and watching Buddha dying with such grace! They forgot completely that this was death. There was nothing of death as they had always conceived it. It was such an extraordinary experience.

So much meditative energy was released that many became enlightened that very day, that very moment. Those who were just on the verge were pushed into the unknown. Thousands, it is said, became enlightened through Buddha's beautiful death.

We don't call it death, we call it *mahaparinirvana*, dissolving into the absolute — just like an ice cube melting, dissolving into the ocean. He lived in meditation, he died in meditation.

It is because of Yoka that I have chosen this title "Walking in Zen, Sitting in Zen." In this simple phrase, the whole experience of all the awakened ones is condensed.

Yoka also says:

> *The fearless thought of Zen is like the power-*
> *ful roaring of a lion,*
> *Striking terror into the hearts of all other ani-*
> *mals. Even the king of the elephants runs off,*
> *forgetting his dignity.*
> *Disciples of good heart, they alone, like the*
> *old dragon hear that roaring with calm*
> *delight.*

Yes, Zen is like the roar of a lion. All other religions speak in a way that does not hurt so much. They are compromising; they compromise with your sleep. Zen is non-compromising. It does not care about your sleep and your beautiful dreams. It shocks you, it shatters you. Its whole effort is to wake you, whatsoever the cost. Yes, it is like a lion's roar.

> Only *disciples of good heart, they alone, like*
> *the old dragon hear that roaring with calm*
> *delight.*

It can be heard only with a deep love for truth. It can be heard only by those who are real inquirers, not just curious, not just spectators, not just philosophers, but who are really ready to go through a radical transformation — who are ready to die and be reborn. It is only for those few people who have guts and courage, because it is not a Sunday religion like Christianity, that each Sunday you go to the church and your paradise is assured. It is not like Mohammedanism, that you pray five times, go on repeating like a parrot the same words, which are not your words, which are not spontaneous to you, which have been imposed by others on you — you may not even know their meaning.

It is such a stupid world! Mohammedans pray in Arabic, which they don't understand; Hindus pray in

Sanskrit, which they don't understand; and now Buddhists pray in Pali, which they don't understand — for the simple reason that priests have been very much insistent on keeping the dead language because those prayers are very poor if they are translated into the language which *you* understand. You will be at a loss — you will not be able to see what there is to pray in them; they will lose all the mystery. The mystery is because you don't understand them. Hence Latin, Greek, Arabic, Sanskrit, Pali, Prakrit — dead languages which nobody understands anymore. Priests go on insisting that prayers should be in those dead languages.

You are saying something the meaning of which is not known to you. What kind of prayer is this? To whom are you addressing it? You don't know anything about God. And what you are saying is not arising out of your heart, you are just being a gramophone record — His Master's Voice.

Zen is not interested in such compromises. It wants you to really wake up. And it is hard work, a thankless job. A Zen Master has chosen something for which nobody is going to thank him. Everybody will feel sabotaged by him and everybody will feel hurt by him. Everybody will feel he is disturbing their sleep. Only very few people, who are real inquirers, who are ready to risk all, will be able to understand, because Zen says your *whole* life has to be transformed, not just a part of your life.

When you are in the temple, in the mosque, in the synagogue, you become religious, and when you are outside of it you are irreligious, just the old self. Then your being in the temple is a pretension. It divides you, it creates a schizophrenic humanity, it creates people who have split minds. If you go and see them praying in the mosques, in the temples, you will say, "How beautiful they are!" And the same people in the marketplace become so ugly. And the same people will kill each other with such cruelty you could not have conceived of it! If you had seen them praying in the mosque, in the church, you would not have believed that they would butcher each other so cruelly, so mechanically.

Christians have killed thousands of Mohammedans, Mohammedans have killed thousands of Christians, Hindus have killed Mohammedans, Mohammedans have killed Hindus, Hindus have killed Buddhists, and so on and so forth. All these religions have been enemies to each other. They talk of love, but that is only mere talk; the reality is totally different. And why is it so? — because their prayer is false.

Zen wants you to be religious, not in a formal way, but to be really religious in your day-to-day life. Zen does not divide your life into the mundane and the sacred, it says *everything* is sacred. So eating, be meditative. Walking, be meditative. Whatsoever you are doing . . . taking a bath, be meditative. Wherever you are, you *are* in the temple. This whole existence is God's temple! Behave as you would like to behave in a temple. God is present everywhere.

Zen does not talk about God at all, but only of godliness: a certain quality, a fragrance which is everywhere. Only when you have the capacity to learn will you be able to see it. All that is needed on your part is the capacity to be silent, receptive, welcoming, open.

The second question

Bhagwan,
It is claimed that we learn from chaos.
How much more does man need to awaken?

Sol Lewis,

CHAOS IS NOT THERE OUTSIDE — the outside is a cosmos

—but inside there is a chaos. And it is because of the chaos inside that people don't look inwards. They are afraid to look, very frightened of looking in. They keep themselves occupied in every possible way so that there is no time left, no space left to look in. They go on listening to the Buddhas, who say, "Know thyself." They understand what is meant by "knowing thyself", but they don't make any effort to know themselves. They are afraid of the chaos.

Inside there is chaos. Outside there is no chaos. The stars are moving in a rhythm, the whole existence is rhythmic, it is in absolute accord. It is just man's mind which is in a chaos. And if you see any chaos outside, that is man-made, man-created.

Man remains a chaos unless he becomes a no-mind. Mind is a chaos — mind is bound to be a chaos — and you have become identified with it. What is mind? Past plus future. The present is not part of the mind at all, the present belongs to existence — and the present is an absolute harmony. The past is no more and the future is not yet, and your mind consists of these two non-existential things: memories and imaginations, memories and desires, memories and hopes. It is because of this that you are living in a mad state.

Everybody is insane inside. We don't call anybody insane unless he moves too much to the extreme; but the difference between insane people and the so-called sane is only of degree — and anything can trigger it. You are just boiling somewhere near ninety-nine degrees; just one degree more — your business fails, you go bankrupt, your wife dies — and that one degree is added to your ninety-nine degrees, and you start evaporating; you are insane.

The psychiatrists, the psychotherapists, all function only to keep you within limits. They keep you normally abnormal — that is their function. They are the agents of society, just as in the old days, priests were the agents of the society. Psychotherapists are the new priests, a new priesthood which functions to keep this society running, which keeps this society believing that everything is okay.

Nothing is okay. Everybody is on the verge of a breakdown and anything, any accident, can push you into the world of the insane. You are getting ready, you are always getting ready. The more sensitive you are, the more alive you are, the greater the possibility that you may go insane.

At the funeral of his wife Perelli made a terrible scene, so terrible and heart-rending, in fact, that friends had to forcibly restrain him from jumping into the grave and being buried with his beloved Maria. Then, still overcome with grief, he was taken home in the rented limousine and immediately went into complete seclusion.

A week passed and nothing was heard of him. Finally, worried about the poor guy, his late wife's brother went to the house. After ringing the doorbell for ten minutes — and still worried — the brother-in-law jimmied the front door, went upstairs and found his dead sister's husband busily banging the maid.

The bedroom was a mess — empty champagne bottles everywhere.

"This is terrible, Perelli!" the brother-in-law declared in shocked tones. "Your dead wife, my sister, has been dead only a week and you're doing this! You're doing *this!*"

So busy in the saddle was Perelli that he managed only to turn his head. "How do I know what I'm doing?" he said. "I got such grief! I got such grief!"

People are in a mess! They are just keeping face somehow, managing a facade, pretending that everything is okay. But nothing is okay.

You ask me, Sol: *It is claimed that we learn from chaos.*

Yes, it is true. But we learn from chaos only if we go inwards, if we enter into the chaos consciously, deliberately, knowingly. If we encounter the chaos, of course, we learn — there is no other way of learning. It is really out of this chaos that stars are born. It is out of this chaos that Buddhas are born — but you have to encounter it.

And we go on doing just the opposite: we go on hiding it, covering it. We don't want to show it to anybody and we don't want to see it ourselves. We are so frightened, we are so scared. We are afraid that we may not be able to manage. We are afraid that if we go in we may not be able to come back. So we cling to anything on the outside; any excuse is enough to cling. We go on clinging to something or other — we just go on avoiding ourselves.

The person that you are avoiding the most in your life is *you.* Your whole life is managed in such a way that you never come across yourself. You have been trained, brought up, educated, cultured, civilized in such a way that you will never meet yourself. You will meet everybody except yourself, you will be introduced to everybody except yourself for the simple reason that the society does not know how to cope with the inner chaos.

It is only in the presence of a Master, in a Buddhafield, that people gather courage to face themselves. And in the beginning it is a breakdown, but if you are moving into it consciously, soon the breakdown becomes a breakthrough.

To transform breakdowns into breakthroughs is the whole function of a Master. The psychotherapist simply patches you up. He puts a few bandages on you, a little ointment here and a little ointment there. He helps you to stand on your own two feet again, back in the old way. He makes you your old self again. You start functioning, you start doing the old things that you have always been doing. That is his function. He is not there to transform you.

You need a metapsychology, the psychology of the Buddhas.

It is the greatest adventure in life to go through a breakdown consciously. It is the greatest risk because there is no guarantee that the breakdown will become a breakthrough. It does become, but these things cannot be guaranteed. Your chaos is very ancient; for many many lives you have been in chaos. It is thick and dense. It is almost a universe in itself. So when you enter into it with your small capacity, of course, there is danger. But without facing this danger nobody has ever become integrated, nobody has ever become an individual, indivisible.

Sol, the claim is absolutely right: we learn only from chaos. But we learn only if we go through the chaos, and we have to go through the chaos in a particular way, with a style, with a method. Just going into chaos without any method will be a breakdown — you will go mad.

Zen, or meditation, is the method which will help you to go through the chaos, through the dark night of the soul, balanced, disciplined, alert. The dawn is not far away, but before you can reach the dawn, the dark night has to be passed through. And as the dawn comes closer, the night will become darker.

This is really the function of religious communes, because alone you may not be able to do it, but in a commune where many people are ahead of you, many people are behind you, with a Master who has attained to the dawn, who goes on calling you forth, who goes on saying to you, "Don't be worried, the goal is not far away." . . . And there are people ahead of you who say, "Don't be worried. We have passed through such a state and you will also pass through it. Just a little more perseverance, a little more awaiting, a little more patience!"

And there is the Master like a shining star. And he goes on helping you in every way, holding your hand in moments when you would like to run away, to escape, to go back to your old world, to forget all about it because it is such a nightmare.

Yes, Sol, one learns, but one learns the hard way; there is no shortcut.

You say: *How much more does man need to awaken?*

It is not a question of how much more, it is not a question of quantity; either you are asleep or you are awake. No one is more asleep than anybody else. The people who are asleep are asleep in the same way. It does not matter how deeply you are asleep — it is not a question of quantity — you are asleep, that is enough. And the same is the case with awakening: if you are awake, you are simply awake. Nobody is more awake or less awake.

For centuries theologians have been discussing . . . theologians always discuss stupid things. In India they have been discussing for centuries "Who is more awake, Mahavira or Buddha?" Jainas say Mahavira is more awake, Buddha's followers say Buddha is more awake. And the whole point is nonsensical, the whole argument is foolish. There is no question of more or less: if somebody is awake, he is awake. Buddha is awake, Mahavira is awake. The night is over; the chaos has been transformed into a cosmos.

And this is the miracle: when you are perfectly awake your very chaos becomes a cosmos, because it starts settling into an orchestra; the noise becomes music.

Suddenly, all that was insanity, madness, is transformed into Buddhahood, into enlightenment — the same energy! Chaos means energy — energy of which you are unconscious. If you become conscious, the very phenomenon of consciousness is a transforming phenomenon. You need not do anything else; just being conscious is enough.

The spring has come. Suddenly, buds start opening, flowers bloom — thousands of flowers; the inner world becomes full of fragrance.

Man is absolutely asleep.

The drunk Mulla Nasruddin noticed one parrot perched atop a farmhouse gable. Attracted by the bright plumage, he ran to fetch a ladder, climbed onto the roof, and was about to clap his cap over the bird when the parrot fixed him with a beady eye and asked, "What the hell do you think you're doing?"

"Gosh, I didn't mean nothing!" said the Mulla, "I thought you was a bird!"

People are not in their senses! You think you are awake, and that is one of the greatest mistakes — it keeps you unawake. The very idea that you are awake is a deception. If you think you are already awake, then there is no need to do anything to be awakened.

You have to realize that you are drunk, drunk with many things: with greed, with lust, with anger, with ambition, with ego. These are all drugs! It is a very strange world: ordinary drugs, which are not so harmful, are prohibited. People are continuously talking against smoking, which is not very harmful. It is a kind of *pranayama*: breathing in, breathing out — of course, a little foolish because you can breathe pure air and you are breathing dirty smoke, and paying for it, but it is nothing much to be worried about. Or people are against alcohol. Once in a while a little bit of alcohol is not bad, it is fun! And it is purely vegetarian! You are not harming anybody. But there is so much antagonism against alcohol and smoking.

And the new drugs are far better than alcohol. For example, LSD is far better, less harmful than alcohol. Taken in right doses, with a right guide, in a right atmosphere, it can reveal many things to you. It can become a method of encountering yourself. It can give you new visions, new insights into your being and into existence itself. But people are against it, although they are not against greed, they are not against ego trips, they are not against ambition.

Just a few months ago Morarji Desai was the Prime Minister of India. He is very much against alcohol, obsessed; he wanted absolute prohibition. But he is not aware that he is more alcoholic than anybody else. He is such an egoist — very rare to find — and so full of greed and ambition. He has been trying to occupy some post or other his whole life. Now he is eighty-five, but still, a few days ago he said, "If people want me again, then I will stand in the elections." It is a well-known fact that he was even willing to become Chief Minister of Gujarat — after being the Prime Minister of India he was ready to be just a chief minister of one of the small states. Such power-hungry people!

But nobody thinks that these are all intoxicants: ambition, greed, lust for power. These are keeping humanity in a chaos. These are the people — and they are not alone. We are all in the same boat. A few are very madly after power, a few are not so madly after power, but everybody thinks in terms of power, money, prestige, respectability. These things go on keeping you drunk. And then a person can do anything.

Morarji Desai wants to live as long as he can. Maybe deep down he thinks that he can become physically immortal by drinking his own urine! He is against alcohol, but not against drinking his own urine. Now, alcohol is pure fruit juice — far better than drinking your own urine! But he does not call it urine, he calls it "water of life".

Just the other day Indira moved into the Prime Minister's house. For two, three months, she didn't move. Why? For the simple reason that the whole house had to be cleaned because Morarji lived there for two, three years! Every utensil had to be cleaned and changed and the bathroom tiles had to be removed and demolished. The whole house was stinking!

I have heard that when he went to America he was very puzzled. Wherever he went — he was invited to many parties — ladies would always gather in the other corner of the room. He inquired, but nobody was answering. People politely tried to change the subject, but he insisted. Finally somebody said, "Sir, if you insist, then we have to say: those ladies are afraid that if you suddenly feel thirsty, then? So they keep aloof, a little far away."

These people have been dominating humanity — ambitious! Now he wants to live. For what? Just to have more power, to have more power for a longer time.

Man is not destroyed by other small things — marijuana, LSD, etcetera — he is destroyed by something far deeper. Ambition is the most poisonous thing. We *are* unconscious.

Sol, unless we become very aware of our inner poisons we will not be able to transform our beings from darkness into light. We will remain dark holes — and we have the capacity to become eternal light.

Three Irishmen, none too sober, were talking together in a bus terminal. They got so engrossed comparing their bowling scores that they didn't notice the bus had pulled in. As the driver sang out, "All aboard," they looked up, startled, and dashed from the platform. Two of them managed to hop on the bus, but the third didn't make it.

As he stood sadly watching the bus depart in the distance, a stranger tried to cheer him up, saying, "You shouldn't feel too bad. Two out of three made it and that's a pretty good average."

The Irishman shook his head. "But *they* came to see *me* off."

And it is not only so with the people who are drunk, it is not only so with the people who are politically drunk, it is so with your so-called religious people too. Those who think they are helping mankind — great missionaries, public servants — they are the most mischievous people for the simple reason that they themselves are in chaos and they are trying to help others. They double your chaos, they multiply your chaos.

The world would be far happier and far saner if there were no missionaries, no public servants. If people are left to themselves they will come to their senses sooner. But there are public servants; they cannot leave you, they cannot leave you alone.

A man was beating an old woman on the street. A crowd gathered. The man was very strong, tall, muscular, but finally somebody in the crowd gathered courage and asked, "What's the matter? Why are you beating that poor old woman?"

He said, "I want to help her to go to the other side, but she insists on not going. And I am here to help old people to cross the road. The traffic is dangerous."

That's what is happening: missionaries, public servants, are bent upon helping you!

Jake the barber, passing by a tenement house in the pre-dawn hours of the morning, saw a man leaning limply against the doorway.

"What's the matter?" he asked sympathetically. "Drunk?"

"Yeah, I'm afraid sho."

"Do you live in this house?"

"Yep."

"Want me to help you upstairs?"

"Yeah, shank you."

"What floor do you live on?"

"Shecon'."

With much difficulty, Jake half dragged, half carried the wilting figure up the dark stairway to the second floor.

"Is this your apartment?" he asked.

"Yep," affirmed the man, his eyes already closed in alcoholic slumber.

Jake opened the unlocked door and shoved the drunk inside. He then groped his way back downstairs. But as he was going through the vestibule, he made out the dim outline of another man, apparently in worse condition than the first, staggering in front of the house.

"What's the trouble, mister?" he asked. "Are you drunk, too?"

"Yesh," came the feeble reply.

"Do you live in this house also?"

"Yesh."

"Don't tell me you live on the second floor, too?"

"Yesh."

Again Jake half carried the stranger to the second floor. He pushed open the same door and shoved the man inside the darkened room.

As Jake was emerging from the building he discerned yet a third man, evidently worse off than either of the other two. This poor fellow was dishevelled and bleeding from cuts and bruises on his head and face. He was about to approach him and offer him assistance when the object of his solicitude darted into the street and threw himself into the arms of a policeman.

"Offisher," he gasped, pointing a quivering finger at

Jake, "perteck me from this man. All night long he's done nothin' but drag me upstairs an' throw me down the elevator shaft!"

Sol, it is not a question of how much more man needs to awaken; man simply needs to be awake. And the only way to be awake is through meditation; there is no other way. Zen is the only way . . . "Walking in Zen, sitting in Zen."

The third question

Bhagwan,
After listening to you the other day and
hearing sex is stupid, we tried it right away.
We don't understand! What do you find stupid?

Ritmo and Deva Mastanando,

I HAVE BEEN TELLING you of other things. Have you ever tried them right away? I am telling you about meditation every day and you go on postponing it! And sex you tried right away! You did me a great favor — you did not try it here! That shows its stupidity.

Sex is not stupid, *you* are stupid! It is because of you that poor sex also becomes stupid. And you will never know unless you rise a little higher. Unless you become a little more alert, you will not see the stupidity. You can't see it remaining on the same level — nobody can see it.

Go to the madhouse, ask any madman, "Are you mad?" He will be mad at you! But no madman will accept that he is mad. He will say, "What are you talking about? The whole world is mad except me. I am perfectly sane." No madman accepts he is mad. If a madman accepts he is mad, that is a sure sign that he is getting out of his madness, he is becoming sane.

20

You will not be able to see the stupidity of it unless you learn a little more meditativeness so that you can observe, so that you can remain detached, so that you can see from a vantage point, so that you can have a little perspective. Right now you don't have any perspective; you are too close.

Just stand very close to the mirror, your nose touching the mirror, and you will not be able to see your own face. That is not the fault of the mirror. You have to give it a little space, then the mirror can reflect you. You are too close.

Sex seems to be the greatest obsession. The priests have to be given all credit for it. For centuries they have been condemning sex as sin and they have made it an obsession.

I don't call sex a sin, I simply call it stupid. I am not saying that you will suffer hell — what more hell do you need to suffer? You are already suffering in it. And what does it go on giving to you? It just keeps you engaged — engaged in the other so that you can avoid yourself. That is its basic stupidity: it keeps you ignorant because it keeps you ignoring yourself. The man is interested in the woman, the woman is interested in the man. Everybody is interested in the other. It seems as if the other has all that you need, and the other is also thinking that you have all that he or she needs. Both are beggars — and believing that the other has the kingdom.

Sooner or later you feel frustrated, but your frustration never teaches you anything. It is very difficult to learn anything. If one woman has failed you you start looking to other women. If one man has not been up to your standards — and no man can be, no woman can be, because that is not possible, that is not in the nature of things — then you start looking to other men.

And all kinds of perversions are there, but if you ask any perverted person, he will not say that he sees any stupidity in it.

A Frenchman was making love to someone's wife when the husband returned two days early from his business trip. Quick as a wink, the Frenchie scrambled out of the sack and took off like a big big bird. However, the angry husband was just as fast on his feet and he grabbed a rifle and shot the Frenchman's balls off. Not at all perturbed, the Frenchman stuck out his very long tongue and shouted, "Missed me!"

Now if you ask this Frenchman, he will not say that he is doing anything stupid; he is doing the most fantastic thing in the world!

Three woodcutters came down to the town after a long four-month work period, during which they had not seen or heard a thing except trees and their axes. Within hours they were totally drunk and decided to visit the local whorehouse.

The madam of the institution found herself in a fix, as she could only offer two girls and didn't want to lose her third customer. So she told one of the girls to put the inflatable tailor's dummy into one bed.

While two of the woodcutters were escorted to the beds with the real girls, the most drunk of them was put to bed with the dummy.

As the three met the next morning, they exchanged the reports of their experiences. When the turn to share his experience came for the one who had been in bed with the air-filled rubber woman, he said, "First it was really nice, but she was too quiet. Then, when I bit her nipple, she gave one big fart and flew out the window."

Ritmo and Mastananda, you will not be able to see what you are doing. Be a little more meditative and don't be in such a hurry: that I told you and right away . . . It seems it was just an excuse. You believed that you were experimenting, you believed that you were doing something in order to know. People can believe all kinds of things — but you cannot deceive me! People can go on rationalizing. You think you did it because I said sex is stupid? You would have done it anyway! Even if I had said that sex is very intelligent, then too you would have done it. If I had not said anything about sex, then too you would have done it.

Have a look at your mind. Try to understand how you go on rationalizing and deceiving yourself. And you cannot understand what I am saying unless you rise a little higher from the state of consciousness where you are right now. If you want to see more you have to rise a little higher.

It is as if you are standing on the road and I am sitting on the treetop. I say to you, "A bullock cart is coming down the road." You say, "I don't see any bullock cart. There is no bullock cart." But I can see; my perspective is greater because I am on a height. You will only see the bullock cart when it comes very close to you, and then after a few yards it will disappear again. And I will say to you, "It has not disappeared. It is still there on the road." You will say, "It is no longer there, it is gone."

The higher you rise, the more you can see. And when you reach the ultimate height, Buddhahood, you can see everything. Then there is no past and no future; then there is only present. And in that clarity, sex is the most stupid thing because it keeps you in bondage the longest. I am not condemning it, I am simply stating a fact. It is your bondage. It keeps you unconscious. It does not allow you to see what you are doing. You are possessed by it.

Back in the early 1960's when France was fighting its last colonial war, a draft-dodger from Paris pretended to have poor eyesight during his physical at the army induction center.

The army doctor didn't buy that, so he sent for a gorgeous young nurse and told her to take off her clothes.

"Describe what you see, young man," the doctor asked.

"All I see is a blur, doctor," the slacker replied.

Said the military M.D., "Your eyes may not be as good as they should be my lad, but your prick is pointing straight toward Algeria!"

That's why I call it stupid: it keeps you unconscious, it keeps you in a kind of possession. It is hormonal, it is chemical. It is not you; it is just your biology that goes on forcing you to do certain things. If you watch, you will be surprised: What are you doing? And why are you doing? If you watch you will be surprised: What are you gaining out of it? What have you gained up to now? And in your saner moments you know perfectly well what I am saying, you understand it; but those saner moments are very superficial — they come and go — and soon you are back in the same trap again.

Mastananda, go back again, do it right away, but be watchful, be meditative. And I will be there, standing by your side, and let us see what happens. Either you will not be able to do it at all or you will find that it is a biological compulsion, it is an obsession, it is not you. Your consciousness will remain floating up; deep down in the valley it will happen, but you will remain detached, unconcerned, cool. And that will give you the insight.

Sex becomes a tantric experience when meditation is added to it.

The fourth question

Bhagwan,
Why do wives always close their eyes during love-making?

Gyanesh,

Tʜᴇʏ ᴄᴀɴ'ᴛ ʙᴇᴀʀ to see their husbands having a good time!

And the last question

Bhagwan,
I am sure my husband is deceiving me. Last
night he came home with lipstick on his shirt,
but when I asked him about it he said it was
tomato juice. What should I do?

Vandana,

Aꜱᴋ ʜɪᴍ, "Who is this tomato?"

2

The first question

Bhagwan,
What is Zen?

Sagar,

IT IS ALMOST IMPOSSIBLE TO ANSWER because Zen is not
a philosophy, it is not a doctrine. It is an experience, an
experience of your own interiority, of your own subjectivity — not an objective experience. If it were some
object outside you, there would be a possibility of describing it, of analyzing it, of defining it. It is indefinable
by its very nature; it is not within the grasp of intellect.
It is an experience of dropping out of your mind, disappearing from your mind into your being, slipping out
of the mind and entering into your being.

The mind is a false entity; your being is your real face,
your original face. The mind is created by the society,
hence there are different kinds of minds — Hindu mind,

26

Christian mind, Jewish mind — but the being is one; it is neither Christian nor Hindu nor Mohammedan. Being is not even individual, it is universal.

It is like a dewdrop slipping into the ocean. It disappears as a dewdrop; nothing remains of it as a dewdrop. It dies, but, on the other hand, it is reborn. It becomes the ocean. But there is nobody to say what has happened and there is no way to say it; no words are adequate enough.

I can tell you how it happens, but I cannot tell you what it is. I can indicate towards it . . . fingers pointing to the moon . . . but fingers are not the moon. And there are millions of people who go on worshiping the fingers. The more attached you become to the fingers the less capable you will be of seeing the moon. The fingers have to be forgotten. Once you have got the point where to look, then forget the fingers and look at the moon.

Zen is one of the purest spiritual experiences, uncontaminated by any thought, any theology, any speculation. It is non-argumentative, it simply is.

Listen to Yoka. Yoka says:

> *Dear friend, do you know the true man of Zen? He has forgotten the intellectual understanding of what he has learned in order to reach profound understanding.*

> *He lives in equanimity, calm and content. He is free from all care, and he acts naturally and reasonably. He does not struggle to avoid illusion nor does he seek for satori.*

> *He knows that illusion is unfounded and that satori is none other than himself.*

> *He sees the real nature of not-knowing as the nature of the Buddha and he sees that the reality of his illusory body is equivalent to . . . the eternal body of the Buddha.*

27

When he fully realizes the body of the Buddha, the body of the universal law, *he has nothing.* He becomes nothing.

He himself is the source of all things and his ordinary life is another name for the eternal Buddha.

If you live in this understanding, you can change in a single moment. You can transform yourself absolutely, without wasting any time.

Beautiful hints. First, you have to forget all that you have learned. All your learning is a barrier. Put it aside. Zen cannot be learned and cannot be taught, but you can imbibe it, you can imbibe the spirit of it.

Living with a Master you can drink, you can drink the invisible nectar, you can be filled with it, but you will have to fulfil one condition: you have to put the mind aside.

Gayan has written to me that while listening to me she feels like dancing. That's how the disciple is bound to feel: something inside you starts dancing, singing. Something inside you rejoices. Something inside you immediately falls in tune with the Master; a deep synchronicity happens. It cannot be taught, it cannot be learned, but it can be transferred. That transfer is beyond words and beyond scriptures. It needs a totally new art: the art of surrender, the art of total let-go.

The first condition is: forget all that you have learned. The second condition is: be calm, quiet, contented. Desire keeps you away from the present moment, far away. And Zen is the taste of reality here and now. It is the *feel* of the here and now. Zen is not concerned with any God after death, Zen is concerned with the godliness that surrounds you right now.

These sounds, these birds, these trees, these people, this silence . . . three thousand people disappearing into a silence, losing their identities, egos . . . and suddenly

Zen is there! It becomes almost tangible. You can touch it, you can eat it, you can drink it. But there is no way to convey it through words. You have to be calm and quiet and contented so that you can be in the present. You have to be free of all care.

Care simply means you are not trusting existence; you are trying to be careful on your own. You are afraid. You are not yet aware that existence cares for you, that it mothers you, that it fathers you. Once you start feeling the mothering, the fathering that surrounds you, in the air, in the sun, in the moon, in the stars, you drop caring for yourself. There is no need to be worried. You start flowing with existence. You drop pushing the river. And then, Sagar, you will be able to understand what Zen is. You have to live naturally and reasonably.

Remember, the society has made you absolutely artificial. It has given you ideas, it has imposed certain moralities, characters upon you. It has destroyed your spontaneity. You have to regain it, you have to reclaim it. That is the most essential thing to be done.

Once you have claimed your naturalness, Zen starts welling up within you. Zen is your nature, your very nature. When you are spontaneous and responsible, responding to reality moment to moment without any ready-made formulas, reflecting reality like a mirror, you *are* living the life of Zen. And that is the reasonable life — not rational, remember, but reasonable.

A reasonable man is not rational. They are not equivalent, they are not synonymous. The rational man is never reasonable, the rational man tries to deny all that is irrational. And life consists of both the rational and the irrational. The reasonable man accepts both. He accepts the paradox of life: he accepts the rational, he accepts the irrational; he sees no inconsistency in them. Hence he remains undivided; nothing can divide him. No division exists in his being and he sees no division anywhere. Life and death are one to him, summer and winter are one to him, men and women are one to him. He knows that divisions are superficial; deep down everything is one. He knows the oneness of life, hence he is not disturbed by any contradictions.

The man of Zen contains all contradictions. He is vast enough, he can contain contradictions. He enjoys paradoxes. He does not make life a problem. He looks at life as a mystery. He is not interested in solving it, he is interested only in living it — living it to the uttermost.

He knows that illusion is unfounded . . .

Hence he is not worried like the Hindu monks who escape from the world because the world is illusory. Do you see the stupidity of it? If the world is illusory, why are you escaping from it? For what? If it is not, if it is not really there, then why are you escaping?

If you see a man running and you ask him, "Where are you going?" and he says, "There is a rope which only *appears* to be a snake — it is not a snake — and I am running away from that appearance of a snake," you will say, "You are stupid! If you know it is a rope, then stop running. And if you know it is not a rope, then stop saying that it is illusory, that it is only an appearance."

But that's what Hindu monks have been doing for thousands of years: calling the world *maya*, illusory, and yet renouncing it. Renounce your wife because the wife is illusory, renounce your children because they are illusory, renounce your day-to-day, ordinary life because it is illusory. Escape to the Himalayas — everything is illusory. But then why are you escaping? From what?

That is the beauty of Zen. Zen says:

He knows that illusion is unfounded and that satori is none other than himself.

He knows that all is illusory so there is no need to escape. It is unfounded, you need not be worried about it. It is a rope — it *appears* to be a snake. So why escape?

Why renounce? Let it appear to be a snake, let it be there as a rope. Whatsoever it is, the appearance is unfounded, hence there is no need to renounce.

Zen does not teach renunciation. It teaches understanding, awareness, alertness, the capacity to see things as they are. And then there is no need to escape from anywhere. Wherever you are, Zen helps you to relax.

And there is no need to search for God, to search for *satori, samadhi,* enlightenment — the very search is a barrier. We search for things only if they are not within our being; if they are within our being, there is no need to seek and search. Just relax! In that very relaxation you have found them. *Satori* is our nature. *Samadhi* is our nature. God is our nature. Hence, the man of Zen goes nowhere; he simply rests in himself.

> *He sees the real nature of not-knowing as the*
> *nature of the Buddha . . .*

To function from the state of not-knowing is to function in the present. If you function from the state of knowing you are functioning out of the past. All knowing is from the past. Knowledge means the past: your experiences, your memories. If you function through them you are not responding to reality. The only way to respond to reality is to be utterly innocent.

When you function from the state of not-knowing, your response is total and always adequate. It always brings fulfilment, it is liberating. Hence Yoka says it is: "the nature of the Buddha".

And when you realize this totally, you are nothing. Not that you become an enlightened soul, no; you disappear. The ego is found no more. There is nobody to become enlightened: that is enlightenment. According to Zen, when there is nobody to be enlightened, enlightenment has happened. When you are just a pure nothing, a silence so profound, so unfathomable that there is no way to measure it; so virgin, so pure that

31

nobody has ever walked into it — even you cannot enter into it — only when you disappear, is it there.

This nothingness is the ultimate truth. Buddha calls it *shunya*, the void. And if you can live in this nothingness, then your ordinary life is another name for the sacred life.

That is one of the greatest messages of Zen. It does not destroy your ordinary life, it enriches it. All other religions have been destructive, they have been poisoners, they have been condemnors. They have been condemning your ordinary life and praising some ideal life which exists nowhere. They condemn that which is and they praise that which is not.

Zen says: This is all. There is no other life, there is no other existence. This ordinary existence is beautiful. There is no need for any other world; this world is more than enough. Zen is the greatest alchemy. It transforms your ordinary, mundane life into a sacred, holy life.

A Zen Master, Rinzai, was asked, "What did you used to do before your enlightenment?"

He said, "I used to do the same as I am doing now. I used to carry water from the well for my Master and I used to chop wood for my Master and for the commune. I continue to do the same: I carry water from the well and I chop wood for my disciples."

The man said, "But then what is the difference between an enlightened man and an unenlightened man?"

Rinzai said, "The unenlightened man thinks that this is an ordinary life — chopping wood, carrying water from the well — and the enlightened man knows this is holy, this is sacred, this is divine."

And the last thing to be remembered, Sagar, is that Zen does not believe in a gradual process. It says: Because your nature is Buddha, because your very nature is enlightenment, you can get it right now. There is no need to wait even for a single moment. Zen believes in sudden enlightenment, hence Yoka says it can happen in a moment.

All other religions are postponements. Hindus say you will have to be born many many times; only then can you get enlightened. Why? — because first you have to undo all the bad karmas that you have done in your past lives. Now, you have lived for millions of lives, how long is it going to take to undo those karmas? And while you are undoing those karmas you will be doing other karmas, so again you will be accumulating bad karma. That means it is impossible to become enlightened or next to impossible.

Zen says: Whatsoever you have done has been done in a dream. Wake up, and it is finished. It is not that when you wake up you first have to undo what you have done in your dream; just by waking up all dreams are finished. Knowing that they were dreams is to end them. You have lived your sleepy life for many lives and whatsoever you have done has been done in your sleep. It is nothing very important: it is of the same stuff that dreams are made of.

Just wake up!

The second question

Bhagwan,
Why do all the awakened ones say that man is asleep? I don't agree. I think I am fully awake. What do you say?

Niraj,

IT IS IMPOSSIBLE TO UNDERSTAND what the awakened ones say unless you are also awakened. They speak your language — they have to speak your language out

of sheer necessity, because there is no other language —
but their meaning is totally different.

When the Buddhas say that you are asleep, they don't
mean ordinary sleep. Of course, you are not ordinarily
asleep, you are awake. You go to the marketplace, you
go to the office, you do your things. Of course, in the
night you sleep. But Buddhas say you are asleep twenty-
four hours a day. Certainly they are not using the word
"sleep" in the same sense which you are acquainted with;
they mean something else, something totally different.
They are talking about a metaphysical sleep. They are
talking about an inner state of unconsciousness.

You walk, you talk, you do a thousand and one
things, but like a zombie. You live mechanically. You
don't live in awareness. When you listen to the awakened ones you are listening again through all the barriers
that you have created in your sleep, through all the
layers of your sleep. You go on misinterpreting them.
Of course, you are right — you are awake, Niraj. In that
sense, all the Buddhas are wrong. They too know it. But
when they say you are asleep they mean something
more fundamental, not the ordinary sleep, not the ordinary awakening.

When they tell you, "Wake up!" they mean: Be totally
conscious so that nothing unconscious and dark remains
in your being, so that no nook or corner of your being
remains dark and unconscious. Right now only a very
small part is conscious — one-tenth — very fragile; nine-
tenths of your being is unconscious. You are just like an
iceberg: just a little fragment of it shows on the surface
— one-tenth, exactly one-tenth — and nine-tenths is underneath the water.

When you listen to the awakened ones you will have
to learn to understand their language, not according to
you but according to them.

As the Prime Minister was waiting to board the special plane that was taking him to the capitals of Europe, the Home Secretary, who had come along to see him off, whispered, "What is your advice on the Homosexual Bill?"

"Oh . . . yes . . . hmm," said the Prime Minister. "Tell him we'll pay him off when I get back!"

You listen according to yourself. You don't listen silently. You don't listen having put your mind aside.

"Have you ever had an X-ray before this?" the doctor asked the sexy Italian girl.

"No, doc," she said, "but I have been ultraviolated a couple of times."

Your mind is constantly distorting; it is giving its own color to everything that it hears. Your mind is making you stupid, although *you* think your mind is making you intelligent.

Listening to the Buddhas needs a certain space, a different kind of space. You have to listen very silently, you have to listen without any thoughts. You have not to listen with any prejudice, you have not to decide for or against. You are not to be in a hurry to decide whether they are right or wrong. Just listen without being for or against. Don't be in a hurry, otherwise you will do something stupid.

The Polish rapist is standing in the "line-up" of criminals at the police station. Bright lights blaze in his face. There are sleazy characters to either side of him.

The police bring in the rape victim, and he jumps forward and shouts, "That's her!"

Keep your stupid mind silent. Tell the mind, "Please be quiet." It is okay in the ordinary world but not with the Buddhas, not with the awakened ones.

Whenever new disciples used to come to Gautam the

Buddha he would say to them, "For two years just sit by my side silently, then something will be possible. Then I can say something to you and then you will be able to understand."

Once a great philosopher, Maulingaputta, came to see him. He had thousands of disciples of his own. He was a well-known philosopher, very much respected, a great scholar. When Buddha said to him, " For two years be here and be silent, then there will be a possibility of something transpiring between me and you," of course he was offended.

He said, "Do you think I am an ignorant person that cannot understand you? You can say whatsoever you want to say right now; there is no need for me to wait for two years. I can understand the Vedas, the Upanishads, the Gita — why not you?"

Buddha said, "If you have understood the Vedas, the Upanishads, the Gita, why have you come here? For what? Your questions are answered! If you have understood the Upanishads, then what is left? Then don't waste my time. You know already. So get lost!"

He must have felt very shocked. He had come with five hundred disciples; they were also shocked. But he must have been a man of great guts — he understood the point. He said, "That's right. If I had understood — really understood — then there would have been no need to come to you. I have come to you because my questions have not yet been answered. I know all the Vedas and the Upanishads, but they have not transformed my being."

Then Buddha said, "Follow what I am saying. For two years no asking of questions. Unlearn everything. For two years keep quiet and be silent and sit here."

When this was happening, Sariputta, one of Buddha's great disciples who was sitting there, started laughing.

Maulingaputta said, "Why is this man laughing? Is he crazy or something?"

Buddha said, "You ask him."

Sariputta was asked. Sariputta said, "I am laughing because this man is really very cunning"—he is talking about Buddha—"I came just like you and he told me to be quiet and silent for two years. And in those two years all my questions disappeared. Now I have nothing to ask! And he goes on asking me, 'Sariputta, why don't you ask now?' So my suggestion to you is: if you want to ask, ask now; if you don't want to ask, then listen to him. Then be silent for two years."

And this happened. After two years Buddha asked Maulingaputta—exactly after two years—"Where are your questions?"

And he laughed, bowed down, touched his feet, and he said, "They have disappeared in silence. Just watching you, just seeing you, slowly slowly my clarity became more and more transparent. The mind disappeared and I could see you with a no-mind. A totally different kind of relating has happened. Something has transpired. There are no questions, no answers either, but I am utterly contented. I have arrived home."

A man says to his friend, "When you get to New York, call up my college chum, Jimmy Sexover. He is now working at the XYZ Company."

When the out-of-towner reached New York he phoned the XYZ Company and asked the receptionist, "Have you a Sexover there?"

"Sex hour? Hell!" she replied. "We don't even have a coffee break!"

You say, Niraj: *Why do all the awakened ones say that man is asleep?*

Because man *is* asleep! It is a simple fact. Watch yourself and you will find the truth of it.

You say: *I don't agree.*

You *can't* agree. You will have to disappear for the agreement to happen. If you persist, agreement is not possible. Both things are not possible: you and the agreement. Either the agreement is possible, then you will not be there, or *you* are possible, then agreement will not be there.

You also say: *I think I am fully awake.*

If you are awake there is no need to think that you are awake. When you love a woman you don't say, "I think I love you." If you say that she will slap your face! If you love her you love her. What is the point of saying, "I think"? When you are thirsty you don't say, "I think I am thirsty." If you are thirsty you *are* thirsty. You simply say, "I am thirsty."

You say: *I think I am fully awake.*

You are fully asleep! Maybe dreaming in your sleep that you are awake . . . that is possible. That's what thinking is all about: dreaming, dreaming with open eyes.

Listen to the Buddhas. Be more silent, quiet, calm. In your silence you will disappear, and then the agreement, then the harmony. . . It is not a question of agreeing philosophically, it is a question of being harmonious with the awakened one, falling in tune with his being. That's what real agreement is.

Niraj, if you go on thinking like this you will miss me totally. Here, thinking is not required, non-thinking awareness is required. It is hard to put thinking aside because we are so much accustomed to thinking and we think it is very clever to think about everything. There are things you cannot think about; either you know or you don't know. And the things I am talking about belong to that category: either you know or you don't.

If you are fully awake, what are you doing here? Such a nice guy, what are you doing here? If you are fully awake, go and help other people to be fully awake. But you are *not* awake. I know you, I know your sleep — it is deep. You need a real hammering on your head. Unless your skull is broken you will not awaken, you will not be able to wake up.

Ordinary alarms won't do. I am creating extraordinary alarms. So I go on sending you from one group to another group. That means being pulled and pushed and beaten and shaken and shocked. We don't leave any opportunity for you to remain asleep. Only when a little bit of awakening happens to you will you understand what is happening here, what is transpiring here between me and the mad people who have gathered here.

The third question

Bhagwan,
Can affirmations be helpful for deconditioning the mind?

Anne Halpa,

DECONDITIONING IS POSSIBLE only through negations, never through affirmations. Affirmation is the way of conditioning the mind. You have to negate: *neti neti.* The Upanishads say: "Neither this nor that." You have to go on negating till nothing is left to negate. When there is absolute emptiness and no content is left to be negated anymore, this is the state of a deconditioned mind.

A deconditioned mind is not a mind at all, it is a no-mind. And how can you achieve a no-mind through affirmations? Affirmations mean that you are repeating something constantly, creating an atmosphere of auto-hypnosis. That's what people have been doing for thousands of years. Go on telling the child, "God is. He created the world," again and again and again — and the whole society goes on repeating it in the home, in the school, in the church — everywhere you go on repeating it — and the child becomes conditioned. Then he starts thinking as if he knows that God is. He is simply a gramophone record! It has become imprinted on his mind that God is. If he had been born in Soviet Russia the situation would have been just the opposite, because there they go on repeating, "There is no God."

One of my friends visited Soviet Russia. He was a teacher, and he was very interested in the Soviet system of education, so he visited schools, colleges, universities — many schools. And he told me that even small children laugh at the idea of God.

On his first visit he went to a small school and asked the small children, "Do you believe in God?" They all laughed. They said, "Do you?" And he said, "Yes, I believe in God." And they said, "In the past, primitive people used to believe in God, ignorant people used to believe in God. Now nobody believes in God." These children are conditioned to believe that there is no God.

Just because of the word "no", don't think that it is a negation — it is an affirmation. Affirmation can be of belief, affirmation can be of disbelief.

Real negation means helping people to get rid of all kinds of beliefs and disbeliefs, helping them to get rid of all the conditionings that the society enforces upon you.

Adolf Hitler in his autobiography writes: "There is only a very small difference between truth and untruth. Truth is untruth repeated many times, that's all."

And he is right in many ways. Repeat any untruth, just go on repeating it, and sooner or later people will start believing it. People have believed in all kinds of things for the simple reason that the people who were in authority were believers, they believed in these things. If they believed in God, then the masses believed in God. People look up to the authorities: the priests, the politicians, the rich people, the scholars, the professors. If they are all believers, then there must be a God. If they believe that there is no God, then the masses start following them. The masses are simply imitators. And the society — every society — creates a certain atmosphere of conditioning. No society exists in the world yet which does not live through this process of conditioning.

And the whole process of conditioning is harmful, poisonous, because it destroys the freedom of the individual. It destroys his capacity to inquire into truth. It destroys his adventure into life. It destroys his initiative to explore what is. Before he ever asks a question, the answer is imprinted upon him. And the people who go on doing this have vested interests. The priests would like you to believe in God. The communists would like you *not* to believe in God. There is *nobody* who is interested in you; they are all interested in their vested interests.

So, Anne Halpa, affirmations cannot be helpful. All affirmations are conditionings. You need total negativity.

That's what Zen is: it negates. It says there is no God, it says there is no soul, it says there is no paradise, it says there is *nothing.* It leaves you nothing to believe in. Even if you start believing in nothing, the Zen Master is going to hit you hard.

It happened:

A disciple of Bokuju would again and again bring his new experiences — that he had experienced energy rising in his spine — and he would be beaten. And Bokuju said, "Get out of here! Don't bring such nonsense to me! You are not it. You are the watcher who watched the energy rising. So don't get identified with it, otherwise it is again a new identification, a new ego: the birth of a new ego, a spiritual ego, which is far more dangerous than ordinary egos."

Then he came one day and said, "You are right. Now I am seeing great light. I am full of light, all is light!"

He was beaten again and he was told, "You are not light either, you are the watcher. Who is seeing the light? You are the seer."

And it went on this way again and again for years. After ten years he came really happy, fell at the feet of the Master and said, "Now you will be happy with me — no need to beat. I have experienced nothingness!"

And this time the Master was so angry! He threw him physically out of the window — of a two-story house. He fell on a rock, and the Master looked from the window and said, "How are you feeling now?"

And the hit was so hard that it really brought him to his senses! He started laughing. Lying down there on the rock he started laughing. The Master also jumped from the window, embraced the disciple and told him, "Now I am happy, really happy!"

The other disciples asked, "What has transpired? It is so mysterious!"

Bokuju said, "To say, 'I have experienced nothingness,' is wrong because then you have made an object of nothingness. Nothingness has again become your affirmation — a thought, a content. You have to get rid of nothingness too! When he laughed, then, in his laughter, I could see nothingness. There was nobody who was laughing, there was simply laughter — no claim, no claimer, just simple laughter, pure laughter. There was nobody who was laughing."

And that very moment the Master felt connected with the disciple for the first time. Otherwise, all those experiences were creating barriers.

Affirmations can't help. All affirmations are conditionings.

"Cats, my dear," said the spinster, "I hate the very sight of them. I had a sweet little canary and some cat got that. I had a perfect parrot, and some cat got that. I had an adorable fiance, and — oh, don't mention cats to me!"

This is how things become conditionings. Now the very word "cat" has become associated with many many bad experiences. The word "cat" has nothing to do with those experiences.

It is said of Napoleon that he was defeated because of cats. The enemy general brought seventy cats in front of the army because he came to know that the moment Napoleon saw cats he went crazy. He would lose all balance, he would lose all intelligence and become very nervous.

And that was a truth, because when Napoleon was only a six-month-old child, a wild cat had jumped on his chest, and since then, although he could fight with lions, don't mention cats! That had become a very deep conditioned reflex.

Behaviorists all over the world are trying to manipulate this process of conditioning in order to create a robot-like humanity. Skinner says that we can change the whole of humanity within a few years. There is no need for a Buddha or a Jesus or a Mohammed to change humanity — and they have not changed it. For centuries they have been teaching, and nothing has happened; humanity has remained the same. We can change humanity very easily. All that is needed are methods of conditioning people.

If you want somebody not to steal there is no need to put him into prison for ten years. That is not going to help; in fact, that will condition him to be a bigger thief than he ever was, because he will be living with thieves. He will be living with greater experts than himself and all that he is going to learn is why he got caught in the first place. Next time he is not going to commit the same mistake.

That's why once a person goes to jail he becomes a regular. Then he comes again and again. Then the jail becomes his home — he becomes a jail-bird. He goes outside only to practice his art, and he comes back again to do the homework. The homework he does in the jail.

Skinner says there is no need to waste time, just give him electric shocks and within two, three weeks we will condition him. He will never think of stealing. Even the idea of stealing will be enough, and he will start trembling and he will fall down on his knees. Just the very idea will be enough to make him so nervous. . . All those electric shocks will be remembered by him.

He proposes that every vice can be dropped from humanity just by giving electric shocks or with methods like that, and all virtues can be established by giving rewards, beautiful rewards.

For example, they have found that in your head there are different centers for different experiences. There is a pleasure center: when you are making love, the pleasure that you derive from it has nothing to do with your genital organs, it happens in your head. The genital organs simply trigger a process. In fact, the pleasure happens in your head, in your brain.

Now, Skinner says there is no need to go into such a long process of courtship and talking nonsense to a woman or to a man and then getting caught and married and having a thousand and one troubles. He says simple things are possible. You just have to keep a small box in your pocket which will be connected with the pleasure center in your head — without any wires, it will be a wire-less connection. So don't be worried that people will see wires coming out of your head and going into your pocket, and everybody will know what you are carrying in your pocket! Just a small box in the pocket, and you can push the button, and suddenly you have a great orgasm and you are all smiles!

Skinner says to reward people for their virtue, for

their good deeds, by manipulating their pleasure center, and then they will keep doing those things.

For example, if whenever you go into the church suddenly you have great orgasms, naturally you will go more often. In fact, you will not leave the church at all! You will have to be forced to go out and do something else.

Skinner was working on a rat. He connected the rat's pleasure center with a small box and taught the rat to push the button. You will be surprised what the rat did: six thousand times he pushed the button; until he fell dead he went on pushing! He forgot everything else. He forgot food, he forgot to drink, he forgot everything else. He just went on and on pushing — six thousand times. Poor rat! Could not bear that much joy! Died, but died in ecstasy!

This can be done to man. This is going to be done because the idea is simple, very simple, and the process is simple. And governments are bound to use it because it is easy to condition people not to do certain things and to do certain other things. Then everybody will be a saint and nobody will be a sinner. But saints or sinners, they will all be robots. They will not have any choice of their own.

Ultimately it can happen that there is no need to have your own small boxes. Just in every country's capital — in New Delhi, in Washington, in London — the prime minister or the president holds the key. And every once in a while he pushes the button and the whole country goes into an orgasmic joy! Then everybody will be obedient. Nobody will break any commandments, nobody will go against them. And the whole country can be punished just by pushing a button, because just as there is a pleasure center in the brain there is a pain center in the brain. Just push the pain center and you are in such agony, you are in hell.

But this is not going to bring freedom to humanity.

This will be the destruction of all freedom and all possibility of freedom. It has to be stopped.

Anne Halpa, affirmations, whether repeated in the old, primitive way or done by a more scientific, technological methodology, are the same. Man needs to be totally free of all conditionings. And that is possible only through absolute negation. Only pure consciousness is left and everything else is negated. Just the watcher is left and nothing to watch. The seer is left and nothing to see. The experiencer is left and nothing to experience.

That's what we in the East have called "the witness". And that is transcendence — transcendence of all bondage, transcendence from body, mind, and all the limitations that body and mind impose upon you. *Nirvana* is possible, absolute freedom is possible, but only via the negative.

The fourth question

Bhagwan,
What is compassion?

Anand Shama,

WE KNOW WHAT PASSION IS, hence it is not very difficult to understand what compassion may be. Passion means a state of biological fever — it is hot. You are almost possessed by biological, unconscious energies. You are no longer your own master, you are just a slave.

Compassion means you have transcended biology, you have transcended physiology. You are no more a slave, you have become a master. Now you function consciously. You are not driven, pulled and pushed by unconscious forces, you can decide what you want to do with your energies. You are totally free. Then the same energy that becomes passion is transformed into compassion.

Passion is lust, compassion is love. Passion is desire, compassion is desirelessness. Passion is greed, compassion is sharing. Passion wants to use the other as a means, compassion respects the other as an end unto himself or herself. Passion keeps you tethered to the earth, to the mud, and you never become a lotus. Compassion makes you a lotus. You start rising above the muddy world of desires, greed, anger. Compassion is a transformation of your energies.

Ordinarily you are scattered, fragmentary. Some energy is being absorbed by your anger, some energy is being absorbed by your greed, some energy is being absorbed by your lust, and so on and so forth. And there are so many desires surrounding you that you are left without any energy; you are left hollow, empty.

And remember what William Blake says — there is great insight in it — he says, "Energy is delight." And you don't have any energy left; all your energy keeps on going down the drain. When all these energies are no longer being wasted they start filling your inner lake, your inner being. You become full. A great delight arises in you. When you start overflowing, you have become a Buddha and you have come upon an inexhaustible source.

Compassion is a key word, but you will understand it only if you go deep into meditation. Meditation is the key to transform passion into compassion. You will have to become more conscious. Right now you are unconscious — notwithstanding what you think, you *are* unconscious.

A girl taking a job in an office is asked by her intended employer how much she hopes to earn.

"Twenty dollars a week," she answers.

"Twenty dollars?" he says. "I'll give you that with pleasure."

"With pleasure, that will be thirty dollars," she replies.

Watch what you do, what you say, what you think, and you will be surprised: without taking any alcoholic beverages, without taking any drugs, you are in a mess.

Mrs O'Brien was berating her husband for his drunken behavior at the party the previous night.

"Sure, and you were making an ass of yourself," she asserted, "cavorting around like that!"

"I was not cavorting or nothing!" O'Brien defended himself. "I was walking as straight a line as any man there . . . till all those people started stepping on my fingers!"

Just look at what you have been doing to yourself, to your life. What have you made of yourself? What have you gained? What meaning have you attained? What significance have you experienced? People don't ask such embarrassing questions because then they feel very depressed. But these questions have to be asked. Unless you ask these questions you are not going to change.

An Irish immigrant walked up to a vending machine, put in a coin, and pressed the button labelled "Coffee, double cream, sugar". No cup appeared. Then two nozzles went into action, one sending forth coffee, the other, cream. After the proper amounts had gone down the drain where the cup should have been, the machine turned off.

"Now, that's real automation!" the Irishman exclaimed. "This thing even drinks it for you."

Man goes on living like a robot, functioning well, efficiently. In fact, the more like a robot you are, the better you function, the better the society feels with you — because it is a society of robots. To be awakened, alert, conscious here is dangerous. It is a society of blind people; to have eyes is to invite danger.

But without creating consciousness you will never be able to know the beauty, the blessing that God has bestowed upon you. You will never know the great opportunity that has been given for you to grow, to become. You can be sunlit peaks and you are just dark holes!

"Shit!" said Polaris. "I got a real jolt in court this morning. The judge fined me five hundred dollars for attempting to rape some broad I met on the subway. And then when he took a good look at her he fined me an extra ten dollars for being drunk!"

If you become alert to at least one thing — that you are not alert — that's a great beginning.

A big Irishman said to a homely woman on the subway, "My God, you're looking lovely tonight."

"Oh, thank you, sir."

"But don't mind what I say, I'm drunk."

Even if you are aware of that much — that you are drunk — you are not absolutely drunk.

Socrates says, "If you know that you don't know, that is a great beginning. Then it is possible for you to know." To be aware that "I am ignorant" creates the possibility of seeking, searching in your own interiority for the truth — for *your* truth.

Compassion is the ultimate transformation of passion. You are in passion, but you go on thinking that you are right as you are. You go on defending yourself. And anything that disturbs your comfortable, mechanical life, you go against.

One visitor has written to me: "Your medicine seems to be too bitter. Are you sure, Bhagwan, that you are a physician and not a horse doctor?" When I look at all the monkeys and the donkeys and the Yankees surrounding me, I wonder myself! I must be a horse doctor.

The medicine *is* bitter and it is difficult to push it down your throat.

I have heard:

Mulla Nasruddin went to the horse doctor and said, "My horse has become so lazy that something has to be done. He does not run. He does not even walk! What to say about running? So give me something really vital."

The doctor said, "We have the medicine, but it is very bitter and the horse may not take it, so you will have to use a certain device. Take this bamboo pipe, it is hollow within. Fill it with the medicine — it is a powder." He gave the powder. "Put one end of the pipe into the horse's mouth and the other in your own mouth and then blow so that it will go down the horse's throat."

Everything went well up to the last moment . . . the horse blew first! Nasruddin, an eighty-year-old man, jumped the fence of his garden and ran so fast that no Olympic runner would have been able to compete with him.

His wife rushed to the horse doctor. She said, "Give me a double dose immediately because I have to catch him! He has escaped!"

Looking at you, I can only say that I must be a horse doctor. But I take every care so that you cannot blow before I blow!

The medicine is bitter because the first thing to be understood is that you don't know anything. It is bitter to accept. The second thing: you are a machine. It is very bitter to accept. The third thing: you are just living in mud, crawling into dark holes, while you are meant to be flying into the sky towards the sun. It is hard to accept. You want lullabies, you want me to sing beautiful songs to you so that you can fall asleep, so that you can dream better dreams.

When you come to me you don't come to be awakened, you come to me so that you can dream beautiful, sweet dreams. That is *your* purpose in coming; that is not *my* purpose in being here. Once you are here you are caught. Then, slowly slowly, I start taking your dreams away. Then, slowly slowly, I go on destroying your illusions. Once your illusions are dropped, your dreams shattered, a great awakening is waiting for you — a great awakening which makes you a Buddha.

And when you are a Buddha, only then will you experience what compassion is. It is cool love — not cold, mind you — cool love. It is a sharing of your joy with the whole of existence. You become a blessing to yourself and a blessing to the whole existence. That is compassion. Passion is ugly, compassion is beautiful. Passion is a curse, compassion is a blessing.

The last question

Bhagwan,
I wrote twenty questions and tore them all up.
I realized that all I wanted was to say, "Hello,
Bhagwan. I am still here," and to hear you say
my name in lecture.

Hello, Deva Mohan. How do you do?

3

The first question

Bhagwan,
You say: Go beyond the mind. Do not listen to
its chatter. Discipline it and make it a
servant. Do not be its slave. But how to
know when the mind is being disciplined and
when it is being repressed?
Also, when I took sannyas the other night you
said not to get hooked on you. I have to tell
you that you are closing the stable door after
this particular horse has already bolted.

Prem Lisa,

THE DIFFERENCE IS SO GREAT that it is impossible to miss it. Repression happens through fighting with your mind. Discipline happens through being watchful, aware, alert. In discipline, there is no fight implied. In discipline, there is no condemnation, no evaluation. One simply looks at the mind silently, seeing the whole traffic, without saying what is right and what is wrong, what should be and what should not be, just as, standing by the side of the road, you watch the people walking by — saints and sinners, beautiful people, ugly people, good people, bad people — but you are unconcerned. It has nothing to do with you; you are out of it.

That's exactly the meaning of the English word "ecstasy". Ecstasy means to be out of the mind. You are just looking, as one looks at the clouds moving in the sky or at the river flowing by — cool, detached. Neither are you trying to cling to something nor are you trying to push something away from you.

This is pure awareness: you are only a mirror. And in just being a mirror, the miracle happens — the miracle of discipline. Slowly slowly, the traffic starts disappearing. Less and less thoughts are moving on the road, less and less pictures are appearing on the screen, less and less memories, fantasies. Gaps start appearing.

A mother was telling her child, "Be very careful when you go to school because the traffic is dangerous at rush-hour time."

The child said, "Don't be worried. I always wait by the side of the road. When a gap comes by, then I cross the road."

"When a gap comes by. . ." As you are looking at your mind you will be surprised: gaps come by, intervals when there is nothing to be seen. The observer remains alone and because it is alone it is no longer an observer either. You can't call it an observer because there is nothing to observe. The mirror is there, but it is not reflecting anything. There is no duality of the seen and the seer. In these intervals discipline arises.

The word "discipline" is also beautiful. It is sometimes very significant to go to the roots of words. "Discipline" comes from a root which means learning. When you are looking at a gap, learning happens. Learning about what? Learning about yourself, because there is nothing else. You are full of awareness. You are just full of your own being, overflowing. And this experience of just being yourself, overflowing, undistracted by anything, undisturbed by anything, is the greatest learning, the greatest possibility of knowing the truth. This is discipline.

From the same root comes the word "disciple." "Disciple" means one who is becoming capable of being utterly silent in the presence of the Master. The disciple is one who allows the interval to happen when he is with the Master. With the Master you are bridged only through silence; when there is nothing in your mind you are bridged. Something then transpires between the Master and the disciple. A flame jumps from the Master into the heart of the disciple. The unlit candle of the disciple suddenly becomes lit. All is joy and light and love, and a great dance arises.

Lisa, discipline can never be misunderstood as repression. Repressions are totally different. In repression you have already decided what is wrong — *a priori* decisions. In fact, others have decided for you what is wrong and what is right. Now you are simply trying to impose the ideas and opinions of others upon yourself. You will have to repress your nature. You will have to force that which is wrong — or which you have been told is wrong — deep into the unconscious. There will be a fight, great turmoil. Instead of bringing silence to you, every method of repression brings more turmoil.

That's why the so-called religious people are more restless, more worried. You are worried only about this world, they are worried even about the other. You are worried only about this life, they are worried about many many past lives and future lives. Your worries are nothing compared to the worries of the so-called religious people. And they are sitting on a volcano, because whatsoever is repressed *is* there; it is not destroyed. Repression never destroys anything; you are simply sitting on top of it. And the danger is that you cannot sit on top of it for twenty-four hours a day; you have limitations. You will get tired, you will need some rest. And whenever you will be tired and you will need rest, repressions will start arising in you.

Hence, even your greatest saints go on thinking, fantasizing, dreaming about all those things that they have repressed.

Mahatma Gandhi has written in his autobiography: "I have been able to control my sexuality as far as my *day* is concerned, but in the night, in my dreams, it comes with a vengeance." This he was writing at the age of seventy . . . a whole life of repression!

Yes, in the day you can somehow manage, but in the night, in the dreams, that which you have repressed in the day is bound to take revenge. It will come back, it will explode in you.

Hence, down the ages your saints have been very much afraid of sleep. They go on cutting down on their sleep — five hours, four hours, three hours, two hours. And the less they sleep the greater the danger, because all their repressions have to come in those two hours in a very condensed way. Then they are crowding in from everywhere. And people worship them! The less a saint sleeps, the more people worship him. They say, "Look how much he has sacrificed! What a great austerity he is doing — he is not even sleeping! Or he sleeps for only two hours or one hour."

The reality is that he is afraid of sleep. And from where is the fear coming? The fear is coming from the fact that when you are awake you can control, but when you are asleep, who is there to control? The controller is asleep, is in a relaxed state. He cannot sit on top of all the repressions, and they will assert themselves.

So, Lisa, if you are fighting with anything, then it is not discipline. I don't teach fight, I teach awareness. It is useless to fight with the darkness, utterly useless and stupid. Bring the light in. Why fight with darkness? And how can you ever hope to win by fighting with darkness? Bring the light in and the darkness is found no more.

You are surrounded by many darknesses: greed, anger, jealousy, lust, ambition, ego. These are layers of darkness. If you start fighting with all these layers of darkness you are not going to win, because there is no way to fight with darkness directly. Darkness does not exist in the first place; it is only the absence of light. So if you want to do something with darkness, don't try to do it directly, do something with light. If you want darkness, put the light out. If you don't want darkness, put the light on. But do something with the light, forget about darkness. If the light is there, darkness is not there. If the light is not there, you cannot avoid darkness. You can close your eyes, you can try to forget about it, you can become occupied somewhere else, you can take your mind far far away from it, but it is there all the same. And it will show in your acts, in your thoughts, in your behavior. It will come up again and again. You cannot hide it — it is impossible to hide it. The truth of your being, whatsoever it is, is bound to surface.

Lisa, become aware. And I am not saying what is wrong and what is right. I am simply saying: Be aware; or, awareness is right and unawareness is wrong. When you are aware, things will start changing of their own accord, and then the mind functions as a servant. It is a machine, a beautiful machine, one of the most complex machines invented by nature in thousands of years. Man has not yet been able to create anything comparable to it. Even the best computer is not yet so capable.

A single human mind can contain all the libraries of the world. It is almost infinite. Its capacity is great, its *use* is great, but it should be your servant not your master. As a servant it is beautiful; as a master it is dangerous.

Let consciousness be your master and mind your servant. It happens through awareness. And I am not telling you to control it, because all control is repression. I am not telling you to fight, because all fight is a sheer waste of energy. You are fighting with your own servant — you are wasting your energy. You need not fight with your servant, you have simply to say, "I am the master"; that's all. You have simply to *be* the master, that's all, and the servant bows down. The servant immediately understands that the master has come in. And how does the master come in? The moment you become awake, the master comes in.

You ask me, Lisa: *You say: Go beyond the mind. Do not listen to its chatter. Discipline it and make it a servant. Do not be its slace. But how to know when the mind is being disciplined and when it is being repressed?*

It is very simple. Nobody can ever mistake the two, nobody can ever confuse the two. They are so different — just like light and darkness, just like love and hate, just like flowers and thorns, just like poison and nectar. They are so totally different! But if you *think* about them you may get confused. In thinking you cannot make the distinction. Don't think about them — experiment, experience, and the distinction will be absolutely clear.

You also say: *Bhagwan . . . when I took sannyas the other night you said not to get hooked on you. I have to tell you that you are closing the stable door after this particular horse has already bolted.*

Lisa, I am not only a horse doctor but a horse lover too! And when I see a good horse I immediately fall in love. I believe in love at first sight, because it saves time! The moment I saw you, Lisa, the moment I saw tears of joy, love, trust and surrender in your eyes, I accepted you deep down as part of the orange Mafia!

And I say, "Don't get hooked on me," only when I

know that you are absolutely hooked and there is no way to escape! I don't say it to everybody. I say it only to those who are already in. They may not be aware of it; they may become aware of it later on.

I have seen it. You *are* hooked, you are stoned on me. Now there is no going back. Now this is going to be your whole world. *I* am your home. I say it only when I am absolutely certain, categorically certain, that there is no possibility of your going away, when I see that you are melting and merging. Then only, just to be generous, do I say, "Don't get hooked on me." I can afford to say it when I know that Lisa is finished!

The second question

Bhagwan,
What is the essence of Buddha Dharma —
the religion of the Buddha?

Mouna,

Y OKA SAYS:

> *If you reach the Zen of Buddha, at that very moment you accomplish everything.*
>
> *In your dream there are many pathways,*
> *But when you wake up, they are reduced to nothing —*
> *Neither error, nor happiness, nor loss, nor gain.*
> *Do not try to find anything in the essence of your being.*
> *It is a long time since you wiped the dust from your mirror,*
> *Now it is time for you to see its brilliancy perfectly.*

Who can not-think, all is his.
If you practice charity in order to become
Buddha
When will you succeed? Never — a thousand
times never.

Drink and eat according to your true nature.
All things in the universe are impermanent,
and therefore all existence is void.
That is the whole understanding of Buddha.

This is the essence of Buddha Dharma, the religion of
the Buddha. First: it is not a philosophy that you can
understand intellectually; you have to become a Buddha
to know it. Hence Yoka says:

If you reach the Zen of Buddha — the state of
the Buddha — *at that very moment you ac-*
complish everything.

Nothing is missing when you reach the ultimate state
of awakening; all is fulfilled, you are utterly contented.
Life is known for the first time as a great significance, as
a great dance, a celebration. Life is known for the first
time as absolutely perfect. There is no complaint, no
desire, no hankering for things to be other than they are.
One is simply contented, totally contented. All desiring
disappears.

And what is the state of Buddha? What is this "Zen of
Buddha" Yoka is talking about? It is the state of no-
mind. Hence Yoka says:

Who can not-think, all is his.

The greatest thing in life to experience is a state of no-
thought. The greatest art of life is to be able to be without mind. Even if it happens for a single moment — just a
glimpse — you have reached the beyond and you have
crossed the point of no-return.

Don't go on thinking about it — what it is. By thinking you will go on missing it. Thinking is the sure way of missing the Buddha Dharma; non-thinking is the way to achieve it. It is your own nature!

Buddha does not talk about some great mysteries, hidden secrets, esoteric knowledge. He does not believe in mythology; he is not an occultist. He is a very simple man, very ordinary. He believes in the ordinary existence. He says your day-to-day life is all there is. If you can live it joyfully, silently, understandingly, watchfully, there is nothing else to be done. Your very ordinary life starts becoming extraordinary.

Drink and eat, Yoka says, *according to your true nature.*

Just remember: don't distort your nature, remain true to your nature. Listen to your own nature and follow it. Don't follow anybody else.

Buddha says, "Even if you meet me on the way, kill me immediately." He is saying: Don't follow me, just take the hints. Try to understand, imbibe the spirit. Feel my presence and then go on your way. Live according to your own light, howsoever small it is; but if it is yours and you live according to it, it will go on growing.

Buddha says, "Be a light unto yourself." That is his greatest message. Nobody else in the whole world, in the whole history of humanity, has been so respectful towards others as Gautam the Buddha. "Be a light unto yourself."

Buddhas only point the way — fingers pointing to the moon. *You* have to follow, and you have to follow according to your nature. You have to be silent, quiet, so you can listen to the still small voice within you, and then follow it. Wherever it leads it is good. Go in deep trust, following your own voice. Be spontaneous, natural, ordinary. This is the way of being extraordinary. Be ordinary but aware, and the ordinary becomes the sacred.

All things in the universe are impermanent . . .

So don't be worried. All things are impermanent: pleasure and pain, friendship and enmity, poverty and richness, success and failure, birth and death. All is in a flux, all is impermanent, so why be worried? Everything goes on changing. Don't cling — clinging brings misery, clinging shows your misunderstanding. The moment you cling to something you are living with the idea that it can be permanent. Nothing can be permanent, and nothing can be done about it. It is just the nature of things to be impermanent.

You are trying to catch hold of rainbows. They are beautiful, but you cannot catch hold of them — one moment they are there and another moment they are gone. So don't cling to anything because everything is impermanent. And don't desire anything because even if you get it, you will lose it. If you don't get it, you will be frustrated. If you get it *and* lose it, you will be frustrated. Either way you will be in misery, you are inviting misery. So don't desire anything and don't cling to anything.

Whatsoever comes, accept it. Buddha calls it *tathata*, suchness. Just accept it, live through it silently, without being disturbed by it. Misery comes, it will go. Happiness comes, it will go. Everything passes away, nothing abides, so there is nothing to worry about.

Go on passing through all kinds of experiences, and then you will know that one can pass through the world uncontaminated, uncorrupted. One can live in the palaces without clinging, then he is a sannyasin; and one can live in a hut and can cling to the hut, then he is not a sannyasin.

That's why I don't tell you to renounce the world, I

simply say: Be watchful. That is the essence of Buddha's message.

People ask me, "But Buddha *renounced* the world. Why did *he* renounce?" He renounced when he was not a Buddha. He renounced when he was as ignorant as anybody else. He renounced in ignorance.

When he attained the truth, when he experienced the truth and came back home, his wife asked him only one question. "Just tell me one thing," she asked. "Whatsoever you have attained . . . I can see you are a transformed being. You have become luminous, you are no longer the same person. The old is gone, you are reborn. It is so clear to me — even a blind person like me can see it. But just answer me one question. Whatsoever you have attained, was it not possible to attain it living here with me in this palace?"

And the story is: Buddha remained silent, looking downwards. The wife was right. He didn't say anything.

In the East, not saying anything is thought to be a sign of agreement: *Mounam sammati lakshanam.* "To be silent means I agree with you." It says more than Buddha saying yes. His silence says more, it is more pregnant with meaning.

He immediately felt it: "She is right." Whatsoever he had attained could have been attained anywhere. There was no need to go into the jungle.

There is no need for you to go anywhere. Wherever you are you can assert your Buddhahood, you can become awakened.

The essence is to slip out of the mind, to get out of the mind. The mind is the world. The mind is full of desires, full of clingings, attachments, longings. Get out of the mind! Create a little distance between you and the mind. Be a watcher, a watcher on the hills, and you will be surprised: as you watch the mind, the distance becomes bigger and bigger. As you watch the mind, as you become more and more established in watching, the mind recedes farther and farther away. One day it happens: you cannot hear the chatter of the mind; it is no longer there. It is simply, absolutely silent. In that silence, truth descends in you. In that silence, you encounter yourself, you encounter your innermost core. And that is the innermost core of the whole existence. Your being is the being of all.

We are separate as minds, as bodies, but not as consciousness. In consciousness we meet, we are one. That consciousness is God. That meeting, that oneness where all differences dissolve, where we are no longer separate ice cubes, where we have melted and disappeared into the universal, Buddha calls *nirvana.* The word is beautiful; it means cessation of the ego. When the ego ceases you are God, you are a Buddha, you are a Christ. It is the ego that is giving you a limitation. It is the ego that is making you live in a prison. Get out of the ego! And nobody is preventing you — it is your own clinging, it is your own attachment. You have become too attached to your chains, you have become too attached to your prison cell. You think it is your home, and it is not. Come out of it! Wake up!

To be awake is to be a Buddha. And Yoka is right. He says:

> *If you reach the Zen of Buddha* — the state of Buddha — *at that very moment you accomplish everything.*

The third question

Bhagwan,
When you speak of religions, you usually
mention Christians, Mohammedans and Hindus,
but not Jews. Is there a reason for it?

Veet Ateet,

T HERE IS A REASON: I am the only Jew in India!

Once I was taken in a Cadillac car; the owner wanted to sell it. I was interested — I have used all kinds of cars except the Cadillac. It was a beautiful car, specially made. I loved it.

He asked me, "What do you say? How did you feel in it?"

I said, "I felt just like a Jew! I will not purchase this car — this will show my identity. I am already in more trouble than a man can manage. Now to declare myself a Jew will be inviting even more trouble. Jews are experts at inviting trouble!"

One old Jew was praying to God for years and never asking for anything. God became fed up. If you ask for something, something can be done and he can get rid of you! But he was not asking for anything; he was just praying and praying and praying.

So one day God said, "Listen! What do you want? Why don't you say exactly what you want? I am ready to fulfil it."

The old Jew said, "Is it true that we are your chosen people?"

God said, "Yes, that's true."

The Jew said, "Now please choose somebody else. For three thousand years, just because of you, we have suffered so much. Enough is enough! Now you choose somebody else!"

Veet Ateet, you must be a Jew also, otherwise why this question? Jews are always thinking, in every possible way, about Jews.

The Friends of the Elephant Society — a society created to help sick, old or homeless elephants — decided that although most people knew what an elephant was, there had never been any serious, definitive study conducted about the huge animal. They therefore decided to hold a competition with a prize of a thousand dollars to be given for the best book on the subject of the elephant.

An Englishman enters his book entitled: "The History and Statistics of the Elephant."

A German enters a three-volume set entitled: "The Anatomy and Physiology of the Elephant."

A Frenchman enters a slim, hundred-page volume entitled: "The Amorous Affairs of the Elephant."

An Italian seriously considers the project for about five minutes, then drops it and joins his friends for some spaghetti.

And a Jew enters an epic effort entitled: "The Elephant and the Jewish Problem."

Now, Ateet, why does this question come to your mind? I don't say much about Judaism because in India there are no Jews. Hindus are there, Christians are there, Mohammedans are there, Jainas are there, Buddhists are there; only Jews are missing, so I don't mention them much. Of course, Jews are not missing here. This must be the only place in the whole of India where you can find thousands of Jews — but they are no longer Jews.

Ateet, this must be a hangover with you. Do you know what your name means? *Veet ateet* means going beyond the past. You still seem to have a hangover of being Jewish. And having thousands of Jews here, it is better not to talk about them because they are very argumentative people.

A Christian visiting the Holy Land struck up a conversation with an Israeli.

"I am really surprised that you and the Arabs can't get together peacefully."

"My dear man," said the Israeli, "the Jews are a very

argumentative people. The only thing you can get two Jews to agree upon is what a third Jew should give to charity."

That is true.

Jimmy finally got Sadat and Begin together for a resumption of the Mid-East peace talks.

Afterwards Sadat said, "I'm glad we buried the hatchet. In the future I wish you everything you wish me."

Begin answered, "See, you're starting up again."

That's why, Ateet, I don't mention Jews very much. It is dangerous! Surrounded by thousands of Jews it is better not to mention Jews at all.

And, moreover, Judaism is a dead religion, just as Hinduism is. In fact, there have been only two source religions in the world: Hinduism and Judaism. Both are dead. Jainism and Buddhism are offshoots of Hinduism, but because the root is dead the branches are dead too. And Christianity and Islam are branches of Judaism, and because the root is dead the branches are dead too. These are dead phenomena. I am not much concerned with the past.

Yes, something beautiful has happened in Judaism, too, and that is Hassidism — and I have talked about it a lot. Just as I love Zen people in the tradition of the Buddha, I love Hassids in the tradition of Moses and I love Sufis in the tradition of Mohammed. These three are still alive in some small way because these three have never become established religions; they have always been anti-establishment, they have always been alternatives to the established religion, they have always been rebellious.

Hassidism is worth talking about, not Judaism — and I have talked about Hassidism. I have been approaching Hassidism with my own experience. I have been bringing Hassidism up to date, trying to make it part of the twentieth century. Hassidism is the essence of Judaism, the very fragrance of it.

And I have something of the Hassids in me, that's why I sometimes call myself a Jew. The Hassids love life, they are life-affirmative. They don't believe in renunciation, they believe in rejoicing. They believe in dancing, singing, celebrating — and that's exactly my approach too.

My religion is something of a meeting of Zen, Sufism and Hassidism — and something more thrown in.

The fourth question

Bhagwan,
Actually, I love to philosophize. What to do
with that ability in a place like this?

Deva Anurati,

Philosophy is a sheer waste of your energy. The same energy can become your meditation, the same energy can become your awakening. Philosophy is like dreaming: you can dream beautiful dreams, but dreaming is dreaming. You can think of God, but to *think* of God is not to know God. To know *about* God is not to know God. The word "about" means around. You can go on around and around . . . you will be moving in a circle and you will never reach the target, because the target is the center not the circumference.

Philosophy is circumferential, peripheral. It can deceive you; it has deceived millions of people because it talks about love, about God, it even talks about meditation. It philosophizes about everything.

But philosophy means that your mind remains your master; it is *mind* that philosophizes. You have to go beyond mind, Anurati — and it is not going to happen through philosophy. It can happen only through meditation.

Now you must be philosophizing about meditation: what it is, how to define it. There are thousands of definitions and you can be lost in the jungle of definitions.

And I can understand your difficulty. You must be feeling a little out of place, because here philosophy is debarred. I am creating a non-philosophical atmosphere. The whole effort here is to help you go beyond mind. I don't want you to think about love, I want you to love. I don't want you to think about God, I want you to *know* God, to *be* God.

What is the point when you are thirsty to go on thinking about water? Even if you discover by your thinking that water consists of H_2O, that is not going to quench your thirst. And that's what philosophy is: H_2O. You are thirsty, and philosophy says, "Don't be thirsty. Water is simply H_2O. Just write H_2O on the paper and eat the paper!"

Philosophers go on eating the papers. They eat great things: Upanishads, Vedas, Korans, Bibles. They have a great appetite for paper! That's why there is such a shortage of paper in the world: there are so many paper-eaters. Crazy people!

Yes, once in a while philosophy may be good, just for a change.

Molly Landau was learning to drive a car. Regrettably, as it turned out, she thought she already knew how, so she dismissed her driving instructor and ventured forth upon the public highway, unaccompanied by either an experienced hand or a driver's license.

As she wobbled in an uncertain course along Southern Boulevard in the Bronx, a milkman driving a well-behaved horse turned a corner. Mrs Landau tried simultaneously to do several things: apply the brakes, avoid a collision, turn out, turn in, veer left, veer right, speed up, slow down, and who knows what else.

The "what else" was that she banged squarely into the side of the milk-wagon, leaving it turned over on its side in the middle of the street, with the horse and driver entangled in the wreckage.

The lady, losing her head, at the same time lost control of the car. She sped away, swerved out of sight and on squealing tires she circled the block. A minute later she reappeared at the scene of the accident, still wrestling with the steering wheel. The dairyman, who had managed to extricate himself from the mess, was cutting his struggling horse loose from the twisted harness when he heard the clatter and roar of an approaching, wide-open engine. He looked up to see the same car and the same woman again bearing down on him. Just in time to save himself, he jumped aside.

There was a second crash and once more the green motorist proceeded on her devastating way. But now the capsized wagon was a total loss. The milkman was a natural-born philosopher. As he stood in the midst of the ruins, he shrugged his shoulders and remarked to the curious citizens who had gathered around, "About that lady's driving, I can't say she's an expert. But you have to give her credit — she's thorough!"

Yes, in such situations, a little philosophy is good: it helps you to keep cool. But more than that it is of no use, Anurati. You will have to learn a new way of being. If you *are* here — and you *are* here — stop philosophizing. Start experiencing, because it is only through experience that one comes to know the truth.

Truth is not a conclusion arrived at by logical argumentation, truth is not arrived at through syllogism, truth is an experience of a silent, still consciousness.

Learn to be more silent and still.

This is the first question from Anurati that I am answering. She must have asked hundreds of questions — I go on throwing them away. The moment I see Anurati's name, the question goes into the wastepaper basket for the simple reason that I don't want to nourish her philosophical mind. If I start talking about her philosophical problems she will get more and more into them.

She goes on asking me, "You answer everybody's question. Why don't you answer my question?" So today I decided that at least one question should be answered.

Philosophy is a disease — and I know it first-hand! I have been a professor of philosophy — you can trust me! I have suffered from it and I know it is very chronic. Once it enters into your system it is very difficult to throw it out. I have every sympathy for Anurati, but if the right effort is made you can get rid of it; it is not incurable. And because it never gives you anything. . . It promises much, but it never supplies any goods.

Just look back. What has it given to you? It makes people great bullshitters, that's all! They go on talking about great things they know nothing of. It may give you a very polished ego, but this is the problem that has to be solved, it is not the solution.

Anurati, wake up from your philosophical dream! Howsoever sweet it is, it is a dream. And it is so useless that you can always find an argument for anything. Philosophy is a prostitute: it can go with anybody.

Meditate on Murphy's maxim: To every Ph.D. there is an equal and opposite Ph.D.

You can argue for, you can argue against. Philosophy has no anchor. It is a game, like chess: it keeps you occupied and gives you a sense of doing something great. But remember, it is all dreaming.

One night Zorba the Greek dreamed that he had to leave his island. So he went down to the port and stepped aboard a boat.

The captain stopped him and said, "You'll have to pay one hundred drachmas."

"That's sheer robbery!" exclaimed Zorba. "I won't give you more than fifty drachmas."

"One hundred or you will have to swim!"

"Is that so?" Zorba said. "You better take me for fifty drachmas or I'll wake up and you'll lose everything!"

Anurati, please wake up! But people are afraid to wake up. The fear is they will lose everything because all that they have is nothing but dream stuff. Their philosophy is their dream, their religion is their dream, their knowledge is their dream, their ego is their dream. In their dream they have gathered many things, hence they are afraid to wake up, because the moment they wake up all is lost.

One night Mulla Nasruddin dreamed that a man wanted to give him some money. He was very generous, but Mulla was insistent, "Give me a hundred rupees."

And the man was saying, "Take ninety . . . ninety-one . . . ninety-two . . . ninety-three."

But Mulla was insistent on a hundred rupees because Mulla could see that the man was so generous, he looked so kind that he might agree on a hundred rupees, so why settle for less?

The man said, "Listen. For the last time, take ninety-nine."

Mulla said, "One hundred!" But he said it so loudly that he woke up. He opened his eyes — the man had disappeared and the money had disappeared.

He immediately closed his eyes and he said, "Okay, okay. Give me ninety-nine!" But now there was nobody there. He said, "Don't be so angry. Ninety-eight . . . ninety-seven . . ." But there was nobody there at all. It was all a dream.

You are dreaming beautiful dreams. Philosophy is a very clever dream.

Anurati, get out of it! And this is not the place to philosophize; you can do it anywhere else. Such stupid things can be done anywhere. For such stupid things you need not come from America to India! Do something real, do something authentic. Do something that will transform your life, that will give you a new birth.

"Unless you are born again you cannot enter into my kingdom of God."

The fifth question

Bhagwan,
I have traveled all over India, but I have
never heard an ill word spoken of this town,
Poona.

Naresh,

PERHAPS IT IS because one should not speak ill of the dead!

The sixth question

Bhagwan,
Why are you against the Greeks? Why do you
call them the "goddamned Greeks"?

Veera,

THE GREEKS ARE GREAT PEOPLE — I love them. I love Socrates, I love Pythagoras, I love Heraclitus — and, of course, I love Mukta. But they are "goddamned."

A Russian can be cheated only by a gipsy, a gipsy by a Jew, a Jew by a Greek, and a Greek only by the devil.

The seventh question

Bhagwan,
I am British. Anything I can do about it?

Mark,

THIS TIME IT IS TOO LATE. Next time be a little more careful in choosing your parents!

The eighth question

Bhagwan,
Can children understand the truth?

Raj,

CHILDREN CAN UNDERSTAND THE TRUTH but cannot understand that they understand it. They understand more clearly than you can understand because they are more clean, more innocent; but they are so innocent that they cannot understand that they understand.

Hence you need another childhood, a second childhood. First you have to lose your first childhood. That is the whole meaning of the biblical story of Adam and Eve losing paradise: that is losing the first childhood. It is a tremendously significant story. It has so many meanings, it is such a multi-dimensional parable, that I don't think there exists any other parable comparable to it.

You can look at it from many aspects. It is losing the

first childhood — which is inevitable. Adam and Eve are not committing a sin. In fact, the word "sin" comes from a root which means forgetting, and that is a beautiful meaning: they are simply forgetting something.

Every child has to forget his innocence. Every child has to get lost in the world. Every child has to go astray, has to make many many mistakes, has to suffer, has to pass through pain and pleasure and all kinds of dualities so that one day he can again start feeling a great longing to go back home. Lost in the deserts of the world, a longing arises one day to go back home.

That longing is sannyas, that longing is religion. And then one consciously comes back again to one's childhood; this is the second childhood. Now one understands and also understands that one understands. The first childhood is very innocent; it is bound to be lost because it is a natural gift, God's gift. The second childhood is never lost because it is your earning, you have become worthy of it. It is no longer a gift; you deserve it. It is growth, not a gift. It is your maturity.

Adam and Eve lose their first childhood, and it is in people like Buddha and Jesus Christ and Zarathustra and Moses that the second childhood happens. In Christ, Adam starts moving back towards paradise. If Adam is the going away from paradise, Jesus is the coming back home.

But if you watch children you will see how clear they are about things — far more clear than you are. You are very much confused; you have so many thoughts to confuse you. Children are not confused — they don't have any thoughts to confuse them. Their flames are burning bright with no smoke. They are full of wonder and awe, and the moment they see something they immediately understand, because there is no barrier.

If we can help children to be meditative we can change the whole world — its energy, its consciousness.

But we teach them something else, never meditation — geography, history, and all kinds of nonsense which is absolutely useless. Now, what does it matter where Timbuktoo is? *I* don't know; I simply love the name Timbuktoo — wherever it is! But children are being taught about stupid kings — Genghis Khan and Nadir Shah and Tamburlaine. For what? Why are you filling their heads with rubbish?

This is the moment to make them aware because they are naturally aware. If we help them to understand their awareness and their innocence, the first childhood can become a movement into the second childhood.

A French farmer's son missed a day in school and explained to the teacher that he was absent because of important family business.

"I had to take the bull to the cows," he explained.

"But couldn't your father do that better?" the teacher wanted to know.

"I suppose my father is a pretty good lover," the French lad said, "but in this case I think the bull does it better."

They are more clear about things than your so-called knowledgeable people.

California is full of crazies. Even the doctors are crazy. A troubled young lady went to consult an M.D., complaining that she was having trouble with her menstrual cycle.

"No problem, chick," said the medico. "Why don't you just trade it in for a Honda?"

During a visit to the zoo a youngster asked his mother, "Mom, how do lions screw?"

She replied, "I really don't know, dear, most of your father's friends are Rotarians."

"My new husband is a sex maniac," complained the young lady to the judge. "Ever since the honeymoon he has been making non-stop love to me. I can't get no rest day or night. I want a divorce."

"All right," said the judge, "but first you'll have to file your application."

"File my application!" exclaimed the lady indignantly. "Why, that poor thing is so sore I can't even bear to touch it!"

A schoolteacher bent too low over her desk to mark a paper and little Johnny in the front seat said, "Teacher, I see something."

"That's very rude, Johnny. Tomorrow don't come to school," the teacher admonished.

A week later, the teacher bent down to pick up a piece of chalk. Johnny, still in a ringside seat, got up and started to walk to the door. "Where are you going?" asked the teacher sternly.

"Teacher, my schooldays are over."

Children see very clearly; their eyes are transparent. But soon they have to lose their innocence. We *force* them to lose it. We fill their heads with such rubbish that their eyes stop seeing. Every parent is trying, every society is trying, every church is trying to fill the child's mind with stupid things before he starts becoming aware on his own; otherwise he will be a rebel. So by the time you are three or four years old, things have already started being poured into you. You are sent to the church, you are being taught religion — as if religion can be taught.

Religion cannot be taught, it can only be caught. You can catch it only when you are in the company of a man like Jesus or Buddha. When you are in the company of a man like Yoka, Rinzai, Bodhidharma, you can catch it; it is infectious. But it cannot be taught. A religion that is taught — it is rubbish. But we are very interested in making our children Christian, Hindu, Mohammedan as soon as possible.

In a better world, in a more human world, at least up to the age of twenty-one, children should not be taught any Christianity, Hinduism, Jainism, Judaism, no. Up to the age of twenty-one — when they become capable of voting — they should be left to inquire on their own. And I assure you, Christianity, Jainism, Buddhism, Judaism, Mohammedanism, will all disappear from the world. Just leave children to themselves up to their twenty-first year and then try to teach them Christianity! They will raise such questions that even you will start suspecting whether Christianity is of any worth. But you force poor children three years of age. . . They cannot resist, they cannot protect themselves. They depend on you for their survival, so you can do anything.

And this is the greatest crime that can be done to children. Parents have been criminals throughout the whole past, and the greatest crime is that you condition your children's minds and you don't allow them the freedom to seek and search and inquire for themselves. Of course, parents have not done it knowingly; their parents had conditioned them and they were simply repeating a pattern. And they were thinking that they were doing it for your own good. In fact, the greatest crimes have been committed for your own good. Whenever somebody says, "I am doing it for your own good," beware, because nobody needs to do anything for your own good.

Yes, parents need to feed you, to clothe you, to support you, to make you strong in body, to support you in your inquiry, in your questioning, to give you every kind of support and protection so that you can freely inquire. The whole world will be full of agnostics, inquirers, and that will be the beginning of a true religion on the earth. And it has to happen from the very childhood because it is such a stupid waste of time to first destroy their minds, because then it becomes very hard, very difficult to uncondition them. They start resisting because then they start getting identified with their own minds.

Every day I receive questions — rude questions, ugly questions — because whenever somebody feels hurt, immediately his conditioned mind reacts and he writes something in anger.

I am trying to help you to be on your own, to be free, and you get angry because you don't want to be free. You have become accustomed to being slaves. But you don't think it is slavery; you think it is knowledge, it is wisdom. You think you know the Bible, you know the Gita, you know the Koran. And when I go on destroying, negating, you become scared. If all your knowledge is taken away, what is left? You are very afraid of nothingness — and that is the true beginning, that is the beginning of a new birth.

Everybody has to become again a nothing, again a child, again innocent; only then will you be able to understand truth.

Children *are* capable of understanding it, but they are not capable of understanding that they understand it. For that you have to wait a little. But we can prepare the children. We can use their capacity to understand to make them more free, to make them more adventurous, to make them more courageous.

If you really love your children you will help them to go on an adventure so that they can find God by themselves. It is beautiful to find truth; it is ugly to carry somebody else's truth on your shoulders. It is simply a dead weight. It cripples, kills; it poisons you.

The last question

Bhagwan,
There's no question about it, Sarjano is
my LSD: a Latin-seducing-Don Juan.
The ashram seems to be the right environment
and I know you are guiding me through the trip,
but what's the right dose to take him in?

Satya Bharti,

SARJANO IS a ladies' man, so don't waste your time in thinking about the right dose to take him in because tomorrow he may not be available. Eat him totally if you can! There is just one thing you have to be aware of: if you don't like spaghetti, then eating him is going to be a torture — it will be all spaghetti!

What did the cannibal say after he ate the Italian? "The meat's a little on the greasy side."

So eat him while he is available and don't waste time in thinking about right proportions — how much and how much not.

Sarjano is like the wind: today he is here, tomorrow somewhere else. And remember perfectly well: eat him before he eats you, because these Italians are really dangerous people!

Just the other day there was a question: "What is more dangerous than an Italian?" Of course, two Italians!

4

The first question

Bhagwan,
The vision "neither this nor that" feels so
negative. How can I be accepting or even
creative with this? I feel totally confused.

Prem Helmut,

MIND LIVES IN THE DUALITY of the positive and the
negative. It lives like a pendulum, moving from yes to
no, from no to yes. It cannot live in the absolute yes, it
cannot live in the absolute no. Absolute yes means now
there is no possibility for the pendulum to move anywhere. Absolute no also means the same: no space for
the mind to play games. Anything absolute is a death
for the mind.

There are two possibilities of killing the mind, of transcending the mind: either absolute yes or absolute no.
The Upanishads have used the first possibility, absolute
yes, and Buddha has used the second possibility, absolute no. But look deeply and you will find they are not
different, they are bridged by the same phenomenon —
absoluteness. Anything absolute becomes the grave of
the mind; it needs duality to exist.

That's why you are so afraid of the absolute negative, because in the absolute you start disappearing. You are your mind. Of course, there is something more in you than your mind, but you are not aware of it. And as you start disappearing, fear arises, confusion arises; one is scared, one wants to cling to whatsoever is available to cling to.

It is because of this miracle of the absolute that God has been synonymous with the absolute. God means the absolute. Either say absolute yes and your mind disappears, or say absolute no and your mind disappears.

Why has Buddha chosen to say absolute no, why not absolute yes? For a certain reason: with the absolute yes there is one danger. The danger is that you may not understand the absoluteness of the yes; you may still go on thinking that it is your old positivity. With the absolute no that danger is not possible. With the absolute no, death seems so clear that you cannot miss it — hence the confusion.

This confusion is good. Don't try to escape from it, go deeper into it. Soon it will become a chaos — not just confusion but chaos. When all that you have known about yourself is shattered, when all that you have believed in has evaporated, when all that you were identified with has slipped out of your hands — the very earth beneath you is no longer available, you are falling and falling into a bottomless abyss — that is chaos. And only out of chaos are stars born. Out of chaos is creativity.

You ask: *How can I be accepting or even creative with this?*

There is no question of accepting because every acceptance means that deep down there is rejection. Otherwise, why the question of acceptance? Why in the first place do you think of accepting? You must be rejecting somewhere.

I don't accept life because I don't reject it in the first place. It is simply there, neither rejected nor accepted. It is so. Buddha calls it *tathata,* suchness.

A man came to Buddha and asked, "What should we do with death? Should we accept it?"

Buddha said, "There is no question of accepting or rejecting. Death is! It is so. Such is the nature of things: they are born one day, one day they die."

Why do you think of rejecting or accepting? If you try to accept, that simply means a kind of repression. First you must have rejected; you must be still rejecting and you are covering up your rejection with acceptance. Deep down you are angry and on the surface you are smiling, you are all smiles. Deep down you are sad; on the surface you are laughing and trying to hide the fact not only from others but from yourself too.

Friedrich Nietzsche has said, "I laugh because I am afraid that if I don't laugh I will start crying and weeping. I go on laughing just to avoid the possibility of crying and weeping. I don't want to cry and weep. I want to forget that there are tears in me."

But this is just a cover-up; this laughter is not true. This is not the laughter of the Buddhas — it can't be. It is the desperate effort of a split mind. This is schizophrenia: one part wants to cry, another part is trying to hide it. You are in conflict. But we are brought up in conflict, we have learned how to live in conflict — this has become our very life style. It is not a question of accepting.

True acceptance is not an acceptance at all. You will be surprised by my statement: true acceptance is not an acceptance at all. True acceptance is absence of rejection and acceptance. One simply knows that this is how things are — the suchness of things, *tathata.*

Hence one of the beautiful names of Buddha: Tathagata. The Buddhist scriptures always use the word *tathagata* for Buddha: one who lives in suchness, neither rejecting nor accepting, simply seeing whatsoever is the case, only reflecting.

And you ask me: *How is creativity possible out of this absolute negativity?* You don't know anything about creativity. Creativity comes only out of total negation, it comes out of absolute emptiness. The whole world has come out of nothingness and the whole world will one day move into nothingness.

Now the scientists have stumbled upon one of the most important discoveries ever: the discovery of the black hole. They say there are a few spots in existence, which can be called black holes, where if anything comes close it is sucked in by the black hole and it disappears, it becomes nothing.

But this is only half the story; the other half has still to be discovered. I can predict it will be discovered soon: the white hole, the other side of the black hole, from which things start coming out of nothingness. Existence goes into rest, then nothingness prevails. When the rest is over, existence again becomes active, manifest; then creativity prevails. Creativity comes out of nothingness.

The more you are a nobody, the more you know that there is no ego in you, the more creativity will flow through you. You will become a vehicle, you will become a passage. Songs will pour out of you — and music and love and joy. And whatsoever you touch will be transformed into gold, and whatsoever you say will have something poetic in it, and whatsoever you do will have grace, will have something divine about it, something sacred and holy.

Creativity is nothing that you have to do; *you* are the barrier — it is because of you that creativity is prevented. Make way. Don't stand in between. Move yourself away and let your void, your inner void, face existence.

And the inner void will reflect the existence and, out of that reflection, creativity is born.

But I am not talking about ordinary creativity: that you compose a poem or you paint a small painting or you sculpt. These things can be done without being creative; all that you need to know is the art, the technique of doing them. Out of one hundred so-called creators it is very rare to find even one or two who are *real* creators; ninety-nine percent are only composers, not creators. They know how to put words together, they are clever, they are cunning, they are crafty; what they are doing is not creativity. They are putting things together — maybe in new arrangements, but there is nothing original.

The original always comes from an egoless state, it always comes when you are absent. When you are absent, consciousness is present, God is present. And then something miraculous starts happening, not by you but *through* you. It gives you a great feeling of humbleness and gratitude.

So don't be worried about absolute negativity; that is one of the most beautiful spaces to be in. One can be in that space through absolute positivity also, but there is a danger: your mind can play tricks with the absolute positive. But it cannot play tricks with the absolute negative. With the absolute positive it can still hope to remain in some way or other; the positive seems to be sheltering, safe.

Hence, except with Gautam the Buddha, every other religion has used the positive. It is only Buddha who has used the negative. But you must know that more people have become enlightened through Gautam Buddha's approach than through all the other approaches put together for the simple reason that with the absolute negative there is no safety, no shelter at all for the mind, for the ego. It is total death.

That's why you are confused. I am happy that you are confused. I will be more happy if your confusion becomes a chaos. I will be still more happy if you disappear into a black hole, because then the only thing possible is that you will come out of a white hole. You will be resurrected.

Crucifixion is the way of resurrection. Death is the way of being reborn.

The second question

Bhagwan,
What is satori and how to attain it?

Pratima,

SATORI IS EXACTLY YOUR ORDINARY NATURE; it is not anything special. Hence there is no question of attaining it — it is already the case. You *are* in it, you have just forgotten. You have become too occupied with the outside world. You have forgotten your own kingdom, you have forgotten your own treasure, you have forgotten yourself. You have become too concerned with others. You are too much in the world and you don't give any time, any space for your inner nature to have a dialogue with you, to whisper a few things to you. You have become artificial.

You have created a false ego because nobody can live without a center. You have forgotten your real center, and nobody can live without a center, so you have created a false center as a substitute. That's the ego. Ego simply means living with a false center.

Satori is dropping the false, entering into the real; just being yourself, your natural self, your ordinary self.

The word "ordinary" has to be remembered because

the mind is not interested in the ordinary at all; it wants
to be extraordinary, it wants to be special. It is through
being special that the ego survives. It is constantly striv-
ing to be more special, more special. It wants to be more
rich, more powerful, more respectable; it is ambitious.
Hence the word "ordinary" has no appeal for the mind.
And that is the beauty of the word "ordinary" — because
it has no appeal for the mind.

Mind is an achiever and the ordinary need not be
achieved; it is already the case. The extraordinary has to
be achieved, the extraordinary becomes the goal. It is
far away; you have to make all kinds of efforts, you
have to struggle for it, you have to fight for it because
there are so many competitors.

To be ordinary . . . and there is no competition at all.
You can just be ordinary, nobody has any objection.
People will simply feel sorry for you that you have
dropped out of the competitive race. One competitor
less — they will feel good but sorry for you. They will
say, "Poor fellow! What happened to him? Why did he
have to drop out?" The dropouts are not respectable
people.

Buddha is a dropout. All real Masters are dropouts.
To be a sannyasin means to be a dropout. To drop out
of the rat race is to drop in, because when you are in the
race you cannot enter in. When you are no longer in the
race there is nowhere to go. You start moving inwards
because life is a flow: if there is no outer direction it
takes the inner direction. If the goal is not there far away
in the future, then you start moving into your nature in
the present. That is *satori.*

Satori is very ordinary. *Satori* means your nature.
You have come with it; it is your original face — all other
faces are masks.

Yoka says:

> *A disciple speaks in accordance with the ulti-*
> *mate, the absolute truth.*
> *Remember that one should cut the root and*
> *not the branches and the leaves.*

What is the root of your misery? The root is your
ambition, desiring. One wants to be this and that, one
wants to possess this and that, one wants to be somebody, one wants to be significant.

Yoka says: *Cut the root . . .* only then are you a
disciple. And the moment you cut the root — not the
branches, not the leaves — you attain the ultimate truth.
The ultimate truth is not far away; it is the *immediate*
truth, it is *your* truth, it is your very being.

> *Most people do not recognize the perfect*
> *jewel, the jewel of supreme wisdom, satori.*
> *It is hidden in the secret place of Tathagata,*
> *awaiting its discovery.*

It is to live in your suchness; it is hidden in your suchness. Whatsoever you are, live in it. Don't create any
conflict, don't live through the ideal. Don't be an idealist, just be natural.

But everybody is being taught to be an idealist: "Become a Jesus" or "Become a Buddha" or "Become a Krishna." Nobody tells you just to be yourself! Why should
you be a Jesus? One Jesus is enough and one Jesus is
beautiful — he enriches the existence. Many Jesuses just
carrying crosses, and wherever you go you meet them
. . . It won't look beautiful, it won't add to the beauty
of existence; it will make the whole world ugly. Wherever you go you meet a Mahavira standing naked. . . .

It is because of this that God never creates the same
person again. He never repeats; he is original. He always
creates a new person. You have never been before, and
there is no one who is like you, and there will never be

anybody else like you again. In the whole of eternity you alone are just like you. Look at the beauty of it and the glory of it and the respect that God has shown to you! What more respectability do you need? See the uniqueness of yourself. There is no need to be unique; you are already unique, just as everybody else is unique. You are unique in your ordinariness, in your suchness.

> *Satori is hidden*, says Yoka, *in the secret place of your suchness, awaiting its discovery.*

It has not to be created, it is already there; you just have to discover it. Go in and discover it! It is waiting and waiting. And centuries have passed and many many lives have passed, and you have become addicted to extroversion. You never move in.

The first step towards *satori* is meditation. *Satori* is the ultimate experience of meditation when meditation is fulfilled, when meditation has reached to its ultimate flowering.

Yoka says:

> *The world is complete illusion, yet nothing exists which might be called illusion.*

The world that you have created *through your mind* is illusory, but there is another world which is not your creation. When your mind disappears you discover that world: the world of suchness. That is a totally different experience. No words can describe it. Thousands of mystics have tried to describe it, but nobody has ever been able and nobody *will* ever be able to describe it. It is so mysterious, it is so beautiful that all words fall short. No poetry reaches to its level, no music even touches its feet.

> *The perfect light of this wisdom enlightens one.*

The moment you have put your mind aside — mind

means ambition, the ego trip of being this and that — the moment you have put the whole mind aside, a great light explodes in you and you are enlightened. This is *satori.* It does not come from the outside: you are not delivered by somebody else, you are delivered by your own being, by your own nature.

> *That is possible only by practicing zazen beyond speculation. You can see clouds naturally in the mirror but to hold on to the reflection is impossible.*

That is possible only by practicing zazen. . . Satori is possible only by practicing zazen. Zazen means:

Just sitting, doing nothing,
The spring comes and the grass grows by itself.

You are simply relaxing into your own being, not doing anything at all. It is not a question of doing, it is simply a question of being. You go on relaxing into your being. A moment comes when *you are* in your utter purity, in your utter simplicity, in your utter innocence. That is *satori.*

Zazen is a beautiful word. It simply means just sitting — not even doing meditation. In fact, you cannot *do* meditation. Meditation is just sitting silently; it is not a question of doing. If you are doing something you are disturbing your meditation.

Somebody is chanting a mantra; he is disturbing his meditation. Somebody is focusing on something; he is disturbing his meditation. Somebody is concentrating, somebody is praying, somebody is thinking of God: they are disturbing their meditation. All these are the doings of the mind, and if the doing continues the mind continues. Stop doing, and where is the mind? When the doing disappears, mind disappears. And the disappearance of the mind is *satori.*

It is *beyond speculation,* says Yoka. You cannot think

about it, you can only experience it. It is the ultimate experience, and the immediate experience, too, of truth, of beauty, of love, of bliss, of God, of *nirvana.*

The third question

Bhagwan,
I still don't believe that sex is stupid.

Yogesh,

It is not a question of your believing or not believing it; such is the case. What can I do? Sex *is* stupid. I feel sorry for you, but I have to tell the truth some day or other. Yes, I have been telling you, "From sex to superconsciousness," and you have been very happy — you only hear "from sex," you don't hear "to super-consciousness."

And this is the case with those who are against me and with those who are in favor of me — the same. Man is almost the same; friends and enemies are not very different. I am being misunderstood by the opponents, and that is understandable, but I am also being misunderstood by the followers; that is not understandable at all. The opponents can be forgiven, but the followers cannot be forgiven.

Because I said, "Sex is stupid," many angry questions have come to me. One of my sannyasins, Maya, has written to me: "You have some nerve to say that sex is stupid!" She must have felt hurt. And I can understand: when you are living in a certain way you don't want it to be described as stupid. Nobody wants to be called stupid. It is not over the question of sex that you are disturbed, it is your life. If it is stupid and you are living it, then you are being stupid. That hurts. But I have to say it even if it hurts because that is the only way to make you aware that there is something more in life, something higher, something greater, something far more blissful, far more orgasmic.

Sex is only a beginning but not the end. And nothing is wrong if you take it as a beginning; if you start clinging to it, then things start going wrong. If I say anything against homosexuality, immediately the homosexuals start writing to me. If I say anything against *anything*, there are people who will start writing. If it hurts *your* ego, then you are immediately ready to defend — not only to defend but to attack.

Yogesh, whatsoever you are doing is going to be stupid because unless something comes out of meditation it remains stupid. It is not only a question of sex. The way you eat is stupid, the things that you eat are stupid, not for any other reason than the simple reason that whatsoever you are doing is being done without any awareness. Stupidity is sleep. Stupidity is unintelligence.

Just watch people — what they are doing, what kinds of things they are doing. And whatsoever they are doing they are doing with the feeling that this is the right thing to do, that this is the most intelligent thing to do.

Abby, a well-stacked coed, was undressing when her roommate, Jean, said, "Do you know there is the impression of a large M on your stomach?"

"My fiance is in town this weekend," confided Abby, "and he likes to make love with his football-letter sweater on."

"Which school does he attend, Michigan or Minnesota?" questioned Jean.

"Neither," giggled Abby, "he goes to Wisconsin."

But tell her fiance that this is stupid and he will hit you on the head!

An ugly-looking little Italian guy always succeeded in picking up the best-looking girls in his favorite bar every night. The other guys in the car just couldn't understand how such a creep could be so irresistible to women.

One night they asked the bartender, "The guy's scoring so much — what is his secret?"

"Well," said the bartender, "I don't know if the guy's hung, but he's the only guy who comes in here who can lick his eyebrows with his tongue."

But nobody can tell the guy, "You are stupid."

Whatsoever you are doing seems to be the most intelligent thing in the world to do. Whatsoever space you are in seems to be the right space. Everybody else may be wrong, but not you. You have to become aware of this phenomenon; this is one of the greatest illusions of humanity. You have to be watchful. You have to learn to see that, yes, there are many things that *you* are doing which are stupid. How can it be otherwise? You are not meditative.

Yogesh, you are not a Buddha, you are not awakened. How is it possible that you can do something which is *not* stupid? So whatsoever you are doing is bound to be stupid — it is out of unawareness. You go on doing things, not exactly knowing why. How did you learn them? From whom did you learn them? Why did you learn them? There are millions of stupid people just like you, and you go on imitating them, you go on learning things from them.

Sex is one of the greatest intoxicants. It is in your very biology. It releases a certain drug in your very bloodstream and you become possessed; you are no longer in your senses, you don't know what you are doing. You are being forced to do it. Some unknown force — call it nature, biology, chemistry, hormones — whatsoever you want to call it — some unknown force, XYZ, forces you to do something. In your saner moments you also know that this is stupid: "What was I doing, and why? And what have I gained out of it?" And you know those saner moments also.

That's why, after making love, many women will cry and weep, for the simple reason that the whole thing seems to be so meaningless. Why? It may be a titillation for the moment, but the same titillation again and again is a repetition; you are not reaching anywhere. And the man immediately goes to sleep after making love, for the simple reason that he wants to avoid the saner moment so he need not think about it. And by the morning he will have forgotten all about it.

After making love, at least for one hour sit in zazen and you will see what I am saying. You will understand what I mean when I say sex is stupid. After making love make it a point to sit in zazen for one hour just watching what has happened. Were you the master of it or just a slave? If you were the master of it, then it is not stupid. If you were a slave, it is stupid, because by repeating it you are making your slavery more and more strong, you are feeding your slavery.

Yogesh, it is only through meditation that you will be able to understand what I have been telling you. It is not a question to be decided by argument, it can only be decided by your own meditation, your own understanding, your own awareness.

The fourth question

*Bhagwan,
I'm in Vipassana. Tell me a joke!*

Anand Sundardas,

I DO FEEL FOR YOU! *Vipassana* is really serious! Buddha invented it so that you can pass through hell on this earth and you need not go to the real hell. It is a process of cleansing you of all your past karmas. Better finish it! It is a torture because you don't know how to sit silently for so long. Your mind goes on thousands of trips. Sitting, sitting, sitting. . . . You feel sleepy and that is not allowed. And if you start dozing, a hit comes on your head — a really good hit to bring you back to your senses! You cannot escape either because I go on praising *vipassana* so much, saying that without *vipassana* there is no *satori*, no enlightenment.

So you say, "Okay, somehow I will pass through it. It is only a question of a few days. And one thing is certain: that many have survived, so there is no danger to life." Yes, your knees hurt and your body aches and you feel very restless and you are not allowed to move; you have to sit just like a Buddha-statue, doing a very stupid thing — watching your breath. Now what kind of thing is this for an intelligent man to do? And thousands of doubts arise: "What are you doing? Such a nice guy, sitting and watching your breath?" You would have made love to your girlfriend, you would have done a thousand and one things. And delicious foods appear . . . and it looks far better to sit in the Blue Diamond than to sit in zazen! "Why am I sitting here? What am I doing here?"

The mind goes on questioning you and there really seems to be no escape because it is all voluntary; nobody has forced you. Not only that — you have to pay for it! Have you ever heard of anybody paying to suffer in hell? But when you have to pay for it, then you think it is worth the suffering.

Mulla Nasruddin was saying that when he came to India for the first time, he was feeling very hungry. As he entered through the Himalayas he came across a man selling some strange fruit, very red, very beautiful. He asked the price. The man said, "Just two paise for the whole bucketful." So he purchased the whole bucket and then he started eating it — and it was fire! Tears were rolling down.

And a man was watching and he said, "What are you doing? This is not a fruit. You will kill yourself! This is a medicinal herb; it has to be taken only in very small amounts for particular diseases. What are you doing? You will go mad!"

He said, "Whatsoever happens, happens, but since I have paid two paise for it, I have to eat it!"

And he said, "I went on crying and tears went on flowing, but I finished it. I ate the whole bucketful of that nasty thing!"

When you pay, then you cannot escape. And we don't leave any loopholes; we make every effort so that nobody can escape.

The man was in jail for rape, murder, kidnapping and blackmail.

The lawyer said, "I found a loophole in your case. According to Abramovitz vs. Arcaro, January 6, 1911: Book III, Section II, page 6, paragraph 13, I think I've got the answer. Don't worry, I'll get you out. Just leave it to me. Now I'm leaving for Washington on Monday and I'll be back Friday. Meanwhile — try to escape!"

We don't leave any loopholes in the first place. There is no possibility to escape either, because whenever somebody escapes from Vipassana I send him back again. Vipassana has to be suffered for the simple reason that it makes you encounter yourself, it *forces* you to encounter yourself — your fidgetiness, your restlessness, your ugliness, your madness. It forces you to see all the rubbish that you are carrying within yourself. And that is one of the most essential steps to go beyond.

If you want to go beyond anything, first you have to encounter it. Without encountering it there is no transcendence. There is no shortcut, there is no way of by-passing it.

It is not that Buddha is a sadist and he is trying to torture you; he is simply making you aware of what you are. And you can never become aware if you remain occupied in your day-to-day business, in your day-to-day engagements. You are so engaged from morning till night that you don't have any time, any space to look within, to feel yourself, to see who you are, where you are, what you are doing.

Vipassana forces you — there is nowhere to go. You have to watch your breath, you have to look at your thoughts day in, day out.

After the seventh day, something starts settling. If you persist, if you persevere, if you are patient enough, your body learns to settle, your mind learns to settle, your breathing becomes calm and cool, almost invisible. But you can feel that something has changed; the climate is different: you are not fidgety, you are not restless. And suddenly, as if the sun had risen, all that neurotic fight disappears. The hell is over. A great peace descends on you, the silence that comes after the storm, and everything seems to be clean, very clean, spotlessly pure, innocent, as if a layer of dust has disappeared from your consciousness. Your consciousness seems to be transparent. You can see for the first time the green, the red, the gold of the trees. You can hear for the first time the song of the birds — as if something which was in your ears blocking them and something which was in your eyes like a curtain has disappeared. Suddenly you feel light, very light.

It is said: Angels fly because they take themselves lightly. You suddenly feel like light, so full of light and so light, that you can fly, almost fly. Gravitation has disappeared. You have entered into a different world: the world of grace.

And then, Sundardas, you will know a different quality of laughter arising in you. It will not be painted on the lips, it will be coming from your depth. And you will be laughing for no reason at all; you will *be* laughter. That is Zen laughter — unmotivated, out of sheer joy, out of sheer delight, out of sheer insight into things.

Yes, you need a beautiful joke!

After a day of long discussions at the World Religions Conference in Geneva, Rabbi Zuckerman found himself seated at the same dinner table as Father O'Malley.

The rabbi was partaking of koshered veal, while the priest was cutting into a thick slice of ham.

"Would ya like to try some of this ham, Rabbi?" asked the priest. "It's really good!"

"Ach, no," replied Rabbi Zuckerman, "it is against our religion."

"Ah, but it's so delicious! Are ya sure ya wouldn't like a taste?"

"Thank you, no," said the rabbi. "Since the time of Abraham, the flesh of the swine has been regarded as unclean by our people, and pork in all its forms is forbidden to us."

"Ah! Ya don't know what you're missin', Rabbi," said the priest, shoving down another mouthful of ham.

"Ach! But you have not tasted the gefiltefish that my wife makes, Father. How about your wife, Father? Is she a good cook?"

"Ah . . . well, Rabbi, that I cannot say, for I am not married."

"Not married? So what do you do for a screw?"

"For a . . . what?"

"I mean — where do you get your sex?"

"Sex?!" said the priest. "Alas, Rabbi, in my religion it is forbidden unto us, the servants of Our Lord, to partake of the ways of the flesh."

"You mean — you've never had sex?" asked the rabbi.
"No, I have not!" replied the priest.
"Oho! You ought to try it . . . it's better than pork!"

The fifth question

Bhagwan,
Do you really think that nothing beautiful
has ever come out of Italy?

Gautama,

I AM NOT AN EXPERT ON ITALY. I have not even tasted spaghetti!

My first Italian sannyasin, Veet Sandeh, once prepared spaghetti for me, but it smelled so awful — it smelled just like the Italians! — that I could not eat it. And Veet Sandeh was one of the most perfect Italians. I don't think she has ever taken a bath in her whole life!

So I don't really know whether anything beautiful has ever come out of Italy or not, but I can tell you what the experts say. They say that two things have come out of Italy, two beautiful things, but both are possessed by Sophia Loren.

The sixth question

Bhagwan,
I must be the most greedy person in the whole
world. What should I do about it?

Kamal,

ARE YOU CONFESSING or bragging? The world is very

big and what do you know about the whole world? It is impossible to be first in anything; not even in greed can you be the first, because people are moving in circles. Nobody is the first. Don't become so concerned with your greed and don't feel guilty either. Everybody is greedy.

Unless you know that you are deathless you will remain greedy; greed comes because of death. You may never have thought about it, but greed exists because we are afraid of death. Because death is there we want to have as much of life as possible; we are greedy. We want to eat more, we want to have as many women or men as possible, we want to have as much money as possible, because death is there. "Soon everything will be finished, so before it happens have all that is possible, don't miss a thing." That's how greed arises. Greed is nothing but fear of death. Greed is out of fear; it is the fearful person who becomes greedy.

The really fearless person is not greedy at all; he shares. He is not possessive, he is very happy to give. He goes on giving whatsoever he has; he goes on giving for the sheer joy of giving.

You will remain greedy, Kamal, unless you experience your eternity: that death is not going to make any dent in you, that death is not going to make any change in you, that death is only of the body, your consciousness continues. Your consciousness is the only eternal phenomenon. Everything else changes, but not your consciousness. But you don't know anything about consciousness, hence the greed.

All the religions of the world have been teaching, "Don't be greedy," but that has not made any difference. That has made people greedy for the other world, that's all. That has made people greedy for heaven and heavenly joys, that's all. But that has not changed their greed; it has even increased their greed.

I don't tell you not to be greedy. I say be conscious, be more conscious, and you will be surprised: as your consciousness grows, greed starts disappearing. Like dead leaves it starts falling; it leaves no trace behind.

Skolnik, the Scarsdale skinflint, awoke one morning to find that during the night his wife had died. After one glance at the stark form lying there beside him, he leaped out of bed and ran into the hall.

"Daisy," he called down to the maid in the kitchen, "come to the foot of the stairs, quick!"

"Yes," she cried. "What is it?"

"Only one egg for breakfast this morning!"

Can you beat that?

When the Internal Revenue Service hauled him in and wanted to know why he claimed his mother as an exemption in spite of the fact that she had been dead for five years, Bernstein said, "Oh, but Mom is still very much alive in my heart."

A Jewish couple went to a shopping center and left their child and carriage with the other carriages in front of the place. After shopping, they started for home. A few blocks later, the wife turned to her husband, who was wheeling the carriage, and cried in panic, "That's not our child!"

"Shut up your big mouth!" he replied. "This is a better carriage."

People are living in greed. Kamal, it will be difficult to be the first! Even to be aware that you are greedy is a good sign: it is a beginning, a good beginning, if you become aware of it. And remember, don't become guilty about it because that is a way of losing your awareness again. Don't start repenting of it because repenting means you are thinking about the past, which is no more. Don't start trying to be non-greedy because what-

100

soever you do will be greed — even the effort to be non-greedy will only be rooted in greed. One can become so greedy about being non-greedy!

I have seen people who have become so greedy about being non-greedy that they go on and on renouncing this and that. Their greed has taken a new turn: it is standing upside down, it is doing a *sirshasan,* a head-stand. Now they are greedy about non-greed; non-greed has become their possession, their money, their power. Now they are respected for their non-greed. They were respected first for their money; now they are respected for renouncing the money. Now they go on renouncing as much as they can — to the fullest extreme. They can renounce clothes, they can stand naked. They can renounce everything, but deep down the greed is there, they are still greedy. It is simply greed and nothing else. Now they are hoping that they will be rewarded in paradise — a great reward is waiting for them.

So don't try to become non-greedy. A greedy person cannot do anything about greed. And that's so about other things also. An angry person trying to be non-angry is not going to change his being. A violent person trying to be non-violent will still remain violent; his violence will now take subtle forms.

The only thing that is possible is to be conscious of your greed. And I am not saying that you will be rewarded in paradise, I am not saying anything about the future. I am simply saying that if you become aware of greed it disappears. And when it disappears, life is bliss *here and now* — not in the future, not as a reward.

Greed cripples you, anger cripples you, violence cripples you. When they all disappear. . . . And they all disappear through one method. A single method is enough — meditation is enough. All the diseases disappear through taking a single medicine.

The words "medicine" and "meditation" come from the

same root. Meditation is the ultimate medicine: it cures you of all ills.

Remember Yoka again. He says: Don't cut the branches, cut the root.

Unconsciousness is the root, Kamal. Cut the root, be conscious, and then, herenow, you are a new person. Herenow, your life is transformed, you become luminous, you radiate bliss, you radiate benediction, you become paradise.

Wherever a man of awareness moves there is paradise. You cannot send a man of bliss, of awareness, of meditation, of *satori*, to hell, because if he reaches hell, hell will be paradise for him. And you cannot send an unconscious man into paradise because wherever he is he will find his hell. If it is not there he will invent his hell — his unconsciousness will project his hell.

Reduced to a simple principle, the whole philosophy of all the awakened ones is: Unconsciousness is hell, consciousness is heaven.

The seventh question

Bhagwan,
I was born on February 29th, hence my birthday
comes only once in four years. Is there some
significance in it?

Gandharva,

JANUARY OR FEBRUARY OR MARCH, February 28th or 29th — these are all arbitrary. These are our imposed ideas. Existence knows nothing of February, March. Even if you were born on April 1st there is no significance in it! You will not be a bigger fool than you are, you will be the same. What significance can February 29th have? But people want some significance.

I have heard about only one accident that has happened on February 29th: that is the birth of Morarji Desai.

Zoo keeper to tourists: "In this cage we see the leopard. This animal has one black spot for every day of the year."
Old lady: "What about a leap year?"
Zoo keeper, thinking fast: "Ah yes — behold, madam, I lift his tail thus — behold the 29th of February!"

And the last question

Bhagwan,
How do you manage to deliver so many
beautiful discourses?

Devakar,

WHAT DISCOURSES? You call this yakkety-yak discourse? Discourse is a serious phenomenon! Discourse is something religious, holy, sacred. It is delivered in churches, temples. This place is not a church. This place belongs to the drunkards — it is a pub! What discourse? I have never delivered any discourse. Yes, I gossip, that is true, but there is no gospel in it and there is no art, no secret in it. It is very simple — my method is very simple.

A great emperor was passing through a village. He was one of the most famous warriors of those days and he was a lover of archery. He loved the people who were perfect archers. Passing through the village he saw on many trees, lampposts, and garden fences, arrows sticking exactly in the middle of circles — exactly in the middle, at the centers, of circles. So many arrows everywhere . . . he was surprised.

He asked, "Who is this man? I have never seen such a

perfect archer! His aim is perfect, he never misses, not even by a fragment of an inch. The arrow always goes exactly into the center. Each target is a proof of it." He stopped his chariot, he called the people of the village. He said, "Who is this man?"

And they all laughed and said, "Don't be worried about him. He is a madman!"

He said, "What do you mean by madman? He may be mad, but he is the greatest archer I have seen."

They said, "It is nothing to do with archery. He knows nothing about archery."

The king said, "But then it is a puzzle. How does he manage?"

They said, "It is simple. First he shoots the arrow at the tree and then he goes and makes a circle around it!"

That's exactly my method. It is simple! Hence you can ask anything. Whatsoever I want to say, I say it. First I shoot the arrow and then I draw a circle around it — just as a finishing touch!

A parish priest was having a few words with his bishop and in the course of conversation said, "It's all right for you, my Lord. When you prepare a sermon you can deliver it to several churches in the diocese, but I have to give two new sermons every Sunday."

The bishop replied, "You should be able to give a sermon on almost any subject at a moment's notice, as I can."

"I'll take you up on that," said the parson. "You come to my church next Sunday and I will put you to the test."

The bishop agreed and in due course went to the pulpit to find a card with the one word "constipation" written on it. Without hesitation he started, "And Moses took two tablets and went out onto the mountain side."

5

The first question

Bhagwan,
It feels that to be a witness is also a kind
of thought. So what is the difference between
the witness and a thought of the witness?

Satyendra Saraswati,

WITNESSING IS NOT A THOUGHT, but you can start
thinking about witnessing, you can make it a thought.
The moment you make it a thought, it is no longer witnessing. Either it is witnessing or it is a thought; it cannot be both together.

When you are witnessing you are not thinking that
you are witnessing. If you are thinking that you are
witnessing, this is not witnessing at all, it is another
kind of thought. If the witnessing is simple, there is no
thought of witnessing at all. If the thoughts are just
passing in front of your vision and you are witnessing
them, and no idea arises in you that "I am witnessing,"
then it is pure witnessing. It is not a thought at all, it is a
state of no-thought, no-mind. You are simply reflecting
whatsoever is passing by.

The moment you say, "Aha! This is witnessing. So I am witnessing. This is what meditation is. This is awareness," you have missed the point. You have fallen back into the mud of the mind. You are no longer a witness. You have become identified. Witnessing cannot be reduced to a thought.

But your problem is significant. It is encountered by almost every meditator. We have become so habituated to witnessing in a wrong way. We *think* that we witness. We judge, we evaluate, but we think that we witness. We think that we witness, and it is not witnessing. We are associated with a wrong kind of witnessing, and that idea lingers for a long time.

Secondly: we have become so conditioned to immediately reducing every experience into a thought. We never allow any experience to remain just a pure experience, even for a few moments.

You come across a beautiful rose flower in the garden. The moment you see it, almost instantly you say inside, "How beautiful!" You can't let that beauty sink in. The thought of beauty becomes a barrier. The moment you say, "How beautiful!" you have already started comparing it with other roses that you have seen in the past. You have started comparing it with all that you have heard about roses. You are no longer seeing *this* rose. You are missing its suchness. You have gone into the past. You are searching in your memory to discover how many roses you have seen before: "And this is the best one." But this rose is no longer there in your awareness. Your awareness has become very clouded. So much smoke has come from the past, so much dust has arisen that your mirror is no longer reflecting the beauty. You are not now-here.

Allow the rose and its fragrance and its beauty and its dance in the wind and the sun to penetrate you. Don't bring your mind in. There is no need to say that this is beautiful. If it is, there is no need to say it; if it is not, then it is false to say it. Either it is or it is not. To create a thought about it in any way is to create ripples in your consciousness. It is like throwing a pebble into a silent lake. Just a moment ago it was reflecting the moon and the stars so beautifully, and your pebble has created ripples, and the moon and the stars have all become distorted.

That's what happens whenever a thought arises in you: your consciousness is disturbed, starts wavering. Waves start arising in you. Now you are not capable of reflecting that which is.

You will have to learn this new art of seeing things without judging, of seeing things without verbalizing, of seeing things without evaluating. See the rose, see the bird on the wing, see the night full of stars, see the river passing by, see the traffic. Listen to the songs of the birds or a train passing by. Start learning a new art of just being reflective, not bringing any thought in, not saying anything at all.

It will take a little time — old habits die hard — but one day it happens. If you persist, if you are patient enough, if you go on and on working at cleaning your inner world, one day it happens. And the benediction of that day is immense. In fact, that day you are born anew. You start seeing the same world with new eyes because your eyes are so clear, your mirror reflects so deeply, so totally, without distortion, that trees — the same trees that you have seen before thousands of times — are far more green than they have ever been. And their greenness is no ordinary greenness: it is luminous, it is radiating light.

It is the same world, the same people. . . . A Buddha walks, a Jesus walks in the same world — the same trees, the same rocks, the same people, the same sky — but they live in paradise and you live in hell. The difference is created by the mind.

It will take a little while to drop this mind. It has dominated you for so long that it is difficult in the beginning to suddenly disassociate yourself from it. It clings. It can't leave its power over you so easily. Hence it goes on coming in from the back door.

You are sitting silently and a beautiful stillness arises, and the mind comes in from the back door and says, "Look, how beautiful this moment is!" And it has taken you away! It came so silently, without making any noise, and you were caught by it in such a subtle way that you could not have been aware of it. You rejoiced, you thanked the mind . . . but it has destroyed your stillness.

When stillness is really true there is no mind to say anything about it. When witnessing is true you are simply a witness. You don't think, "I am witnessing." There is no "I," there is no thinking, there is only the witness, because all thinking, and the "I" — they have all become contents, objects of your witnessing. And witnessing itself cannot be its own object. No mirror can reflect itself. Your eyes cannot see themselves. Your witness cannot witness itself, that's impossible.

Your question is relevant. And you will have to be very very careful, watchful. It is a razor's edge. One has to be very cautious because if you fall, you fall into a deep abyss. The ordinary people cannot fall; they have nowhere to fall to — they are already at the bottom. But as you start moving higher, the possibility of falling down grows every day. When you reach the Everest of your consciousness, just a little slip, just a little wrong step, and you will go rolling down into a deep abyss.

The greater the meditation, the greater the danger of losing it — naturally; only a rich man can be robbed, not a poor man. That's why a beggar can sleep under a tree in the afternoon and the noise of the traffic and the marketplace . . . nothing disturbs him. He can sleep anywhere, he can sleep deeply. He has nothing to lose — no fear.

Once, at night, a king came across a very strange man, a very luminous man, standing alert underneath a tree — so silent, so quiet and so alert. The king was curious: "Why is he standing there?" From his appearance he looked like a monk, one who has renounced the world. The king was a very cultured man and he thought, "It is not right to disturb him." But every night it happened.

That was the routine of the king: to go around the capital at night in disguise to see how things were going — whether the guards were on duty or not; mixing and meeting with people, going into the hotels and the theaters to find out how things were going — whether things were all right or not.

Every night he would come across this man. He saw this man so many times that it became impossible to resist the temptation. One day he approached him and asked, "Excuse me, sir, I should not interfere — you look so silent — but why do you go on standing the whole night? What are you guarding? Is there any treasure underneath this tree?"

The mystic laughed. He said, "Not underneath this tree, but within me there *is* a treasure and I am watching it. And the treasure is growing every day, it is becoming bigger and bigger, hence I have to be more and more alert."

The mystic said to the king, "You can sleep, you have nothing to lose. I cannot, I have much to lose; and if I can remain awake I have much to gain."

The king was very much impressed. He asked him to come to his palace, he invited him. The monk agreed. The king was a little puzzled: a monk agreeing so soon without even refusing once is not thought to be right. A monk should say, "No, I cannot come to the palace. I have renounced the world. It is all futile. It is all dream, illusion, *maya.* I cannot come back to the world. I am happy wherever I am."

But this monk didn't say anything. He was a Zen Master. The king started thinking in his mind, "Have I been deceived by this man? Was he simply standing there every night just to catch hold of me?"

But now it was too late; he had invited him.

The mystic came to the palace, lived with the king. And, of course, he lived more joyously than the king because he had no worries, no cares about the empire, no problems and no anxieties. He enjoyed good food, and the king had given him the best room in the palace — he lived just like an emperor!

Six months passed. Now the king was boiling within himself to ask him, "What kind of renunciation is this? You are enjoying everything — servants and good food and good clothes and a beautiful palace."

One day, walking in the garden, he asked the mystic, "Can I ask you a question? Forgive me if you feel offended. This is my question: What is the difference now between me and you?"

The mystic looked at the king and he said, "Why did you wait for six months? This question you could have asked me the very first night. The moment you invited me and I accepted your invitation, this question arose in your mind. Why did you wait for six months? You tortured yourself unnecessarily. I was expecting it at any moment. There is no question of my feeling offended — it is a natural question.

"There *is* a difference, but it is very subtle. And if you really want to know the difference, then come with me. I cannot tell you here. I will tell you in a certain space, at a certain place. Come along with me."

They both went outside the city. The king said, "Now can you tell me?"

The mystic said, "Come along."

When they were crossing the boundary of his empire — it was evening — the king said, "What are you doing? Where are you taking me? Now this is the end of my empire. We are entering somebody else's kingdom and I would like to be answered. What is your answer? And I am feeling very tired."

And the mystic said, "My answer is that I am going. Are you coming with me or not? I am not going back."

The king said, "How can I come with you? I have my whole empire, my wife, my children. How can I come with you?"

The mystic said, "That's the difference. But I am going!"

Again the king saw the light, the beauty of the man, and fell at his feet. He said, "Come back! I am just stupid. I have missed these six months. I have been thinking things which are really ugly. Forgive me and come back."

The mystic said, "There is no problem for me. I can come back, but you will again think the same. It is better for me now to go ahead — that story is finished, that chapter is closed — so that you can remember the difference."

The witness lives in the world just like a mirror, reflecting everything. He may be in a hut, he may be in a palace; it makes no difference. What difference does it make to a mirror whether the mirror is in a hut or in a palace? What difference does it make to the mirror whether the mirror is reflecting beautiful diamonds or just ordinary stones? It makes no difference to the mirror.

Witnessing is the art of transcending the world. Witnessing is the very essence of Zen, of religion itself. But don't make it a thought — it is not a thought at all. Thoughts have to be witnessed. Even if the thought of witnessing arises, witness that thought. Remember that it is not witnessing, it is only a thought — it has to be witnessed. It is there in front of you. You are not it.

The witness is irreducible to any thought; it always goes on sliding back. You cannot catch hold of it through any thought. It can witness each and every thought, the thought of witnessing included; hence, it can never itself become a thought.

Next time when you are meditating, Satyendra Saraswati, remember it. Don't start enjoying the thought that "This is a beautiful moment. My mind is silent, my being is still. This is witnessing!" The moment you say it, you have lost it.

The second question

Bhagwan,
Please say something more about the man of Zen.

Pratibha,

THE MAN OF ZEN IS VERY ORDINARY, extraordinarily ordinary. He is so ordinary that there is every possibility if you meet him you will not be able to recognize him. He lives just like you, eats like you, sleeps like you. He is in every way just like you. As far as his outside is concerned he is not different from you at all.

The difference is certainly there, but that difference is inner. He has an insight, he has a clarity. He has eyes and you are blind. He is awake and you are asleep. You are drunk: drunk with greed, drunk with lust, drunk with anger, ambition, ego.

The man of Zen is simply not drunk; he is in his senses. He walks consciously, he sits consciously: "walking in Zen, sitting in Zen." He is not in any way special. He is not like other so-called saints. He will not lie down on a bed of thorns or on a bed of nails, he will not stand on his head. He is not stupid, he is not an exhibitionist. He will not walk naked in the streets. He is not mad, he is not neurotic! He lives in the very ordinary way, in the very normal way.

That's why it is the most difficult thing to recognize the man of Zen. You can recognize a saint who walks on water — naturally, it is so obvious that he is special. But a man of Zen does not walk on water. He does not perform any miracles. He does not play any kind of egoistic games. He is not an ego, he is not even a person. He is just a presence, a nonentity. He is absolute nothingness. Only when one is absolute nothingness is one full of awareness. Whatsoever he does, he does with totality. Only a man who is not drunk can do things totally. Otherwise one remains partial; only a part goes on doing something and at the same time other parts may be going against it, being destructive. You may be creating something with one hand and destroying it with the other.

A man who is drunk does not know where he is going. He thinks he is on the right path, but that is only his dreaming.

Barry Higgins, a traveling salesman, was driving home to London one afternoon after a hard-drinking lunch with a prospective customer. Through the rearview mirror he spied the flashing blue light of a police car behind. A shiver went up his spine and he grasped the steering wheel tightly to steady his driving. The blue light approached, a siren wailed, and a police car overtook him with a hand signalling him to pull to a stop.

Barry was nervous as he saw the policeman get out of his car. His breath was heavy and his hands were moist on the steering wheel. He wondered what he was going to say.

The policeman came up and bent to speak through the car window. "Ay, ay, now then, had a few, eh?"

Barry could not stop himself and blurted, "Ohh . . . g . . . good onsternoon, afterble, I . . . I'm not as think as you drunk I am!"

The man of Zen is absolutely conscious — no greed, no anger, no jealousy, no ambition. These are all intoxicants, these are all drugs: they go on keeping you sleepy. It is a miracle how you manage your life with so many poisons running in your bloodstream, in your very being. That is the only difference; otherwise, from the outside, you will not know.

There are other so-called saints who make outside differences because there is no inner difference. They have to stand naked, they have to torture their bodies, they have to go on fasting. They have to distort their bodies, cripple their bodies. They have to do something that makes them more special than you, "holier than thou."

A Zen man is not "holier than thou." He has no idea of being in any way higher than you. He is simply living his nature.

Yoka says: The man of Zen goes alone.

That is his first characteristic. He is not part of a mob psychology. He is not Hindu, he is not Mohammedan, he is not Christian, he is not Jewish. He is not Indian, he is not Japanese, he is not Chinese — he cannot be. He never belongs to any crowd. He is alone. He is a rebel. He lives according to *his* light. He does not follow, he does not imitate. He has reached the goal.

What is the goal? The goal is not somewhere outside you. It is not there, far away like a star; it is within you, it is your own interiority. He has entered his own interiority. And the man who has reached his goal . . .

    . . . *can play on the path of nirvana.*

He is playful, he is not serious. He cannot be serious: the whole of life is a divine play, *leela,* and he is part of

114

it. He is just playing a role. He acts the role as beautifully as he can, as perfectly as he can, but he knows that the whole world is a big stage, a great drama — but nothing more. So he is not serious about it.

> *The man of Zen has natural manners and is*
> *harmonious.*

He does not pretend to be special, he *has natural manners.* He is very human, utterly human. His humanity is superb, intense, absolute. He does not claim any sacredness — and because he does not claim he *is* sacred. He is harmonious. He is not divided within himself, he is not in a constant fight with himself, he is not in a constant civil war. He has a melody, a music. If you sit by his side you will be able to listen to the music.

Navanit asked just the other day: "Bhagwan, whenever I come close to you I immediately smell a certain fragrance. What fragrance is it?" I don't use any perfume — I cannot. Navanit is a doctor, he knows; hence the question has become more pertinent to him. And he says that he always finds the same fragrance whenever he is close to me.

That fragrance has nothing to do with any perfume. It is the fragrance of harmony, it is the music. It expresses itself in a multi-dimensional way. Sometimes you will hear it as a silent sound like a murmur, the wind passing through the pine trees, or the sound of running water. Sometimes you will hear it as music and sometimes you will experience it as a smell, a beautiful fragrance. Sometimes you will see it as an aura, a light, very mysterious.

But the man of Zen simply lives in harmony, and out of harmony all these things are manifested.

> *His spirit is simple, clean, pure and sincere.*
> *His Zen, which no one sees, is treasure be-*
> *yond all value.*

You can see his body, you cannot see his Zen. You cannot see his inner meditativeness, you cannot see his awareness unless you become aware yourself. You can know only that much which you have experienced.

Navanit, you are blessed that you are experiencing a certain fragrance. That means you are reaching to a certain depth, a certain height in your being.

> *His Zen, which no one sees, is treasure beyond all value.*
> *This jewel, rare and of incalculable value, never changes however one uses it.*
> *And others can freely benefit from it on all occasions.*

The man of Zen is always overflowing with joy. You can share it. He is a giver: he gives delight, he gives joy, he gives beauty, he gives truth. He radiates truth, he radiates God, but so silently . . . without any declaration. He goes on pouring his blessings into existence. He is a blessing to the world.

The third question

Bhagwan,
I know my love stinks, so why do I cling to the smell?

Prem Amrito,

WE LIVE according to the past: our lives are rooted in the dead past, we are conditioned by the past. The past is very powerful, that's why you go on living in a certain pattern; even if it stinks, you will go on repeating it. You don't know what else to do; you have become conditioned to it. It is a mechanical phenomenon. And this is not only so with you, Amrito, it is so with almost every human being — unless he becomes a Buddha.

To become a Buddha means to get rid of the past and to live in the present. The past is immense, very huge, enormous, of millions of lives. You have lived in a certain way. Now, being here, you may have become aware that your love stinks, but that awareness is also not very deep, it is very superficial. If it becomes really deep, if it penetrates to the very core of your being, you will immediately jump out of it.

It is like if your house is on fire you will not ask anybody how to get out of it. You will not consult the *Encyclopaedia Britannica,* and you will not wait for some wise man to come and tell you, and you will not consider whether it is appropriate to jump out of the window or not — you won't bother about anything. Even if you are taking a bath naked you will jump naked out of the window; you won't even bother about clothes. When the house is on fire, your life is at risk; now everything else is secondary.

If your love stinks — this has become your experience — then you will come out of it. You will not simply ask a question, you will jump out of it.

But I think that it is just an intellectual idea, because each time you are in love, some misery arises. Each time there is some conflict, some struggle, some fight, some jealousy, some possessiveness. So you have started taking an intellectual standpoint: "My love stinks, so why do I cling to the smell?" Because it is not yet really an existential experience for you.

And it is your own smell. One becomes accustomed to one's own smell. That's why when people are alone they don't experience that smell, they experience it only when they are together with somebody.

When you are in love, then you start showing your real face. Love is a mirror. The other starts functioning as a mirror. Every relationship becomes a mirror. Alone, you don't experience your own smell — you cannot; one becomes immune to it. You have lived with it so long, how can you smell it? It is only with the other that you start feeling that *he* stinks and he starts feeling that *you* stink. And the fight starts. . . . That is the story of all the couples all over the world.

"Where are you going with that goat, Juan?" asked the policeman.

"I'm taking him home to keep as a pet!" replied Juan.

"In the house?"

"Sure thing."

"But what about the smell?"

"So what? He ain't gonna mind the smell!"

Your own smell is not disturbing to you. In fact, if it suddenly disappears you will feel a little jolted, you will feel a little uprooted, you will not feel your natural self; you will feel something has gone wrong.

If you love and there is no jealousy you will start wondering whether you love or not. What kind of love is this? There seems to be no jealousy! You love a man, and if the man goes with another woman once in a while, you don't make much fuss about it. You take it for granted — it is perfectly good for a change. And if your man is happy, why not let him be happy? You love him. If you really love him you will respect his happiness too. And he is not going forever.

In fact, if once in a while couples are allowed a little freedom, they will not separate; the divorce rate will drop in the world. Divorce exists only because marriage is too tight. Let marriage be a little more relaxed and divorce will disappear. Divorce is only a by-product of marriage. The tighter the marriage system, the more divorce becomes an absolute need. And if divorce is not allowed, then you have double lives: one to show to the society and one to live.

It is because of marriage that prostitution exists in the world. The whole blame goes to the marriage system. If people are a little more loving and less jealous and if they understand human nature, it is simple.

You eat the same food every day; you get fed up with it and once in a while you would like to go to the hotel. And the hotel food may be worse than what you get in your home, but even that is good — at least that makes your home food look better. And when you come back the next day you feel so relieved that you are back home, and you are so happy to have the same food again!

The more man's mind is understood, the more and more marriage will have to be relaxed. It is perfectly okay to give a few days off in marriage. The woman should be allowed to have her boyfriends and the man should be allowed to have his girlfriends — at least, just as you have Sunday religion, a Sunday marriage! And you will be surprised that your own wife looks far better. Again a honeymoon starts — a mini-honeymoon. You again start from ABC.

And being with many women and with many men does not destroy marriage — no, not at all. It is a very nonsensical idea that has prevailed over humanity: that it is destructive to marriage and family. It is not so — it is very supportive. It will help the family to be more joyous, less quarrelsome. Otherwise, the woman is constantly spying on the husband and the husband is constantly spying on the woman. And what love can exist between two persons who are constantly at each other's throats?

Yes, your love stinks, as everybody else's love stinks, but you feel it only when you are in relationship. You have not yet felt that it really has something to do with you. Deep down you still feel it must be something wrong with the other. That's how the mind functions: it throws the responsibility on the other. It accepts itself and it is always finding faults in others.

Several people are sitting in the front row of a movie theater. The show has already begun when suddenly there is a terrible smell.

One of the spectators turns to the man sitting beside him and asks, "Did you shit in your trousers?"

The man beside him answers, "Yes, why?"

People accept themselves totally! Whatsoever *they* are doing is right: "Why? What is wrong in it? They are his own trousers, so who are you to interfere? And freedom is everybody's birthright!"

Amrito, if your love stinks, then try to find out what exactly it is that stinks. It is not love, it is something else. Love itself has a fragrance; it can't stink, it is a lotus flower. Something else must be in it — jealousy, possessiveness. But you have not mentioned jealousy and possessiveness. You are hiding them. Love never stinks, it cannot; that is not the nature of love. Please try to see exactly what it is that creates the trouble. And I am not saying to repress it. All that is needed is a clarity about it — what it is.

If it is jealousy, then I would only suggest one thing: be more watchful of your jealousy. When it arises next time, rather than becoming mad, close your doors, sit silently, sit in meditation, watch your jealousy. See exactly what it is. It will surround you like smoke, dirty smoke. It will suffocate you. You would like to go out and do something. But don't do anything; just be in a state of non-doing, because anything done in a moment of jealousy is going to be destructive. Just watch. And I am not saying repress it, because that is again doing something.

People are either expressive or repressive, and both ways are wrong. If you express you become destructive to the other person. Whosoever is your victim suffers, and he is going to take revenge. He may not take revenge consciously, but unconsciously it is going to happen.

Just a few months ago, Krishna Bharti fell in love with a woman. Nothing extraordinary about it, but Deeksha got mad! Deeksha could not accept the idea. For centuries we have been told that if a man loves you or a woman loves you and the man or the woman goes to somebody else, that is a rejection of you.

That is utter nonsense. It is not rejection; in fact, it is just the opposite. If a man loves the woman and he enjoys the woman, he starts fantasizing how it will be with other women. It is really the joy that this woman has given him that triggers his fancy. It is not that he is rejecting this woman; it is really an indication that this woman has been such a nourishment that he would like to see and know how other women are. And if a little rope is given he is not going to go very far, he will come back, because with the other woman it may be novelty, it will be something new, but it can't be that nourishing because there will not be any intimacy. It will have something empty about it. It will be sex without love.

Love needs time to grow, it needs intimacy to grow. It needs a really long time. It is not a seasonal flower that is there within three, four weeks, but then within three, four weeks it is gone too. It is a long long process of intimacy. Slowly slowly, two persons melt and merge into each other; then it becomes nourishing. The other woman or the other man cannot be nourishing. It may be just an adventure, a thrill. But then suddenly the feeling will arise — it is bound to arise — that it is good as fun, but it is not nourishing. And the person will be back.

And Krishna Bharti would have been back, but Deeksha went mad. She behaved just like any other woman! But I was waiting . . . sooner or later she was going to take revenge. Now she is taking revenge.

Krishna Bharti fell ill, he was in hospital, and Deeksha had a little freedom. She fell in love with her own handyman! He really proved handy! Now K.B. is in hell.

There is no need to be so worried about it. I have given K.B. a message: "Wait, don't be worried. Just let her take revenge. And it is good that unconscious burden is finished."

If we understand each other a little more, if we understand human nature a little more, there should be no jealousy. But it is a past heritage of centuries.

So, Amrito, I cannot say you can drop it right now. You will have to meditate over it. Whenever it possesses you, meditate over it. Slowly slowly, the meditation will create the distance between you and the jealousy. And the greater the distance, the less jealousy will arise. And one day, when there is no jealousy, your love releases such a fragrance that no flower can compete with it. All flowers are poor compared to the flowering of love.

But your love is crippled because of jealousy and possessiveness and anger.

It is not love that stinks, remember, because I have seen people who think it is love that stinks so they close up, they become closed, they stop loving.

That's what has happened to millions of monks and nuns down the ages: they became closed to love, they dropped the whole idea of love. Rather than dropping jealousy, which would have been a revolution, rather than dropping possessiveness, which would have been something of immense value, they dropped love. That is easy, that is not much; anybody can do that. To be a monk or a nun is very easy, but to love and not to be jealous, to love and not to be possessive, to love and let the other have the whole freedom is really a great achievement. Only then will you feel love and its fragrance.

The fourth question

Bhagwan,
What do you think? Is Jesus coming back to
earth again as he had promised or not?

Sujata,

ONCE A MAN becomes awakened he cannot come back. He promises out of his compassion, but it is not possible. It is not possible because it is against the law of life. Jesus *has* promised to come back, Buddha also has promised to come back, Krishna has also promised to come back. Nobody has come yet and nobody is going to come back. It is against the law of life. They promise because of their compassion, their love. They promise because they see your misery, they see your sad state of affairs, they see your tears. So they promise, and their promise fulfils a certain purpose. Because of their promise you go on remembering them and that remembrance helps you. Because of their promise you go on connecting yourself to them, surrendering to them, and that surrendering helps. But they cannot fulfil their promise.

Once a man is awakened there is no possibility of his being born again. One can be born only if something in him has still remained unconscious. Life is an opportunity to become conscious. It is a school, a training school, where people become centered, rooted, integrated. Once they have become integrated, once they have attained self-realization, they cannot be allowed back into the school. They disappear into the universal. They become part of God.

So the first thing to be remembered: Jesus, Krishna or Buddha cannot come, but that does not mean that awakened people will not be there. There will be people like Jesus, like Buddha, like Krishna — of the same quality. Maybe their faces will not be the same and their bodies may not be the same. . . .

And who would like to have a body like Jesus? You don't know about Jesus, that's why. He was only four feet five inches, and a hunchback! And it is said in the old scriptures that he was the ugliest man who has walked on the earth. Who would like to have his body?

But his disciples have said he was the most beautiful man. They saw his beauty; that is of the inner, hence there is no contradiction. The disciples saw the inner. They saw the real Jesus, the pillar of his consciousness. They saw his interiority. They communed with his *being.* And, yes, there has never been such a beautiful man.

But the others saw only his body; the others could not see his soul, the others could not see his Zen. Only his disciples could see his Zen, his meditativeness, his love. Only his disciples could feel who he was, his divineness. They could say, "He is the most beautiful man who has ever walked on the earth."

And the descriptions are so contradictory that it has been a problem for the historians how to decide what is right. Both are right; there is no need to decide. It is not a question of choosing this or that.

And, in the second place, even if it were possible for him to come back, do you think he is mad? What did you do with him when he was here? Just remember it: you tortured him as you have never tortured anybody else before him.

Socrates' death was not a torture. He was given poison and within minutes he was dead. His death was a silent one.

The way Jesus was crucified is one of the most violent ways . . . sometimes it takes three days for the person to die. Just nailing a man on a cross cannot kill him immediately. Blood starts oozing from his body slowly slowly. Life starts oozing out, but very slowly. Even the weakest man will take at least six to eighteen hours to die, and if the man is healthy he can take even three days or more. This is real hell! This is real torture!

He was dying on the cross, and people were throwing stones and abuse. Soldiers were poking their spears into his body, and blood was coming out of his body. He was alive, he was thirsty, and they would not give him water. He was crying for water. And one hundred thousand people had gathered to see this torture.

What did you do with Jesus when he was here? I think that was enough to keep him away from this earth forever!

A new arrival knocked on heaven's door. Jesus was on duty and opened the door.

"Who are you?" he asked.

"Adolf Hitler," came the reply.

"Adolf Hitler! You cannot come here. You are a megalomaniac bent on world domination. Get away!"

"But I want to mend my ways!"

"No way! Get out!"

"Ah, if you will let me in, I will give you something."

"Well," said Jesus, weakening a little, "what is it?"

Hitler, in dress uniform, pulled off his special Iron Cross and showed it to Jesus. "Well," he asked, "can I come in?"

"You just wait here. I'll go and ask my dad."

Jesus found God in his study. "Dad, there's a newcomer at the gate who wants to come in."

"Who is he?"

"Adolf Hitler."

"Adolf Hitler! That megalomaniac bent on world domination? He can't come in here!"

"But he has something very special to give me."

"What is it?"

"His Iron Cross."

God thumped his chair. "What do you need an iron cross for? Hell, you couldn't even carry that wooden one!"

You forced poor Jesus to carry his own cross. He was weak; he had not slept the whole night — the whole night he was tortured and questioned and investigated. And then he had to carry that big wooden cross. He fell thrice on the road under the burden of the cross. He was hurt and wounded, but the soldiers whipped him again and forced him to carry his cross.

He was only thirty-three years old. He had not seen much of life yet; in fact, it was just the beginning. Had he lived as long as Buddha, the world would have been enriched far more. Buddha lived eighty-four years, Mahavira lived eighty years, Krishna almost the same age. They died at a ripe old age. They saw the whole of life with all its ups and downs, success and failure, misery and joy, ecstasy and agony. They became mature and ripe. They could give to the world something immensely valuable.

Jesus was allowed only three years. He started his ministry when he was thirty years old and he was killed when he was thirty-three. Just three years! He could not do much. He could have done great work for humanity, but we killed him. And now we are waiting for his next coming.

And if he comes you will do the same again, because you are doing the same again to people of that quality, of that insight. You have always been behaving as inhumanly as possible with the Buddhas.

Jesus is a Buddha. That is exactly the meaning of the word "Christ." "Christ" and "Buddha" are synonymous. Buddha means the awakened one, Christ means the crowned one. It is awakening that becomes your crowning, that makes you an emperor, that takes all suffering away from you and gives you the kingdom of God.

No, even if he *could* come he will not decide to come.

And man has not learned anything. After Jesus, you did the same with Al-Hillaj Mansur. Even more ugly

126

was the behavior with Al-Hillaj Mansur. And the same is the attitude of the masses even today. Nothing has changed. Man seems to be stagnant, stubborn, just living an unconscious life and repeating it.

But, Sujata, why should you be waiting? You can find the awakened ones any time; they are always available. Fortunately, there is always somebody who is a Buddha. And those who are real seekers are bound to find him because he is also seeking and searching for the real seekers. It is not a one-way search.

If you have come here in search of me, I am also searching in my own way for you. It is not one-way. If you are here, you are here only because I have invited you to be here. You are here only because I have called you forth to be here.

Now don't waste your time thinking about whether Jesus will come or not. What do you want with Jesus? I am ready to give you all that Jesus can give to you. Be receptive, be surrendered, because he will ask for the same conditions to be fulfilled. He cannot just deliver you as you are; you will have to fulfil a few conditions. You will have to drop your ego; that is the basic requirement. Fulfil that.

And I am your Jesus. Of course, the body is different, the mind is different, but the consciousness is never different. Two awakened persons are exactly the same. They belong to the same dimension, the same fragrance, the same harmony, the same bliss, the same godliness.

The fifth question

Bhagwan,
Is there a place for competitive sport
in the new commune?

Anand Murti,

In the new commune there will be a new organization called "Athletics Anonymous." When you get the urge to play golf, baseball, or anything else involving physical activity, someone will be sent over to drink with you until the urge passes.

The sixth question

Bhagwan,
I am a Jew, Italian, and a psychologist!
Is there any hope for me?

Anand Shravan,

You are really fortunate! There is every hope for you; in fact, you cannot miss. Even if you want to miss you cannot, because the Jew is going to kill the poor Italian, and the psychologist is going to kill the poor Jew, and when there is nothing left for the psychologist, they almost always tend to commit suicide!

And the last question

Bhagwan,

Are you pushing my pleasure button?
When I sit in lecture I am all smiles
and it takes me hours to wipe it off
my face.

Parmita,

You fool! Why do you try to wipe it off? I make so

much effort to create it and you take hours to wipe it off! Never do it again—so that it becomes something permanent, something essential with you, something natural, something that surrounds you.

But I know people are afraid of smiling, because if you are caught red-handed by others smiling for no reason at all, they think you are crazy. So people repress their smiles. That's why Parmita must have been trying to wipe it off.

But when I push the button I really push the button, and now I am going to push harder! You will not be able to wipe it off even if you make effort for hours or for days! Enjoy it! And what does it matter if people think you are crazy? Why be worried about it? There is nothing wrong in being crazy. Here, at least, everything is crazy!

Just the other day somebody asked, "Bhagwan, there are so many clocks in the ashram. Why do they all show different times?" Just crazy—cuckoo clocks! And if they all show the same time, then what would be the need for so many clocks? Then one would be enough!

Parmita, one joke for you:

A young nurse's first duty on her new job was to bathe the man in room 305. She performed her task and quickly returned to the nursing station.

"How was he?" asked her supervisor, an old, seasoned nurse.

"He was doing fine," she said, "but there was a very strange thing . . . he had the word 'little' tattooed on his prick."

The older nurse was very curious and decided to check it out. She returned forty-five minutes later, hair messed up, clothes askew, and said to the young nurse, "Honey, that tattoo does not say 'little.' It says, 'Little Rock, Arkansas, Pride of the South'!"

6

The first question

Bhagwan,
Why do I want to wake up when, as you say,
awakening only happens when I am not?
This seems very paradoxical.

Deva Satyarthi,

THE EGO IS NOT YOUR REAL SELF; the ego is a false entity, arbitrary. It is the ego that is your sleep, that surrounds you like a darkness, like a cloud. Hidden behind this darkness is your real self, your real being, which wants to wake up, which wants to get out of all this smoke, out of all this darkness, which wants to get out of the prison of the ego.

There is really no paradox, it only appears so. It *appears* paradoxical. Your question seems relevant . . . but you have two selves. One is the real: the one that you were born with, the one that was even before your birth, the one that will be there even when death has happened, the one that is running underneath like a hidden current. And the other is created by you, by your family, by your church, by your society, by your state, by the crowd.

This false one is a pretender: it pretends to be the real self. And the real self wants to come out of this unreal one surrounding it. It is a constant suffering for the real self because the real is being suffocated by the unreal; the real feels imprisoned in a dark cell. The real self is vast and has become confined in a very small space. It is crippling and paralyzing.

So when I say awakening happens only when you are not, I mean when your false ego is no more. And that is the only "I" you are aware of right now — that is the "I" you are identified with. Hence I say whatsoever you know of yourself will not be there when awakening happens. That does not mean *you* will not be there. You will be there, but that "you" will be so new, so utterly discontinuous with *this* "you" that you are living right now, that it is better not to mention it at all.

Hence Buddha is silent about it. Not only that . . . if you insist, he calls your real self *anatta*, a no-self, for the simple reason that to call it also a self may be confusing. The false is known as the self; if the real is also called a self, you may get confused. You are already too much confused! Buddha calls it a no-self.

But don't lose heart. Don't be worried, don't be afraid that you will die completely. *As you are,* you will not be there, but you will be there *as you should be.* Your natural, your spontaneous being will be there.

And Buddha is also right in calling it a no-self because when the real self is there you don't have any idea of "I." The "I" is also a thought. The real self has no idea of "I"; the real self is one with the universal self. It is not separate from existence, it is not an island. The unreal self is separate, the unreal self creates separation, hence, the unreal self creates misery. To be separate from the whole is to be miserable. To be one with the whole is bliss.

And the paradox is only apparent; there is no paradox in reality.

One Sunday morning at the parish of St. Mary's, Little Wakefield, the signboard announcing the subject of the day's sermon read: "And forgive us our trespasses."

A few yards away, stuck into the grass, was another sign which read: "Trespassers will be prosecuted."

Just like that: there is no real contradiction, but it appears to be there. On the one hand, a sign says: "And forgive us our trespasses," and on the other hand another sign says: "Trespassers will be prosecuted." But they are not concerned with the same object; their meaning is totally different.

When I say you will not be there, I am talking about the artificial self — which you are not but which you have come to believe that you are. Your real self will be there — which you *are* but which you have forgotten completely.

The second question

Bhagwan,
Please comment on these words of Yoka:
By zazen we can obtain directly the
ultimate truth.
The scholars like to teach others but have
no deep convictions themselves.
Once you have revealed your prejudices
you can see your true self.
How can you wander off into external struggles?

Anurag,

YOKA'S WORDS are always tremendously beautiful. He is one of the greatest Zen Masters. There have been many Zen mystics, but there is a difference between a Master and a mystic.

A mystic is one who has known the truth, but is absolutely incapable of relating it to others. He has no means, he cannot devise methods, he has no skills. He cannot paint it, he cannot sing it, he cannot dance it, he cannot say it. He is utterly dumb. The experience leaves him almost drunk — utterly drunk. You can see that something has happened, something of tremendous import. You can feel a certain vibe around him. You can try to understand what has happened. But from his side there is no effort to communicate, to commune. He is so dazed by what he has seen, he is in such awe that he has forgotten language. He has entered into the no-mind and he has forgotten the way to the old mind. First he used to live in the mind, then he tried hard to find the way towards the no-mind. Now he *is* in the no-mind, but he has forgotten the way to the mind. He cannot use the mind — he has lost his mind. He is almost, to all practical purposes, mad — absolutely joyous, overflowing with bliss, beauty, grace; something worth seeing, something of the beyond, but of no practical use.

The Master is one who has reached to the ultimate but is capable of coming back down to the world where you are. The Master is one who has reached to the Everest of consciousness but is able to come down back to the dark valley where millions of people are still living, and to communicate to them something about the incommunicable, to make a few gestures towards the highest peak. Maybe one in a million will be able to look at the moon where his fingers are pointing, but even that is more than enough.

The Master is something plus. The mystic knows but cannot help you to know. The Master knows and can help you to know.

Yoka is a Master, a Master of great skill. Hence his words have to be meditated upon — each word is significant. He says:

By zazen we can obtain directly the ultimate truth.

First: *by zazen* . . . zazen means just sitting and doing nothing. That is the most unique phenomenon in Zen; nowhere else has it happened. No other religion has been able to create this device of just sitting. Every religion provides you with something to do: chant a mantra, utter a prayer, repeat certain words from the holy scriptures or go through a ritual, but do something: physical exercises — yoga — or some mental exercises — visualization, concentration, contemplation. But one thing is certain: all the religions have provided you with something to do.

And Zen says — and there is great insight in it — that if you go on doing something, the mind will go on living; you will never be able to transcend it. You may be able to control it, but control is not transcendence. You may be able to make it more virtuous, but to be virtuous is not to know the unknowable. To be virtuous is a choice, and whenever you choose you are choosing bondage. All choices lead to bondage.

Somebody becomes a sinner — he has chosen iron chains; and somebody becomes a saint — he has chosen golden chains, beautiful chains, valuable chains. But chains are chains; whether they are made of gold or of iron makes no difference. In fact, golden chains are far more dangerous, because with the iron chains sooner or later you will get fed up, you would like to get out of them — they are humiliating. With the golden chains you may feel that they are not chains at all, they are ornaments. You may start loving them, you may start clinging to them — they are so valuable! You will be happy that you have them. You will look on others who don't have them as poor people, unfortunate people.

Your saints look on sinners as unfortunate. They feel sorry for them because they think that the sinners are bound for hell and they are going to heaven. Both are in hell!

Hell is divided in two parts — let me tell you the truth! In one part saints live, in the other part, sinners. Sinners live a little more uncomfortable life — a third-class prison you can call it. In India there used to be class divisions during the British Raj: third class for the criminals and first class for the political leaders — for Mahatma Gandhi and Pundit Jawaharlal Nehru, etcetera. Just like that, in hell there are two divisions: one is for sinners, the other is for saints.

Saints are provided with a little comfort. They have already suffered too much in being saintly, hence they have to be compensated. The sinners have enjoyed too much, hence a little suffering will bring a balance, but there is not much difference. Whenever you choose you are in bondage.

Zen teaches choiceless awareness: neither this nor that, *neti neti.* It teaches you absolute negation. And that is the meaning of zazen: doing nothing, neither singing a film song nor saying a prayer, just sitting silently, doing nothing.

The moment you do something the mind becomes powerful, because the mind is the doer. And the moment you are a doer, the ego comes back. The ego is a doer. When you are in a state of non-doing, the mind has to cease, the ego has to disappear.

Non-doing is the death of the mind and the ego: that is the meaning of zazen.

Yoka says:

> *By zazen we can obtain directly the ultimate truth.*

And there is no need to wait, there is no need to grow gradually; one can know the truth directly. Nothing else is needed; one can know the ultimate truth immediately. It is a quantum leap from the mind to the no-mind.

Learn the art of just sitting silently, doing nothing . . . and spring comes and the grass grows by itself.

Zen is a method of sudden enlightenment, not of gradual enlightenment. There is no question of gradual enlightenment, there is no question of degrees. Either you have it or you don't have it. And Zen says: Take the jump, be courageous, and have it in its totality. And it is possible *right now.* It is possible *only* now. Either now or never!

> *The scholars like to teach others but have no deep convictions themselves.*

Avoid the scholars — they don't know themselves. They have learned from the scriptures; they have not experienced it directly, they have not seen it directly. They have not realized it; it is not their own experience. Avoid the scholars.

> *Once you have revealed your prejudices you can see your true self.*

All that is needed is to drop your prejudices. Your mind consists of your prejudices: being Indian, being Japanese, being Italian, being German; being Hindu, being Jewish, being Mohammedan.

That's why I go on hitting the Italians and the Germans and the British and the Indians. Now I am getting so many requests from Spanish sannyasins who are writing letters: "Bhagwan, why are you leaving us out?" And Australian sannyasins are writing: "Have you completely forgotten about Australia?" Wait! Turn by turn I am going to hit everybody! I am not going to leave anybody out.

All your prejudices have to be destroyed, demolished. Then only can you come to your reality.

Yoka says:

> *How can you wander off into external struggles?*

Once you have dropped all your prejudices — your mind — all your extroversion disappears, all your ambitions disappear. Then there is nothing to achieve. You have already found the treasure of treasures, the kingdom of God.

The third question

Bhagwan,
Why can I take almost everything lightly
except my husband, Pravasi? Why do I fight
him so? Why do I always try to change him?

Deva Nirdosh,

It is the most ancient story. It has nothing to do with you or Pravasi in particular. The institution of marriage is an ugly institution — the ugliest, in fact. All other ugly institutions are based on the institution of marriage.

The day marriage disappears from the world, states will disappear, nations will disappear, because they all need the family as a base. Churches will disappear, religions will disappear. The whole past is rooted in family, and the family is rooted in the invention of marriage.

Marriage is ugly because it destroys the freedom of two persons. Freedom is the ultimate value for me. Anything that destroys freedom is against human nature. And when your freedom is destroyed you are angry, you are in a rage. And on whom are you going to throw all your rage? The wife finds the husband, the husband finds the wife. They are close, available, and bound together in such a way that escape is not easy. The society has made it in every way difficult or almost impossible.

Marriage has an entrance but no exit. Or, even if the

137

exit has become possible in a few countries, it is not really respected; it is condemned, a subtle condemnation. Marriage is praised. The priests go on saying, "Marriages are made in heaven," and they go on saying, "This is something sacred." The whole establishment depends on the sacredness of marriage. But it is not sacred, it is really very ugly. It has destroyed the whole of humanity.

And you cannot take revenge on the priest because he is not directly there; he functions in a very indirect way. You cannot take revenge on the politician; he is very diplomatic. All that you can find is the other person — the wife, the husband — tangibly, physically present, so your anger starts pouring on the other.

Husbands and wives are continuously quarrelling, fighting, as if they were enemies. It is very rare to find a couple which is friendly. They show friendliness when they are with others; when guests come, immediately they start smiling. They wear masks before their children, they avoid clashes. They don't fight on the streets, but they are fighting twenty-four hours a day. Their fight takes so many forms; it is multi-dimensional. It dissipates their energy. And then they have to live together, so somehow they have to make it up.

Sex just becomes a method for making things smooth, for making it up. First fight, then, because you have to live with the other person, use sex to show love and tenderness to the other so that for the time being there is peace. But that peace does not last long; it is just a cold war, not peace. Again the war will erupt. In the morning, again the same story will be repeated.

Unless we become aware that something very stupid has been propounded in the name of marriage, Nirdosh, this is going to continue.

My sannyasins, at least, should become aware: your husband has not done anything wrong to you, nor has your wife done anything wrong to you. If anything is wrong it is the very bondage, the very feeling of bondage that is wrong. Drop that bondage. Give each other more freedom. Respect freedom more than anything else because freedom is the highest value — even higher than love. If your love brings freedom, it is good. If your love does not bring freedom, it is not good — it is not even love either.

Your love brings jealousy, possessiveness; it never brings freedom. It destroys all possibilities of freedom. And it started at the very beginning. . . .

Forget what your rabbi told you! What does he know about romance? Here's the way it *really* happened!

"Adam, baby," said Eve as she presented him with a bouquet of forget-me-nots she had picked in the Garden of Eden, "do you absolutely and truly love me?"

"Sure," said Adam. "Who else?"

Nirdosh, your story started then!

I have heard that every day when Adam would come back after his day's adventures, in the night Eve would count his ribs!

It is a very ancient story. In the very beginning, something went wrong.

You may know, you may not know: Eve was not the first woman. God first created Adam and Lilith. And the first night, the honeymoon night — the first honeymoon — and a quarrel started because there was only one bed. And in those days double beds were not available! This is the story of the beginning: there was just a single bed. So who should sleep on the bed and who should sleep on the floor?

Of course, Adam was as much a male chauvinist pig as anybody! He was muscular, more powerful, so he possessed the bed. But Lilith was not willing. She said, "We are equal, we are made equal." She was the founder of the Lib Movement, the real founder!

They fought so much. I don't know whether clothes were thrown at each other or not, but they must have been thrown if there were clothes! In the middle of the night they knocked on God's door and Lilith said, "This cannot go on. Either I have to be accepted as an equal or I am finished with this man."

So the marriage was not consummated.

And God, being himself a man, of course favored Adam. So he dissolved Lilith and he created Eve, taking out a rib from Adam's body to make sure that Eve was always going to be secondary, just a part of Adam's body, not more than that, so that she could not claim equality. She would have to sleep on the floor!

Now what kind of foolishness is this? Just a double bed was needed! Our Asheesh could have done it — it was so simple! But God was very miserly.

Nirdosh, you are simply repeating an old story, an old pattern. Get out of this old pattern! Being a sannyasin, that should be the first thing.

There is no need to take your husband Pravasi seriously. Why that poor man? What has he done to you? If you can take everything else lightly, then why take your husband seriously?

Seriousness is a disease. And when you take somebody seriously, sooner or later you will take revenge, because you cannot remain serious for long. One wants to be happy and take things in fun.

But you alone are not at fault. Pravasi must also be making sure that he is being taken seriously. Every husband has been doing that for thousands of years: he should be taken seriously — he is no ordinary person, he is your husband!

In India, husbands have taught the women that "Your husband is your god." Husbands themselves teaching the wives! And they have forced the poor women to accept them as their gods. But they take revenge — they are bound to take revenge. They cannot accept it. No being can accept such indignity.

But the way of the woman is more subtle. The way of the man is gross: he imposes his superiority by beating the wife. And the wife imposes her superiority by torturing him in very subtle ways — in such subtle ways that he cannot even defend himself.

When somebody is fighting with you, attacking you in a gross way, there is a possibility of defending yourself. You can learn karate — Satchidananda can help you — you can give him a few good kicks. Every woman should learn karate because enough is enough! So when your husband tries to force you, "Take me seriously," you can give him a few good karate kicks! And you should learn karate shouts so that the whole neighborhood knows what is happening!

Life has to be light. Neither the wife has to be taken seriously nor has the husband to be taken seriously. Seriousness is not a good thing. Between two persons, seriousness creates a wall; it destroys intimacy. But if you are bent upon dominating each other, naturally you have to be serious. You cannot dominate playfully. If you become playful and take things in fun, you cannot be dominant, you cannot have any ego trip. Ego functions only in the climate of seriousness.

"Dear," asked the husband, "exactly what is hypnotism?"

"Hypnotism," replied his wife, "is getting a man into your power and then making him do whatever you want him to do."

Snorted the husband, "That's not hypnotism — that's marriage!"

Husbands are trying to force the wives to be just shadows to them. And the wives are trying to force the husbands to be just shadows to them. The whole idea is inhuman, irreligious, insane, neurotic!

If you really want to celebrate life, don't make such demands on life. Take things non-seriously. Remember how long it has been since you laughed with your husband, how long it has been since you danced with your husband informally — not in a formal setting, not at some marriage, or in some Rotarians' meeting or Lions' meeting — not in some formal setting, but just out of sheer joy. How long has it been since you sat silently together listening to music, not arguing, not talking, not nagging, not doing all that nonsense that goes on in the name of marriage?

A wall is created between the wife and the husband. The society perpetuates the wall, and you are so stupid that you go on helping the society to destroy your relationships, to destroy the beauty of your relationships.

Walking down M.G. Road, the middle-aged guy said to his wife, "Hey, did you see that pretty girl smiling at me?"

"That's nothing," said the wife, "the first time I saw you I laughed out loud!"

A Frenchman came home early one day and found his best friend in bed with his wife.

Shaking his head in disbelief, he said, "You know I have to, Pierre — but *you!*"

Mr Schmendrick came home earlier than expected and found his wife in bed with a strange man.

"What are you two doing?" he bellowed.

"See what I mean?" said the wife to her lover. "A schnook!"

The Bravermans married off their last daughter and decided to sell their house and move into a furnished apartment.

Mr Braverman showed his wife the apartment he rented.

"I don't like it," said Mrs Braverman.

"Why not?" asked Mr Braverman.

"There are no curtains in the bathroom. Every time I take a bath the neighbors will be able to see me in the nude!"

"Don't worry," said her husband, "when the neighbors see you in the nude, they'll buy the curtains!"

"Ah, yes, my late wife was a most remarkable woman," the mild old Englishman told one of his cronies on a park bench in London. "A very religious woman," he continued. "Never missed a day in church and at home it was prayers and psalm-singing from morning to night."

"How did she come to die?" the friend inquired.

"I strangled her."

Nirdosh, you say: *Why do I always try to change him?*

Stop! Otherwise, if he strangles you, it will be difficult to save you. Every wife goes on trying to change the husband; that is a subtle strategy to dominate. It is a condemnation: "You are wrong and you have to be put right." And husbands can't defend themselves because they do a few things which they themselves think are bad, so they can't defend themselves.

For example, they smoke and they themselves say that it is wrong, so the wife goes on nagging, "Stop smoking!" In fact, the more she nags, the more the husband has to smoke because he becomes more nervous. And when he is nervous, there is no other escape than smoking. If he does not smoke, he will strangle the wife! So he strangles a cigarette, or he starts chewing gum; otherwise he will chew the wife! He has to do something just to keep himself engaged so that this moment of anger passes by.

And the wife has a good point there: she is just doing it for your sake — for your health, for you to live a long life. And the husband wants to die as soon as possible!

With this woman . . . to live a long life! He goes on smoking more in the hope that smoking really does kill!

He drinks and you are against it — and he is against himself because the whole atmosphere is that he has been told it is wrong and he has accepted the idea. So he cannot say that he is right — he has no guts to say that he is right. He has to accept that the wife is right. And wives don't smoke, they don't drink, they don't gamble, they don't do anything wrong. They are so saintly!

That is one thing good about being saintly: you can torture everybody! In fact, if you cannot torture everybody you will not be a saint at all — the whole joy is lost!

Wives are very holy and very religious for the simple reason that they can torture the husbands, they can torture the children, they can torture everybody. They are so holy! In comparison to them, everybody is a sinner.

The husband comes home shaking, trembling. He knows that he is doing wrong things. And there is nothing wrong in smoking! There is nothing wrong if you drink once in a while; it is absolutely human. Have you ever seen any animal smoking? That makes you distinct! Otherwise, what is distinctive about you? Have you seen any animal drinking, going to the pub, carrying bottles of beer? That makes you human! There is nothing wrong in it.

Just the other day I received a letter. One woman from Vinoba Bhave's ashram had come to see our ashram. . . . She could not see anything else. She writes that she had no time to come and listen to the lecture, no time to participate in the meditations, but she had enough time to go to the Blue Diamond and to other hotels to see what sannyasins are eating. She writes: "I have found that sannyasins are not all vegetarians and they also drink. And, Bhagwan, you should stop them from doing this because if they are religious, if they are meditators, how can they be non-vegetarians and how can they drink?"

I don't see that there is any problem. Jesus used to drink, and he was religious — as religious as Buddha — in fact, a little more religious, because Buddha must have been a little afraid that if he drank, his religiousness might be lost. Jesus must have been absolutely certain about his religiousness: that a little drink here and there did not make much difference. And, as far as alcohol is concerned, it is absolutely vegetarian — nothing wrong in it!

But the woman took note of these things. In the first place, a woman; in the second place, coming from a Gandhian ashram . . . so, doubly wrong! That was all that she could find.

Mohammed was not a vegetarian, neither was Ramakrishna a vegetarian. And I don't think that Krishna was a vegetarian or Rama was a vegetarian or the seers of the Upanishads were vegetarians or the *rishis* of the Vedas were vegetarians. They were not vegetarians, and still they attained to the ultimate. So just what you eat and what you drink can't make much difference.

And I am not telling you to eat meat. I am simply telling you that if it is possible it is cleaner not to eat meat. But it has nothing spiritual about it. It is aesthetic not to eat meat, it is poetic not to eat meat, but it has nothing religious about it. And I am not telling you to become drunkards, but I cannot say that it is unspiritual; once in a while, getting a little ecstatic from a little drink is perfectly okay and human.

My whole approach is human. I don't want you to become sad and serious holy people. We are tired of all these saints!

Please, Nirdosh, don't try to change him. Love means acceptance, accepting the other as he is. These are the ways of hate. . . . Trying to change someone is not love. And don't be after him. He has not done anything wrong in getting married to you! Don't make him suffer too much. He has not done anything wrong, so why punish him so much? Give him freedom. And in giving freedom you will find your freedom too, because we can get freedom only if we give freedom.

And when two persons give freedom to each other, then only can love grow. In absolute freedom, absolute love grows. And when love and freedom are together, their beauty is immense.

My sannyasins have to live freedom, love, meditation, bliss. Drop all these wrong patterns of creating misery for each other.

The fourth question

Bhagwan,
Why are you so much against knowledge?

Pragito,

KNOWLEDGE IS DESTRUCTIVE of something immensely valuable in you: it destroys your wonder. And it is through wonder that one becomes aware of God, not through knowledge. You need wondering eyes like small children. You need the capacity to feel awe before the sunrise, before the sky full of stars, before a roaring ocean. If you cannot feel awe you cannot feel God, because God is a mystery and he is available only to those who are capable of feeling awe, who are capable of being mystified.

Knowledge destroys wonder, destroys the capacity to feel awe. It makes you capable of explaining away everything. It takes away all poetry from life. It takes away all meaning from life. The knowledgeable person is never surprised by anything. He has explanations for everything—why should he be surprised? And, in fact, no explanation is true. Explanations don't explain anything at all. The mystery remains. The mystery is infinite.

But the knowledgeable person becomes so burdened by his knowledge that he loses the mirror-like quality of reflecting the beauty, the benediction, the dance, the ecstasy of existence.

Hence I am against knowledge, because I am in favor of knowing. Knowing is a totally different phenomenon. Knowing means innocence, knowledge means cleverness, knowledge is cunning. Knowing is simply a heart phenomenon, knowledge is a head thing. Knowledge means you have a lot of information, you have gathered much information in your memory; your memory has become a bank. Your memory is nothing but a biocomputer. It does not make you wise — no, not at all; you can repeat only that which has been put into your memory in the first place. Memory can never give you any original experience, any original insight. It takes away many things and gives you nothing — except that you feel more egoistic because you think you know.

Strolling through the card room of a business club, Stimson was surprised to see three men and an Airedale terrier playing poker. Pausing to watch, he commented on the extraordinary performance of the dog.

"He's not so smart," said the Airedale's owner. "Every time he gets a good hand he wags his tail!"

Perkins dropped over to visit Nelson, a new neighbor. They were sitting in the den talking, when a dog came in and asked if anyone had seen the *Sunday Times.* He was handed the newspaper and left.

"That's remarkable," exclaimed Perkins. "A dog that reads!"

"Oh, don't let him fool you," said Nelson. "He just looks at the comics."

Dixon, seated in a movie theater, noticed that the

man in front of him had his arm around the neck of a huge Afghan hound that occupied the seat next to him.

The dog was watching the picture with obvious understanding for he snarled softly when the villain spoke and yelped joyously at the funny lines.

Dixon leaned over and tapped the man in front of him on the shoulder. "Excuse me, but I can't get over your dog's behavior."

"Yeah, I'm surprised too," said the man. "He hated the book."

The knowledgeable person becomes absolutely incapable of experiencing surprise, of experiencing the mysterious, the miraculous. Even if God stands in front of him he will say, "So what?" Nothing can surprise him, hence nothing delights him.

Jesus says, "Unless you are like small children you will not enter into the kingdom of God."

Knowledge has to be put aside so that you can reclaim again those beautiful moments of your childhood when you were running after butterflies and you were collecting seashells and colored stones on the seashore, and you were thinking that you had found a treasure. Those colored stones were far more significant to you than Kohinoors. You have to regain that fairyland. You again have to look with those eyes at the world; then it is full of God. Then the birds singing, and a distant call of the cuckoo, and the flowers . . . then everything is so wonderful that wherever you look, wherever you move, you would like to give thanks, you will feel grateful. You would like to kneel down on the earth and pray. You will not need to go to any church or to any temple; there is no need. The whole existence becomes His temple — it is His temple.

Pragito, I am against knowledge because knowledge hinders your wisdom. Unless you put the knowledge aside, your nature cannot explode into intelligence. Put the knowledge aside and you will be in for a great surprise: you start behaving in a different way, in a spontaneous way.

Knowledge is ready-made; it keeps you tethered to the past. Hence all your responses are out of date, are never to the point, are always falling short, are never adequate, *can* never be adequate. Life goes on changing every moment, it is always new. And your response is not a response, it is a reaction; it comes from the past. You have a ready-made answer. You have not even looked at the situation and you have repeated the ready-made answer like a gramophone record.

Hence you lag behind life. And if you lag behind life you can't have blissfulness in your being. You will always feel you are missing, you will always feel something is missing. And what is that something? You are not in step with life. You will always dream that you are rushing and running towards a station; by the time you reach it, the train is moving away from the platform. That dream is symbolic: that simply shows that you are never alive to the moment, you are always late. It is because of your past, because you think you already know the answers. Hence you never listen to the questions, you never listen to the situation that is confronting you.

A Zen story:

Two temples were traditionally antagonistic to each other. Both priests had a small boy to run errands and both priests told the boys, "Don't talk to the boy from the other temple. We are enemies!" They were afraid that boys being, after all, boys they may start becoming friendly to each other. If the priests had not said anything they may not have thought about it, but when they insisted that they should not talk to each other, of course, the temptation was too great.

So one day, one boy asked the other boy when they met on the road, "Where are you going?"

The other boy said, "Wherever the wind takes me."

Listening to philosophical discussions and discourses, he had also become philosophical.

The other boy was almost dumb. He could not think what to say now. And then he thought, "My Master is right — these people are dangerous! I am asking a simple question, 'Where are you going?' and he is talking metaphysics!"

He went back. He told the Master, "I am sorry that I didn't obey you, but this has happened."

The Master said, "This is very bad — we have to defeat him! It has never been so. We have always been victorious in every argument with the other temple. So tomorrow you ask him again, 'Where are you going?' and when he says, 'Wherever the wind takes me,' ask him, 'And if the wind is not blowing at all, then?' "

The boy was very happy! He arrived a little earlier, stood there, waited, and repeated many times what he was going to say to become perfectly clear about it.

The other boy came and he asked, "Where are you going?"

And the other boy said, "Wherever my feet take me."

Now the answer was irrelevant; whatsoever he had prepared was meaningless. He was again at a loss. He asked the Master again.

The Master said, "Those people are cunning and crafty! Now, whenever he says, 'Wherever my feet take me,' you ask him, 'If you were born paralyzed, then what?' "

Again the boy came. He asked, "Where are you going?"

And the boy said, "I am going to fetch vegetables."

Life is like that. You come with a prepared question and it changes, it says, "I am going to fetch vegetables." No prepared answer is going to help. Knowledge is not going to help as far as life is concerned. The knowledgeable person is almost a dead person; he lives in his grave.

Come out of your graves! Live more spontaneously, more responsibly. Respond to the moment. Listen to the moment and act accordingly. Then your act will be total because it will arise out of the present; it will reflect the actual situation. It will be really meaningful, significant, satisfying, fulfilling. And you will find that you are no longer missing. You are in step with life, you are in harmony with life.

Innocence is always in harmony with life. And to be harmonious is to be enlightened. To be harmonious is the only way to know the ultimate truth.

The fifth question

Bhagwan,
Why do the Jaina monks live naked?

Bhagawato,

THEY SUFFER from clothestrophobia!

The sixth question

Bhagwan,
Whenever I get off on the jokes you crack,
underneath my laughter I get run over by a
bulldozer and end up feeling like a mashed
potato! How long can an over- and over-mashed
potato survive?

Anand Bhagawati,

HAVE YOU SURVIVED YET? Are you still there?

The distraught woman went to the hospital and said, "It is my husband—he was run over by a steam roller. Could you tell me which ward he's in?"

The nurse said, "Ah, he must be the one who is in wards four, five and six!"

Here you see all mashed potatoes! It is very difficult to know who is who—just orange potatoes!

Your question is coming a little too late, Bhagawati. You are finished already! Now nothing can be done. You can't put a mashed potato back together again. That is impossible!

The last question

Bhagwan,
I work for the Shree Rajneesh Ashram, Poona,
India. Please . . . tell me a joke!

Deva Yashen,

Why A JOKE? I am not miserly! I will tell you three jokes!

The Italian bride and groom went into the honeymoon suite. The bride, eager to go but still a trifle bashful, insisted that they turn off the light and undress in the dark.

The bride made it into bed in seconds and she lay there sighing deeply. "Oh, my darling," she said, "I just can't believe I'm really married."

She heard a scuffling sound in the darkness, and she repeated, "Oh, my darling, I can't believe that I'm really married!"

From out of the darkness, the bridegroom's voice said furiously, "If I ever manage to get this zipper unjammed you will!"

The second:

An old philosopher goes to see the doctor and says, "Doc, I've got a question you can probably help me with. When I was a young man in my twenties I used to get an erection once in a while and I'd grab it with both hands and I couldn't bend it. Then later on in my forties I would get a hard-on and I'd grab it with both hands and I couldn't bend it. Now, doc, I'm in my seventies and you know — the other day I was surprised! I got a hard-on and I grabbed it with both hands and I could bend it. Now, doc, does this mean I'm getting stronger?"

And the third:

An American tourist's pretty wife said she didn't feel well and went to consult a well-known French doctor. Worried, the American followed her to the doctor's office to make sure everything was alright. To his anger and dismay, he found her in bed with the doctor when he got there.

"What in hell do you think you're doing?" he raged.

Said the foxy Frenchman, "Do not excite yourself, my friend. I am merely taking the lady's temperature."

"Okay, doc," said the burly American, doubling his big fists. "But that thing better have numbers on it when you take it out!"

7

The first question

Bhagwan,
What is the difference between longing for
the divine and loving another?

Prem Neeto,

THERE IS NO DIFFERENCE AT ALL — all desires are the same. You can desire money, you can desire meditation, you can long for power, you can long for God, but you remain the same. What you long for cannot change you, the object of longing has no effect on your inner being; it is the same game played again with new words, with new objects of desire.

You long for a person, you desire a person. Why? — because you are feeling lonely. In yourself you don't feel sufficient. There is a kind of emptiness in you which you would like to be filled by the presence of the other. You feel meaningless and you want the other to impart meaning to your life. It never happens; it is only a longing and a hope. It is never fulfilled — it cannot be fulfilled in the very nature of things. It is impossible because the other is desiring you for the same reason; he is also feeling empty. Now two empty persons are hoping to be fulfilled through each other: two meaningless lives are hoping from each other to become meaningful and significant.

This is the utmost absurdity. Sooner or later one becomes aware of the phenomenon because again and again there is frustration, again and again there is failure, again and again the hope evaporates and you are left in a far deeper mess than you were ever in before. Again and again you are disillusioned.

It is because of this that Jean-Paul Sartre used to say: "The other is hell." He is unconsciously groping in the dark and has unknowingly stumbled upon a fact, although the way he expresses it is not exactly what it should be. The other is not hell, your *desire* for the other is hell — that's what all the Buddhas have said down the ages — not the other, because when Sartre says, "The other is hell," it seems as if the other is responsible for your misery, disappointment, disillusionment. The other is not responsible, it is your own expectation that has been shattered. The greater the expectation the more will be the frustration.

Hence wherever arranged marriages have disappeared and love marriages have become prevalent there is more frustration. In an arranged marriage your expectations are not very big; it is not a romantic affair at all, you are not hoping to reach to paradise through it. It is a mundane phenomenon, arranged by your parents, grandparents, arranged by the society, the family, the priest, the astrologer, arranged by others. Your dreams are not very involved in it. Hence the arranged marriage moves on far smoother ground: it has no peaks, no ups and no downs. It is just like a plain superhighway — not even an Indian one but a German superhighway. Nothing grows on it, it is dead; made of asphalt or tarmac or cement — utterly dead, but safe. It is not a hilly track. You are not moving in the unknown. You can have a map and there are milestones everywhere, pointers indicating where

you are, where you are moving, how far the destination is, how far you have moved from your place.
Everything is clear; that's how the arranged marriage
functions.

And if the arranged marriage happens when you are
just a small child, with no idea of love, of sex, of romance, then you start taking your wife for granted or
your husband for granted, just as you take your brothers and sisters for granted. Nobody ever thinks of
changing one's mother. If the marriage happens when
you are a child, a small child, then you never think of
divorce. You grow together; the husband and the wife
grow together just as brothers and sisters grow together.
They have lived together so long, as long as they can
remember.

When my mother got married she was only seven
years old. My father was not more than twelve years
old. Now what dreams are possible? What can they
hope for? In fact they were enjoying the whole show of
marriage, they were enchanted with the music, the
bands and all kinds of fireworks — it was a really en-
joyable experience — with no idea of what they were
getting into. And by the time they became aware they
were already rooted; they had become indispensable to
each other.

But in a love marriage it is going to be difficult. In
America, out of two marriages one is going to be shattered. That is the proportion of divorce: one divorce out
of two marriages. And remember, the one marriage that
has not shattered is not moving in a joyous world; it is
not moving, it is simply because of cowardice, security,
safety that people go on clinging. As they become more
courageous, the divorce rate is going to become higher
and higher, it is going to become bigger and bigger.

Why do love marriages fail? — for the simple reason
that there is deep expectation and it cannot be fulfilled.
Soon you have to realize that you have been a fool.

Soon, even before the honeymoon is over, the marriage is over. It may linger on . . . it depends how much courage you have. If you are a coward it may linger on your whole life. If you are courageous and if you can see the point you may divorce immediately after your honeymoon is over because the marriage will also be over, because you will have seen that all those illusions that you were carrying were just illusions. You were living in a world of rainbows, you were living in a world of poetry, not of reality.

Sartre is not right when he says that the other is hell, but in an unconscious way he has come very close to the truth.

The Buddhas say: Not the other but the *desire* for the other is hell. To make the other responsible is a very common characteristic of human beings.

One of Murphy's maxims says: To err is human and to blame the other for it is even far more human.

That's what Sartre has done: you have erred, now you are blaming the other. If you really see the point, then you will see that desire is the cause; if you don't see that, then you will change the other. Then this other is causing you problems — change him. So after one divorce another marriage, and then another marriage and then another marriage. And it is the same illusion you live again and again! And people are so unintelligent, so unaware that they never see the point: that you can go on changing the whole world, again and again you can change the partner, but it will remain the same story because *you* are the same. Wherever you go you will remain the same; your heart is in the same state. There is confusion, there is no light inside you, there is only darkness.

When one becomes too fed up with ordinary relationships with people one starts imagining a relationship with God; that is the longing for the divine. Now God is a little better in the sense that you can never be disappointed because you will never meet him; for the simple reason that there is going to be no honeymoon, the honeymoon can never be over; for the simple reason that there is going to be no living together with God, you can go on hoping. Now you are alone: it is a monologue, it is not a dialogue.

All human relationships fail because the other is there and you start clashing with each other, you start dominating each other, you start being jealous of each other, you start being possessive of each other. You are afraid that you may lose the other. And then one day you see that there is nothing to lose — the other is as empty as you are. One dream is shattered, then another dream. . . .

That is the beauty of the religious dream: you can go on dreaming, it can't be shattered. The relationship with God can never be on the rocks — it is impossible because you are simply alone. When you are praying, what are you doing? Talking to yourself! It is like whistling in the dark — there is nobody to listen.

God is not a person with whom you can have any relationship. God is not somebody in particular whom you can address, whom you can long for. But all your frustrations, all your relationships, which have failed, have not made you alert enough to the fact that it is better to drop the whole idea of desiring the other. Now you are trying to desire something which you are never going to get. One thing is good about it: you can go on hoping for lives. There is never going to be any end to it; the journey is unending. The other does not exist at all; now you are living in pure dreams. First you were living in dreams but the other was there, so between the two realities the dreams were bound to be crushed — and they *were* crushed. But now there is nobody else, you are alone. You can make your God the way you want.

In India people worship God in such ways that one feels sorry for them. Once I was staying with a woman; she was a great lover of Krishna, so much so that she had stopped sleeping with her husband — how can you love two persons? That is a betrayal. She believed that her true husband was Krishna. Her poor husband was really in a very mad state. He could not say that she was wrong because he was also brought up in the same Krishnaite tradition. He could not say it, although he was a doctor, well educated. But in India education makes no difference to people, not at all. Their conditioning is so old and so ancient and so deep rooted that education remains just on the surface. Scratch any educated Indian and inside you will find the whole rotten past. So intellectually he knew that the wife was crazy, but only intellectually; deep down he himself was afraid that she might be right, because Meera used to think the same way: that Krishna is her true husband. She left her own husband.

At least this woman had not left her husband; she simply had stopped sleeping with the husband. She used to sleep in another room; she would lock the room from inside. She would sleep with Krishna's statue.

When I stayed in their home I watched the whole game. In the morning she would sing songs to wake up Krishna. Now Krishna needs to wake *you* up! But she would sing songs to wake Krishna up. And then Krishna would be up and then the whole morning routine: he would take a bath, he would be given a bath, and then breakfast . . . the whole day was devoted to Krishna. And it was just a statue made of silver — there was nobody there! But she used to talk to Krishna. And if you could have seen her you would have been impressed because she would cry tears of joy and she would dance in utter ecstasy — at least on the surface it would look like that.

And the more repressive she became about her sex — because she was not having any sexual relationship with the husband — the more and more obsessed she became with Krishna. Then she started dreaming that Krishna was making love to her in the night. Once she even got falsely pregnant — just hot air in her belly and nothing else.

When I talked to her. . . . It was really cruel of me, but I am a cruel man — I have to be. I had gone for only three days; I stayed there for seven days just to bring her to her senses. And finally she understood the point — she was an intelligent woman. She presented the statue to me and she said, "Now you take it from here, otherwise I can again get entangled into this stupidity. I have wasted my whole life. And I can see the point that I am just living in my own dream. There is no Krishna, nobody comes to make love to me, it is all my dream. It is just sexual repression." And this whole nonsense of waking him up and giving him a bath and then breakfast and then lunch and then Krishna retires for the afternoon sleep and then tea — and everything, as if she were really serving a real person!

The statue remained with me for many days; I think I gave it to Mukta. Mukta must have it even now. But the woman was freed, freed from that stupid monologue.

It is madness. It is the same madness, even a little worse, because when you love a real person there is at least somebody real, good or bad, frustrating or not frustrating. But when you start longing for the divine it is simply living absolutely in the abstract.

Neeto, you ask me: *What is the difference between longing for the divine and loving another?*

There is no difference at all — longing is longing. Then what will I suggest? Try to understand the nature of longing, the nature of desire. When you understand the nature of desire, in that very understanding the desiring disappears. Then you start enjoying your aloneness, you become utterly joyous with yourself. There is no need for the other, there is no dependence on the other.

I am not saying that you will not be able to love then.

In fact you will be able to love then and only then because then love will have a totally different quality, the quality of sharing. You will not be a beggar, you will be an emperor. You will love because you have something to give, not to get something. You will love because you are overflowing with joy and you would like to share it with people. But then it will not be a relationship at all.

I call it relating. You can relate, but there is no need to create any bondage, there is no need to create any marriage. You can relate with somebody, you can relate to the same person your whole life, but tomorrow remains open, it is not closed. Tomorrow is not settled today, you cannot take it for granted; tomorrow you may feel like sharing with the same person, the same person may like sharing or may not like sharing. Even if one of the two decides not to share, then you say good-bye to each other with great gratitude because all that joy and all that has happened before and all that has transpired before one is grateful for. With no grudge, with no complaint, with no quarrel, you simply depart. You know, "Our ways are parting now, we may not meet again," so you depart with a song in the heart, with a smile on the lips; with a hug, with a kiss you depart. You depart in deep friendliness. It is not a divorce because there has not been any marriage at all in the first place. You were not bound to each other so you are not getting free from each other. You had always been free, you had always remained individuals.

Two individuals relating remain individuals; two individuals getting into a relationship lose their individuality. They become a couple, and to be a couple is an ugly thing. That means you have lost your freedom, you are no more yourself; the other is also no more himself or herself. Both have lost their freedom and nobody has gained anything out of it.

That's why Sartre says, "The other is hell." But still I would like to remind you: it is not the other, it is the desire for the other. When you have understood the futility of desire, the utter stupidity of desire, then you relate in a totally different way; a qualitative change happens to you. You are happy with yourself; you are not seeking happiness through the other. You are so happy that you would like to share it with somebody, that's why you relate.

Relationship originates in misery, relating originates in bliss.

And when you start relating with people you also start relating with existence. And that's what true religion is: relating with existence. It is not a longing for God. You can call existence God, there is no problem in it, but it is better to call it existence because once you call it God, all the old associations with the word creep in and you start thinking of an old man sitting somewhere on a golden throne above in the sky looking at you, watching you, and then strange ideas happen out of it.

Carl Gustav Jung remembers in his memoirs that throughout his whole childhood he was obsessed with only one idea: that if God sits above and sometimes he pisses, then? — or shits, then? And his father was a priest so he used to ask his father and the father would get very angry. He would say, "Stop! Never ask such questions!" So he had to repress those questions. The more he repressed them the more they were there. He was continuously obsessed with the idea: what happens then? He must be eating, he must be drinking, and sitting above the head, anytime. . . . Then he started dreaming that God was urinating and it was falling all over the earth and his shit was falling all over the earth. He himself became very guilty, "What am I . . . ?" See! If you think of him above, this is what is going to happen — any moment!

Then stupid questions arise; out of a stupid idea they are bound to come.

God is not a person at all, God is a quality — godliness, not God. Existence is full of godliness. When you are capable of feeling joyous, fulfilled, contented, then meditating on desires, seeing the futility of desires, desires disappear and you are left without desires. Suddenly a great peace descends on you. In that peace your self-nature starts exploding. That is bliss. That bliss radiates as love, it reaches to people, it reaches to trees, it reaches to animals, it reaches to the clouds and the stars. It starts reaching finally to the whole existence. That's what relating to existence is. Then you see the sunset and in the very sunset you see God — not Jesus crucified or Krishna playing on his flute; those are all childish ideas. You see godliness.

Have you ever observed a beautiful sunset? What more godliness can there be? You see a rose flower — what more godliness can there be? Or just leaves of grass swaying in the wind. . . . All this green and the red and the gold! This whole existence is so full, so overfull, overflowing with silence, with peace, with joy, with ecstasy. When you are able to be silent, peaceful, joyous, you start relating with it. That relating is religion.

Religion is not a desire for God, it is an experience of godliness. And the question is not how to find God, the question is how to drop desiring. This has to be remembered, very emphatically remembered: if you start seeking and searching for God you will remain the same person, you will never change. If you start trying to understand the nature of desire you are bound to go through a radical revolution because anybody who is a little bit intelligent is bound to see the utter futility of desire — it leads nowhere. And the moment desire disappears from your being you have arrived.

You have always been there; it was only desire that was distracting you. Sometimes the desire was for money, sometimes for God, sometimes for power, prestige, sometimes for heaven, paradise, but any desire is enough to distract you from your nature. When there is no desire, where can you go? All desires lead you away from yourself. When there is no desire you are simply centered in your being. That very centeredness is bliss, is ecstasy, is *samadhi*, is *nirvana*.

The second question

Bhagwan,
Why are people constantly pouring scorn
on you? Why?

Pradeepo,

I̶T IS ABSOLUTELY NATURAL. If they were not pouring scorn on me, that would have been very unnatural. This is expected, this is how it should be. This is how people have always behaved. They are very predictable; they function like machines. They go on functioning in the same way; their consciousness has not changed at all. Although they are Christians and they are Hindus and they are Mohammedans and they are Jainas and they are Buddhists, these are only words; deep down they are as unconscious as ever. It makes no difference to them what philosophy they believe in, it is only a belief — convenient, comfortable, consolatory — a kind of solace but not a transformation. They don't want any transformation, they are afraid of transformation. Hence, whenever there is a person with whom transformation *is* possible, they naturally behave in a very antagonistic way.

Yoka says:

> *Some men pour scorn on Zen or hold it in*
> *question. They play with fire, trying in vain*
> *to burn the sky. A true student of Zen should*

*hear what they say as if their words were
sweet drops of dew,
Forgetting even their sweetness however
when he enters into the realm of the non-
mental.
I consider hurtful words as virtuous actions
And I treat those who hurt me as good masters, for I feel neither for nor against the man
who insults me.
I do not need to explain the two powers of
perseverance, the understanding of without-
birth and without-death, suchness, nirvana.*

*The Buddhas, as numberless as the sands of
the Ganges, all bear witness to this fact.*

Once you have known yourself, nothing disturbs
you, no insult can insult you. The people who go on
pouring scorn on me will burn their own fingers, they
will suffer, because what they are doing and what they
are saying is absolutely untrue. But we cannot expect
truth from them — they don't know what truth is.

But, Pradeepo, you need not be worried about them
— they are lying. Everybody lies, but it does not matter
since nobody listens. And, remember, a man like me is
bound to be punished. Virtue is its own punishment!
Virtuous actions will never go unpunished, otherwise
why is Jesus crucified? Why is Socrates poisoned? Why
is Mansur murdered? Virtuous actions will never go
unpunished. Why? — for the simple reason that a man
like Socrates is a danger to the society, which is rooted
in lies. A man of truth is dangerous to all those who are
living in lies. A man with eyes living with people who
are blind cannot be tolerated because it is this man who
has eyes who makes the blind people feel that they are
blind. If he were not there they would have never felt
themselves blind. Now his presence hurts them; his very
presence shows them that something is wrong with

them. And of course, there are millions of them and how can millions of people be wrong? Obviously this man must be wrong; the crowds cannot be wrong. The crowds have to defend themselves.

Pouring scorn on me is nothing but sheer self-defense, but it is a good sign — a good sign in the sense that they have become aware that I am here, that I am a danger to them and to their society and to their structures, to their minds, to their philosophies and ideologies. Now they will find every possible way to distract people from coming to me, to prevent people from reaching me. They will do all that they can do.

But truth, even if crucified, becomes victorious, and lies, even if crowned, are bound to be defeated. That is the ultimate law. Buddha says: *Ais dhammo sanantano,* this is the eternal law of existence. So let them do what they want to do.

Pradeepo, don't be worried about what they say; in fact, be happy that they have started taking note of me. The only thing that can be bad is if they ignore me.

Just think, if they had ignored Jesus, if they had behaved as if he never existed, he would have died by himself; there would have been no need to crucify him. He may have lived a few more years, but he was bound to die. If they had ignored him there would have been no Christianity. Christianity exists because they could not ignore Jesus.

If they had ignored Socrates you would have never heard the name of Socrates. Now we don't know who the people were who insulted him, who the people were who gathered together to kill this beautiful man. But Socrates has become immortal, his message has become immortal, his message still resounds, and wherever someone is searching for truth, he is bound to feel tremendous respect for Socrates. No country, no race, can prevent Socrates from penetrating the heart of a true seeker. If they had ignored this man — he was already very old when they poisoned him — he would not have survived more than another five to ten years at the most.

What wrong could he have done in five, ten years? But they could not ignore him, and it is good that they became very antagonistic. They created so much fuss about this single individual with no power that twenty-five centuries have passed and thousands of powerful people have been born but nobody has that power over seekers of truth that Socrates has.

The same is true about Buddha: they could not tolerate his existence. Many times attempts were made on his life. They could not succeed in killing him — that is another matter — but they tried their best. Now nobody knows those people, who they were — they must have been just like people you come across everywhere — the crowds, the mob — but Buddha became the greatest star in the whole history of human consciousness; nobody shines so brilliantly as he. If they had ignored him we would have missed him, we would have missed something of tremendous value.

So, Pradeepo, don't be worried about what people say about me. Be happy that they are becoming interested. And not only in this country, all over the world. . . .

One bishop in England has written to one of my sannyasins who is also a priest — he is a chaplain at the University of Cambridge. The bishop has written to him: "We have heard that you have also become involved with this dangerous man, and this is not right for a Christian priest. Please explain." Our sannyasin — Chinmaya is his name — has written a beautiful letter to the bishop saying: "Listening to this man I became convinced that Jesus was a reality. Coming closer to this man, for the first time I became aware that Jesus is not a myth." Now, from a chaplain at Cambridge University, an important person . . . the bishop must be feeling very disturbed — "What to do with this man?" And now

Dynamic Meditation is being done in his church in Cambridge!

The Protestant Church of Germany has circulated an order to all Protestant churches in Germany that my name should not be mentioned in any church. No books, no quotations should be quoted. That simply shows that they must be being used, people must be quoting me, otherwise why should they get worried? A committee was appointed to investigate and just the other day the West German government published a pamphlet to make people aware of the danger, particularly young people. The pamphlet says: "Although this man says that you need not leave the marketplace, that you need not renounce your home, your job, still people become so magnetized that they leave their jobs. And so many people are missing from Germany that it is not a small problem; it is taking on epidemic proportions."

When a government becomes worried — and a faraway government. . . . Seminars are being arranged all over the world, for and against me. I don't even go outside my room, but they cannot even ignore a man who just lives in his room, who never goes outside. I have even stopped walking in the garden — it may be objectionable to somebody! But this is, in a way, a good sign.

Jesus was only criticized in the small vicinity where he lived. Buddha was critized only in the small province where he moved, Bihar. The name comes from his movement — the name Bihar means "where Buddha moved." So just in that small province he was criticized. I may be the first man who is being criticized all over the world; irrespective of race, country, religion — all are agreed about one thing: "This man is dangerous!" This is really something to make one happy! You should rejoice — something great is going to happen out of it. If the criticism of Buddha in only a small province created so much energy, if the criticism of Jesus in a small area around Jerusalem created such an impact on history, then there is great promise.

The criticism of me around the world is going to affect the whole of humanity, the whole future of humanity. Right now you cannot visualize it because right now you are in the very birth pains of the whole process. The followers of Jesus could have never conceived. . . . When he was being crucified they escaped. And there were not many followers, only twelve apostles, and not more than one hundred people who were deeply devoted to him, and not more than one thousand people who were in some way related to him. Everybody was against him. Who would have conceived that this carpenter's son who was being crucified in such a humiliating way, with a thief on either side, just like an ordinary criminal, would have such an impact on history that history would be divided with his name, that his name would become a demarcation line: "Before Christ" and "After Christ"? Who would have conceived it? It would have been impossible.

You cannot conceive right now what is happening, but I can see. All these things are good tidings. Don't be worried, Pradeepo. Go on continuing in your way, go on living in your suchness, go on living in your meditation, in your celebration. That is the only message that I have given to you: Celebrate life, rejoice in life. Don't be bothered about what others say; that is *their* business.

The third question

Bhagwan,
Sometimes I do not know whether I am stupid
or just mad. What is the difference between
stupidity and madness?

Prem Raquibo,

Y OU CAN'T BE STUPID because the stupid person cannot ask such a question. The stupid person cannot ask any question at all. The stupid person has no curiosity, has no inquiry. He does not live, he vegetates.

This question arising in you, "What is the difference between stupidity and madness?" shows a clear sign of intelligence.

And certainly you are not mad either because a mad person never thinks that he is mad. That is one of the essential qualities of madness, that a mad person never thinks that he is mad; he thinks the whole world is mad except him. The moment the mad person starts inquiring, questioning, "Am I mad?" that is a good sign. That shows that some sanity is happening, that he is coming back to his senses. To know that "I am mad" is to be free of madness.

You can go to any madhouse, ask people; they don't think that they are mad.

Kahlil Gibran remembers one of his friends who went nuts and was put in a mental asylum. Gibran went to see him. He was sitting underneath a tree enjoying himself, singing a song; he was very happy. Gibran sat by his side and said to him, "You must be feeling worried that you have been put inside these walls?"

The man said, "What are you talking about? Sorry? Sad? Why should I feel sorry and sad? In fact I am feeling very happy. These walls are not around me, these walls are around all the mad people of the world. Only a very few, sane people live here. We have left all the insane outside. Since I have come in I have come across such intelligent people, such beautiful people, and outside everybody is ugly."

Naturally, because everybody was telling him, "You are mad"; now nobody here is telling him he is mad. In fact everybody is enjoying everybody else's madness, accepting it. It's perfectly okay, there is no problem in it.

Raquibo, you are neither stupid — otherwise the question could not arise — nor are you mad; you are only asleep. And that is far more dangerous, because a madman can be cured, a stupid man can be helped to become intelligent, but the man who is asleep and is dreaming is really in bad shape because if you try to wake him up he becomes angry — you are disturbing his dreams. He has invested so much in his dreams; he is seeing such great dreams and you are disturbing him.

Now to tell some president that all power is just a childish desire is to shatter his dream. To tell a rich man that money is nothing but an effort to stuff yourself somehow with things, with junk, so that you can feel that you are not empty, will make him angry at you. To tell people that whatsoever they are doing in their lives is nothing but playing with toys will drive them crazy against you; they will jump upon you. How dare you to call their lives sleep? That's why they cannot forgive the Buddhas.

But, Raquibo, you are my sannyasin and you have to forgive me. There is no problem, you are only asleep. And all that is needed is a clear-cut awareness, consciousness, wakefulness, watchfulness that can bring you out of your sleep. But if you want to remain in your sleep, nobody can pull you out; that is impossible. Only you can bring yourself out of your sleep. Madness can be cured by others, but not sleep. Stupidity can be cured, it can be helped, because no child is born really stupid.

Every child learns stupidity from the stupid people all around. He imitates — he has to imitate. If you have to live with stupid people you have to behave like them, otherwise you start becoming separate. And they want you to be part of the collective mind; they don't like individuals. So everybody has to become stupid in some way or other — Catholic stupid or Protestant stupid, Hindu stupid or Mohammedan stupid, but some kind of stupid you have to become. Maybe a communist stupid, an atheist stupid, but you have to bring yourself to some kind of stupidity so that you can belong to a crowd.

But there is a clear-cut difference between madness and stupidity. Mad people are the people who are really more sensitive than others, that's why they go mad. They are more intelligent than others, that's why they go mad. They are so intelligent that they cannot cope with all the stupid masses around and they are so intelligent that they cannot force themselves to behave stupidly. They start functioning like individuals and that creates trouble. They are so intelligent that they can see the futility of many projects that have been imposed upon you.

You have been taught to be ambitious. An intelligent person can immediately see that this is nonsense — it can never give you any joy. Yes, it will destroy many other people's lives — it is violent, it is ugly, it is destructive — and it is not going to give you anything in return. The ambitious person is a stupid person. The intelligent person is not ambitious, he simply lives with no hankering to compete with others because he knows everybody is unique. There is no question of competition. He never compares. The really intelligent person never compares himself with anybody. He never thinks himself higher or lower. He never suffers from a superiority complex or an inferiority complex — which are two sides of the same coin. He simply knows, "I am who I am and you are who you are," and there is no question of comparison. How can you compare a rose with a lotus? All comparison will be wrong from the very beginning. Each individual has such a beauty, and such a *unique* beauty, that there is no comparison possible.

Then what is the point of becoming ambitious? Ambition means I have to be superior, I have to prove that I am superior to others. Now for this you have to lose your intelligence, you have to become stupid. That's why politicians are utterly stupid people, they can't be otherwise. They are all bananas, and rotten bananas at that!

A man was driving along an outer suburban road and was just passing a hospital for the mentally insane when his car got a flat tire.

He got out of his car, got his tools out of the trunk, undid the wheel-nuts and put them in the hubcap in the gutter of the road beside him. Just then there was a burst of thunder and torrents of rain started to fall. In his hurry to change the wheel he knocked over the hubcap and the wheel-nuts were washed down a drain just near him.

Now he was in trouble, but after puzzling for ten minutes or so he heard someone calling to him. Looking up, he saw a head poking over the top of the high wall opposite him. This guy had been watching all that was going on and said, "Why don't you take one nut off each of the other wheels and put the wheel back on and drive to the next garage where you can get some more?"

The driver was pleased and did what had been suggested to him. Then looking over to this man on the wall he said, "Hey, what are you doing inside that place? You're supposed to be mad!"

The guy on the wall yelled back, "Maybe we are mad in here, but we're not stupid!"

A very sensitive person in this stupid world is bound to become mad. He has to learn the art of meditation, otherwise he is bound to become mad. Only meditation can save him from becoming mad.

Now even psychologists are becoming aware of the phenomenon that mad people are very sensitive and vulnerable people, intelligent people who cannot cope with the reality that surrounds them. It is too much and they are too fragile for it. They break down under its weight. If they can be helped through meditation their breakdowns can become breakthroughs.

Meditation is the only hope, otherwise as people become more intelligent, more and more people will go mad. And that is happening.

In backward countries fewer people go mad; in advanced countries more people go mad. Why? For example, in a country like India, utterly poor, dying of starvation, illness, disease, not so many people go mad as they do in America. And the Hindu swamis and the Hindu mahatmas brag about it. They go on talking around the world — the Muktanandas and Maharishi Mahesh Yogis, etcetera — they go on bragging: "Why don't Indians go mad? — for the simple reason that they are religious people." It is not so; the fact is something else, something totally different. The fact is that because India is undernourished it can't have that much intelligence with which to go mad.

The Indian mind is undernourished. How many Nobel Prizes does India get? Such a vast country, one-sixth of the whole globe! Out of six people one is an Indian; one out of six Nobel Prizes should go to India, but how many Nobel Prizes . . . ? Why is it not happening? Why can't Indians be great discoverers? — for the simple reason that their bodies are undernourished; they are lacking the essential ingredients that make intelligence bloom. Intelligence does not grow on an empty stomach. If you want beautiful roses and big roses you have to have a rich soil. You have to give fertilizers and manure and you have to take every kind of care. But in India people are undernourished; what they eat is not sufficient. It does not provide the right vitamins, the right proteins, the right amount of chemicals to their brains. Hence all they can do is stand on their heads and do yoga postures. That does not need any intelligence.

All they can do is repeat like parrots scriptures thousands of years old, which are really irrelevant.

One sannyasin has written that he was in New York and Muktananda was answering questions. All the answers were absolutely patent answers which one can find in the Gita, which one can find in any Hindu book. Only one question was such that the Gita has no answer for it and the Vedas have no reference to it — they cannot have. The question was: "What do you think about Shree Rajneesh and his Tantra?" Now his mind must have ceased completely! My name functions like a sword. The answer was: "We are doing research on this matter. When the research is complete we will answer."

These are the enlightened people! These are the people who go on trotting around the world initiating people. They are doing research on Tantra, on me. The simple reason why he could not answer is because no patent answer is available. And he goes on asking people about me; that's what he calls "research."

Nirgrantha has come. Muktananda saw Nirgrantha walking on the beach in Miami. He called him — he must have seen the mala and the locket — and wanted him to stay with him. Nirgrantha stayed there for two days, and there were long interrogations, three-hour-long interrogations: "Has Rajneesh said this against me?" Nirgrantha said, "They are all openly-said things, they are all published. You need not inquire of me, you can just look in the books." This is the research work that is going on!

They don't have intelligence, they don't even have guts, but they go on telling the whole world that Indians don't go mad, Indians don't commit so many suicides because they are religious. They are not religious — not at all. They are not mad because to become mad first you need intelligence. Have you ever heard of any stupid person going mad? That is impossible. Have you ever heard of any idiot going mad? How can an idiot go mad? To go mad you need some intelligence in the first place; to lose it you have to have it!

Only very intelligent people can commit suicide — and these are the same people who can become sannyasins. The same people who can commit suicide can become sannyasins for the simple reason that they have seen that this life is useless. Now either they have to find another life, another way of living, or it is pointless to continue. And they have courage enough, guts enough.

It does not need much intelligence to see that this life is really futile.

Murphy says: If the shoe fits it is ugly. If you like it, they don't have it in your size. If you like it and it is in your size, it doesn't fit anyway. If you like it and it fits, you can't afford it. If you like it, it fits and you can afford it, it falls apart the first time you wear it.

Just a little intelligence and you will be able to see that's what life is! Then if you have guts, either you commit suicide, you simply say to God, "Enough is enough!" or you transform your being — you become a sannyasin.

Many people ask me, "Why aren't Indians coming to you?" Because they are not religious people, they are not intelligent, they don't have guts and they don't yet have the intelligence to see that life is futile, although they go on repeating like parrots that life is futile, life is illusion, it is all *maya.* But it is just a way of talking. Just as the English talk about the weather, Indians talk about metaphysics! Neither do the English mean anything. . . .

One Englishman was coming from another town where he had gone to visit some friends. His horse, who was pulling his cart, suddenly said, "It is too hot."

The Englishman could not believe his ears! And there was nobody else there, just his dog was sitting in the cart, so he said to the dog, "Have you heard?" He had to say it to somebody! "Have you heard?"

The dog said, "I have heard it many times. Everybody talks about the weather and nobody does anything about it!"

So English horses and dogs also talk about the weather. Indian horses and dogs talk about metaphysics, God-realization; they recite the Gita and the Vedas. But you don't see any intelligence, you don't see any brilliance, you don't see any light in their eyes, you don't see any response to reality.

It is better to be mad than to be stupid. But ordinarily, Raquibo, people are not mad, they are just on the verge of going mad at any moment. If you don't turn your energies to meditation you will go mad.

And the difference between you and the mad people is only one of degree, remember. Maybe you are at ninety-nine degrees and the madman has crossed the boundary of one hundred degrees. And any small incident, any accident, can push you one degree more. Your wife escapes with somebody and that's enough. Your business fails, the bank goes bankrupt, the government nationalizes — anything, just one degree, and you can be mad at any moment. But remember, it is better to be mad than to be stupid.

But there is no need to be mad. Why not meditate? And I have created so many mad kinds of meditations that you can be both together — mad and meditators! Slowly slowly meditation is bound to win over.

Sujata has asked, "Bhagwan, I have three questions to ask you. How did you discover Kundalini meditation?" — the first question. Simple, Sujata: Meditating down by the river upon a hill of red ants!

And second: "And Dynamic?" That is even more simple, Sujata; it was almost impossible not to discover it. I came upon it driving on Indian roads in Indian cars!

And third: "And what about Nadabrahma?" Hm!

And the last question

Bhagwan,
Why am I afraid of you?

Yogesh,

I⊤ IS A GOOD SIGN: it means something is on the way. You become afraid of me only when you start coming closer to me; it is natural. To be close to a Master is to be close to a certain kind of death. Only stupid people are not afraid because they can't see what is going to happen: that I am taking you slowly slowly to the cliff. And once you are there and enjoying a joke, I will push you!

Sitting in an armchair at his club, a retired British-colonial army officer was recounting one of his heroic adventures to a young captain.

"There I was, me boy, stalking through the jungle, when out jumps this enormous great tiger right in front of me."

"Gosh, golly, sir, what happened?"

"It stood there and went 'ROAR'!"

"Gosh, golly, sir, what happened next?"

"I fouled me breeches."

"Great Scot! That must have been incapacitating — what happened next?"

"No, no, no," stuttered the old colonel, "I fouled me breeches."

"Yes?" said the young captain, watching the old man evidently in some discomfort.

"No, no, no, I fouled me breeches when I went 'ROAR'!"

Get it?

8

The first question

Bhagwan,
How is it possible that Gurdjieff needed
another head, an Ouspensky, to work on a
third psychology, the psychology of the
Buddhas, while you work by yourself and
you can be both in the state of mind
and no-mind?

Prem Sanatana,

THERE HAVE BEEN TWO KINDS OF MASTERS in the world. One kind, the first, has always needed somebody else to express, to interpret, to philosophize, to communicate what the Master has experienced. Gurdjieff is not alone in that; he needed P.D. Ouspensky — without Ouspensky he would not have been known at all. Ramakrishna comes in the same category; he needed a Vivekananda — without Vivekananda Ramakrishna would have remained absolutely unheard of.

So has been the case with many Masters, for the simple reason that their whole work concerned the heart center. They became crystallized in the heart center — so much so that it was impossible for them to move to the head and to use their own heads. It appeared far easier for them to use somebody else's head rather than their own.

But there was a difficulty in it. One thing was good about it: the Master himself was not constantly moving between two extremes — from mind to no-mind, from no-mind to mind — there was no movement in his being; he was absolutely crystallized. But another kind of trouble was there: the man who was being used as a medium — Ouspensky, Vivekananda, or others — was himself not an enlightened person. Gurdjieff could use Ouspensky's head, but not exactly the way he would have liked to. Ouspensky's own mind was bound to color Gurdjieff's experience; he was bound to bring his own prejudices, his own philosophy, his own understanding to it. He had no experience of his own, he was simply a medium. But the medium is not just an empty vehicle, he has his own mind, and anything passing through his mind is going to be changed a little bit here, a little bit there.

Ouspensky introduced Gurdjieff to the world, but he introduced Gurdjieff in his own way. One cannot blame Ouspensky. What could he do? He tried his best. I think he was one of the best interpreters that any Master has ever been able to find; but still an interpreter is an interpreter. It can't be the same; it is impossible to be the same. Hence sooner or later they had to part from each other.

In the last days of Ouspensky's life he became almost an enemy to Gurdjieff. He started saying, "Now Gurdjieff has gone mad. At first he was moving in the right direction, but the later Gurdjieff has gone astray." He could not say that the whole of Gurdjieff's teaching was wrong because his own teaching was based on Gurdjieff's teaching, but he divided Gurdjieff in two: the first part of Gurdjieff — when Ouspensky was with him — was right and the later part was wrong. In fact, the later part was the culmination of the first part.

But why did this happen? It was almost bound to happen because sooner or later Ouspensky's own mind was going to become a barrier. When he first came to Gurdjieff he was absolutely surrendered to him — surrendered in the sense that he was fascinated by his personality, fascinated intellectually — because he was a great intellectual — absolutely surrendered in the intellectual sense, not in the existential sense. If he had been existentially surrendered he would have been of no use because Gurdjieff needed a head, he was in search of a head. He had many other followers who were devoted to him from their very innermost core, but they were not going to become his interpreters to the world.

When Ouspensky came to Gurdjieff he was already a world-famous mathematician, a philosopher. His own book, *Tertium Organum*, had already been translated into almost all the great languages of the world. And that book, *Tertium Organum*, is really something tremendous; coming out of a man who was unenlightened it is almost a miracle. Intellectually he managed something which nobody has ever been able to manage. He knew nothing, he had not experienced anything, but his intellectual grasp . . . his intellect was really sharp. He belongs to the topmost intellectuals of the whole history of humanity; there are very few competitors to rival him. Only once in a while. . . .

Socrates had such a man, Plato. Socrates was the heart of the teaching, Plato was the head. Exactly the same was repeated in the case of Gurdjieff: Gurdjieff was the heart, Ouspensky became the head. And if I have to choose between the two my choice will be Ouspensky, not Plato. Ouspensky is simply unbelievable; his insight, without any self-realization, is so accurate that anybody who has not experienced will think that Ouspensky was a Buddha, a Christ. Only a Buddha will be able to detect the flaws, not anyone else. The flaws are there but ordinarily undetectable.

He started writing books on Gurdjieff. He wrote one of his greatest contributions, *In Search of the Miraculous*, then he wrote *The Fourth Way*. And these two books introduced Gurdjieff to the world; otherwise, he would have remained an absolutely unknown Master. Maybe a few people would have come in personal contact with him and would have been benefited, but Ouspensky made him available to millions.

But as those books spread all over the world and thousands of people started moving towards Gurdjieff, Ouspensky also became very egoistic — naturally, because he was the cause of the whole thing. In fact, he started thinking, "Without me, what is Gurdjieff? Who is Gurdjieff without me? Who was he? When I met him he was just a refugee living in a refugee camp in Constantinople, almost starving. Nobody had ever heard about him. I have made him world famous; the whole credit goes to me." This idea went to his head — it became too much for him — and in subtle ways he started to dominate the movement. And you cannot dominate a man like Gurdjieff, you cannot dictate to a man like Gurdjieff. They had to part.

In the last days of his life Ouspensky was so against Gurdjieff that he would not tolerate anybody mentioning Gurdjieff's name to him; in his presence Gurdjieff's name was not mentioned. Even in his books Gurdjieff's name was reduced to only "G"; the full name disappeared. After the break just "G" remained — somebody anonymous, " 'G' said . . .," not "Gurdjieff." And he made it clear, very clear: "We have parted and I have developed my own system." He started gathering his own followers. Those followers were not allowed to read Gurdjieff's books, those followers were not allowed to go and see Gurdjieff. While Ouspensky was alive he was very suspicious of anybody who wanted to go to Gurdjieff or who even wanted to study his books.

But Gurdjieff was aware that this was going to happen. Still, there was no other way; some head had to be used. Gurdjieff's work was such that he was absolutely crystallized in his heart; he could not move to the head.

So was the case with Ramakrishna. Vivekananda was an ordinary intellectual, not even of the caliber of Ouspensky, but he made Ramakrishna world famous. Ramakrishna died very early, that's why Vivekananda and Ramakrishna never parted; otherwise the parting was absolutely certain. But Ramakrishna died and Vivekananda became his whole and sole representative. He dominated all the followers, he dominated the whole movement; he became for them the representative of Ramakrishna. If Ramakrishna had lived, the same thing would have happened sooner or later because Vivekananda was just head and nothing else, nothing of the heart. Even if he talks about the heart it is just head-talk, the head talking about the heart, it is not heart-full. There is no love in it, there is no meditation in it, there is no prayer in it, just intellectual analysis. He knew the scriptures and he forced his ideas on Ramakrishna's ideas. And Ramakrishna had died so there was nobody to say no to it.

Vivekananda destroyed the whole beauty of Ramakrishna. But that was going to happen because Ramakrishna was not a man of the head at all.

But this has not always been the case. Buddha never depended on anybody else. He was capable of moving from mind to no-mind, from no-mind to mind; that is his greatness. That is a far greater achievement than that of Gurdjieff or Ramakrishna because their achievements are in a way limited. Buddha is very liquid; he is not solid like a rock, he is more fluid — like a river.

So was the case with Lao Tzu: he never depended on anybody else, he said whatever he had to say. He said it himself, and as beautifully as it could be said. And their philosophies are bound to be far more pure because they come from the original man, they come from the original realization, from the very source; there is no *via media*. So is the case with Zarathustra, Jesus, Krishna, Mahavira.

This is the second category of Masters. The first category is easier in a way; it is easy to be crystallized at one center. It is a far more complex process, a longer and far more arduous journey, to remain alive at both extremes. These are the two extremes: the head and the heart. But it is possible. It has happened before. It is happening right now in front of you.

I live in silence, but my work consists of much intellectual communication. I live in silence, but I have to use words. But when I use words, those words contain my silence. I don't need anybody else to interpret me, hence there is a far greater possibility that whatsoever I am saying will remain pure for a longer period of time.

And now, since Buddha, many scientific developments have happened. . . .

We don't know what Buddha actually said although he never used anybody like Ouspensky or Plato or Vivekananda; he himself was his own interpreter. But there arose a problem when he died. He spoke for forty-two years — he became enlightened when he was about forty and then he lived to eighty-two. For forty-two years he was speaking morning, afternoon, evening. Now there were no scientific methods for recording what he was saying. When he died the first question was how to collect it all. He had said so much — forty-two years is a long time, and many had become enlightened in those forty-two years. But those who became enlightened had become crystallized in the heart because that is easier, simpler, and people tend to move to the simplest process, to the shortcut. Why bother? If you can reach a point directly, straight, then why go roundabout? And when Buddha was alive there was no need for anybody else to interpret him; he was his own spokesman, so the need was never felt.

There were thousands of *arhats* and *bodhisattvas*; they all gathered. Only those were called to the gathering who had become enlightened — obviously, because they would not misinterpret Buddha. And that's true, they could not misinterpret him — it was impossible for them. They had also experienced the same universe of the beyond, they had also moved to the farther shore.

But they all said, "We have never bothered much about his words since we became enlightened. We have listened to him because his words were sweet. We have listened to him because his words were pure music. We have listened to him because just listening to him was a joy. We have listened to him because that was the only way to be close to him. Just to sit by his side and listen to him was a rejoicing, it was a benediction. But we did not bother about what he was saying; once we attained there was no need. We were not listening from the head and we were not collecting in the memory; our own heads and memories stopped functioning long ago."

Somebody became enlightened thirty years before Buddha died. Now for thirty years he sat there by the side of Buddha listening as one listens to the wind passing through the pine trees or one listens to the song of the birds or one listens to the rain falling on the roof. But they were not listening intellectually. So they said, "We have not carried any memory of it. Whatsoever he must have said was beautiful, but what he said we cannot recollect. Just to be with him was such a joy."

It was very difficult now — how to collect his words? The only man who had lived continuously with Buddha for forty-two years was Ananda; he was his personal attendant, his caretaker. He had listened to him; almost every word that he had uttered was heard by Ananda. Even if he was talking to somebody privately, Ananda was present. Ananda was almost always present, like a shadow. He had heard everything — whatsoever had fallen from his lips. And he must have said many things to Ananda when there was nobody there. They must have talked just on going to bed in the night. Ananda used to sleep in the same room just to take care of him — he may need something in the night. He may feel cold, he may feel hot, he may like the window to be opened or closed, or he may feel thirsty and may need some water or something, or — he was getting old — he may feel sick. So Ananda was there continuously.

They all said, "We should ask Ananda." But then there was a very great problem: Ananda was not yet enlightened. He had heard everything that Buddha uttered publicly, uttered privately. They must have gossiped together; there was nobody else who could have said, "I am friendly with Buddha," except Ananda. And Ananda was also his cousin-brother, and not only a cousin-brother but two years older than Buddha. So when he had come to be initiated he asked for a few things before his initiation, because in India the elder brother has to be respected just like your father. Even the elder cousin-brother has to be respected just like your father.

So Ananda said to Buddha, "Before I take initiation . . . . Once I become your *bhikkhu*, your sannyasin, I will have to follow your orders, your commandments. Then whatsoever you say I will have to do. But before that I order you, as your elder brother, to grant me three things. Remember these three things. First: I will always be with you. You cannot say to me, 'Ananda, go some-where else, do something else.' You cannot send me to some other village to preach, to convert people, to give your message. This is my first order to you. Second: I will be always present. Even if you are talking to some-body privately I want to hear everything. Whatsoever you are going to say in your life I want to be an audience to it. So you will not be able to tell me, 'This is a private talk, you go out.' I will not go, remember it! And third-ly: I am not much interested in being enlightened, I am much more interested in just being with you. So if en-lightenment means separating from you I don't care a bit about it. Only if I can remain with you even after en-lightenment, am I willing to be enlightened, otherwise forget about it."

And Buddha nodded his yes to all these three orders — he had to, he was younger than Ananda — and he followed those three things his whole life.

The conference of the *arhats* and the *bodhisattvas* decided that only Ananda could relate Buddha's words. And he had a beautiful memory; he had listened to everything very attentively. "But the problem is he is not yet enlightened; we cannot rely upon him. His mind may play tricks, his mind may change things uncon-sciously. He may not do it deliberately, he may not do it consciously, but he still has a great unconscious in him. He may think he has heard that Buddha said this and he may never have said it. He may delete a few words, he may add a few words. Who knows? And we don't have any criterion because many things that he has heard only he has heard; there is no other witness."

And Ananda was sitting outside the hall. The doors were closed and he was weeping outside on the steps. He was weeping because he was not allowed inside. An eighty-four-year-old man weeping like a child! The man who had lived for forty-two years with Buddha was not allowed in! Now he was really in anguish. Why did he not become enlightened? Why did he not insist? He made a vow, a decision: "I will not move from these steps until I become enlightened." He closed his eyes, he forgot the whole world. And it is said that within twenty-four hours, without changing his posture, he became enlightened.

When he became enlightened he was allowed in. Then he related . . . all these scriptures were related by Ananda. But who knows? He became enlightened afterwards. All those memories belong to the mind of an unenlightened person; even though he had become enlightened, those memories were not those of an enlightened person. It is not absolutely certain that what is reported is exactly what Buddha said.

But now science has given all the technology. Each single word—not only the word but the pauses in between—the very nuances of the words, the way they are uttered, the very gestures, all can be recorded. The words can be recorded, the gestures can be photographed, films can be made, tapes can be made.

Now the best way for any enlightened person is not to depend on anybody else, although that path is difficult, far more difficult, because you have to do two things together. You have to constantly shuttle back and forth, back and forth. You have to constantly go into wordlessness and come out from that emptiness into the world of words. It is a difficult phenomenon, the most difficult phenomenon in the whole of existence, because when you enter into silence it is so beautiful that to come back to the universe of words looks absurd, meaningless. It is as if you have reached to the sunlit peaks and then you come back to the dark holes where people live in the valley, the slums. When you have touched the sunlit peaks, when you can live there and you can float like a cloud in the infinite sky, to come back to the muddy earth, to crawl again with people who *are* living in mud seems to be very absurd. But there is no other way. If you have compassion enough you have to go into this difficult process.

It depends on many things too. It depends on the whole process by which a Master has reached through many lives. Ramakrishna was never an intellectual in any of his lives. A simple man — in this life he was a simple man. Even if he had wanted to it would have been impossible for him to become a Vivekananda too. It was easier to find somebody who could do that work.

Gurdjieff, when he was very young, only twelve years of age, became part of a party of seekers: thirty people who made a decision that they would go to the different parts of the world and find out whether truth was only talk or there were a few people who had known it. Just a twelve-year-old boy, but he was chosen to join the party for the simple reason that he had great stamina, he had great power. One thing was certain about him: whatsoever he decided, he would risk all for it. He would not look back, he would never escape; even if he had to lose his life he would lose his life. And three times he was almost shot dead — almost, but he pulled himself back into life somehow; the purpose was still unfulfilled.

Those thirty people traveled all over the world. They came to India, they went to Tibet and the whole Middle East, all the Sufi monasteries, all the Himalayan monasteries. And they had decided to come back to a certain place in the Middle East and to relate whatsoever they had gained; after each twelve years they were going to meet. At the end of the first twelve years almost half of them did not return; they must have died somehow, or forgotten the mission, or become entangled somewhere. Somebody must have got married, fallen in love. A thousand and one things can happen — people are accident-prone. Only fifteen people returned. And after the next twelve years only three people came back. And the third time only Gurdjieff was there, all the others had disappeared. What happened to them nobody knows.

But this man had very great decisiveness: if he had decided then nothing was going to deter him. He was almost killed three times; the only thing that saved him was his mission, that he had to go back, and he pulled himself out of his death. It needed great inner power.

He had no time to become an intellectual. He was moving with mystics — from one monastery to another monastery, from one cave to another cave, from one country to another country. He came to India, he went to Tibet, he went up to Japan; he gathered knowledge from all over the world. By the time he himself became enlightened there was no time left for him to intellectualize it, to put it into words. He knew the taste, but the words were not there. He needed a man like Ouspensky.

My own approach has been totally different. I began as an intellectual — not only in this life but in many lives. My whole work in many lives has been concerned with the intellect — refining the intellect, sharpening the intellect. In this life I began as an atheist with an absolute denial of God. You cannot be an atheist if you are not supraintellectual, and I was an absolute atheist. People used to avoid me because I was doubting each and every thing and my doubt was contagious. Even my teachers would avoid me.

One of my teachers was dying; I went to see him. He said, "Please . . . I am happy that you have come, but don't say a single word because this is not the time. I am dying and I want to die believing that God is."

I said, "You cannot. Seeing me, the doubt has already arisen."

He said, "What do you mean?"

And the thing started! Before he died, just after twelve hours, he died an atheist. And I was so happy! I had to work for twelve hours continuously. Out of desperation he said, "Okay, let me die peacefully. I say that there is no God. Are you happy? Now leave me alone!"

My university professors were always in difficulties. I was expelled from one college, then another, and then thrown out of one university. Finally one university admitted me with the condition — I had to sign it, a written condition — that I would not ask any questions and I would not argue with the professors.

I said okay. I signed it and the Vice-Chancellor was very happy. And I said, "Now, a few things. What do you mean by 'argument'?"

He said, "Here you go!"

I said, "I have not written that I would not ask for any clarification. I can ask for a clarification. What do you mean by an 'argument'? And if I cannot ask a question, what is the point of your whole department of philosophy? — because all your philosophers ask questions. The whole of philosophy depends on doubt; doubt is the base of all philosophy. If I cannot doubt your stupid philosophers, your stupid professors, then how am I going to learn philosophy?"

He said, "Look at what you are saying! You are calling my professors, in front of me, stupid!"

I said, "They *are* stupid, otherwise why these conditions? Can you think of somebody being intelligent and asking his students not to question him? Is this a sign of intelligence? A professor will *invite* questions. An intelligent professor will be happy with a student who can argue well."

That remained a problem. My whole approach from the very beginning was not that of a Ramakrishna. I am not a devotional type, not at all. I have arrived at God through atheism, not through theism. I have arrived at God not by believing in him but by absolutely doubting him. I have come to a certainty because I have doubted and I went on doubting till there was no possibility to doubt anymore, till I came across something indubitable. That has been my process.

That was not the process of Gurdjieff. He was learning from Masters, moving from one Master to another Master, learning techniques and methods and devices. He learned many devices, but he learned in a very surrendered spirit, that of a disciple.

I have never been anybody's disciple; nobody has been my Master. In fact, nobody was ready to accept me as a disciple, because who would like to create trouble?

One of my professors, who is now dead, Dr. S.K. Saxena, loved me very much. The only man out of all my professors . . . because I came across many professors; I had to leave many colleges and many universities. Rarely does one come across as many professors as I came across. He is the only man that I had some respect for because he never prevented me from doubting, from questioning, even though a thousand and one times he had to accept defeat. I respected him because he was capable of accepting defeat even from a student. He would simply say, "I accept defeat. You win. I cannot argue anymore. I have put forward all the arguments that I can muster and you have destroyed them all. Now I am ready to listen to you if you have something to say."

He was very afraid. . . . When I was doing my final M.A. examination in philosophy he was very afraid because he loved me so much. He wanted me to get through the examination, but he was afraid — afraid that I might write things which were not according to the textbooks or were against the textbooks. I might say things which were not acceptable to the ordinary professors. Just to save me he gave all the papers to such people all over the country as were his friends and he informed them: "Please take care of this young man, don't be offended by him; that is his way. But he has great potential."

Only one thing he could not manage, that was something to be decided by the Vice-Chancellor himself: the verbal examination, and that was the last thing. And the professor had invited a Mohammedan professor from Aligarh University, the head of the department of philosophy there, a very fanatic Mohammedan. My professor was very worried. He said to me again and again, "Don't argue with this man. In the first place, he is a Mohammedan — Mohammedans don't know what argument is. He is very fanatical; if he cannot argue with you he will take revenge. And I know he cannot argue — I know him, I know you. But you just remain quiet because this is the last thing. Don't destroy the whole effort that I have made for you." He said to me, "It is not *your* examination, it seems that *I* am being examined!"

I said, "I will see."

And the first question the Mohammedan professor asked was: "What is the difference between Indian philosophy and Western philosophy?"

I said, "This is something stupid. The very idea! This is nonsense. Philosophy is philosophy. How can philosophy be Indian? And how can philosophy be Eastern or Western? If science is not Eastern and science is not Western, then why philosophy? Philosophy is a quest for truth. How can the quest be Eastern or Western? The quest is the same!"

My professor started pulling my leg underneath the table. I said, "Sir, you stop! Don't pull my leg! Forget all about the examination — now this thing has to be decided!"

The Mohammedan professor was at a loss. What was going on? He said, "What is the matter?"

I said, "He is pulling my leg. He is telling me that you are a Mohammedan — and a fanatic Mohammedan. And he says that if you cannot argue well with me you will take revenge! So do whatsoever you want, but I have to say what I feel. I don't believe in all these distinctions. In fact, to me the very idea of somebody being a philosopher and yet a Mohammedan is simply illogical, it is ridiculous. How can you be a real inquirer if you have already accepted a certain dogma, a certain creed? If you start from *a priori* assumptions, if you start from a belief, you can never reach the truth. Real philosophy starts in a state of not-knowing. And that is the beauty of doubt: it destroys all beliefs."

For a moment he was shocked, felt almost dumb, but he had to give me ninety-nine marks out of a hundred. I asked him, "What happened to the last one?"

He said, "This is something! In my whole life I have never given anybody ninety-nine marks out of a hundred, and you are asking me, 'What happened to the last one?' "

I said, "Yes! Since you are giving me ninety-nine I have every right to ask why you are so miserly. Just one! Make it a hundred — at least be generous for once!"

He had to make it a hundred.

My whole approach has been a totally different approach than that of Ramakrishna and Gurdjieff. I have arrived through doubt, I have arrived through deep and profound skepticism. I have arrived not through belief but through the denial of all belief and disbelief too, because disbelief is belief in a negative form.

A moment came in my life when all beliefs and all disbeliefs disappeared and I was left utterly empty. In that emptiness the explosion happened. Hence it is not so difficult for me, so I can argue easily. I can even argue against argument; that's what I am going to continue to do. I can argue against intellect because I know how to use intellect.

Ramakrishna had never used his intellect; he started from the heart. And the same is the case with Gurdjieff. Buddha could use the intellect because he was the son of a king, well educated, well cultured. All the great philosophers of the country were called to teach him; he knew what the intellectual approach was. And then he became fed up with it.

The same happened with me. I know what can be achieved through intellectual effort: nothing can be achieved through it. When I say it I say it through my own experience.

But it has been beautiful in one way. It did not result in giving me truth — it cannot give truth to anybody — but in an indirect way it has cleansed the ground, it has prepared the ground. It has not helped me to realize myself, but it has helped me to communicate whatsoever I have realized.

I can communicate with you very easily, with no problems. You can ask all kinds of questions, you can ask, you can doubt, because I know that all these questions and doubts can be quashed, they can be destroyed. And it is good that you should ask because then I can destroy your questions. Once all your questions are destroyed, the answer arises in your own being. In that utter emptiness something wells up; it is already there.

I am not in favor of repressing doubt by believing. You are not here to believe in me, you are here to bring out all your disbelief. Your doubts, your questions, all are respected, welcome, so that they can be taken out from you. Slowly slowly a silence, a state of not-knowing arises. And the state of not-knowing is the state of wisdom, is the state of enlightenment.

The second question

Bhagwan,
I belong to the legal profession and have a
very legal mind. Can I also become a sannyasin?

Devakar,

Sannyas places no conditions on you. Everybody is welcome — sinner and saint, legal experts, lawbreakers, virtuous people, criminals — all are welcome. Sannyas makes no precondition, although it will be a little difficult for you. But that is your problem, not my problem. If you belong to the legal profession and have a very legal mind then it is going to be a little difficult for you. So what? Accept it as a challenge! Let it be difficult! In fact, the more difficult it is, the more challenging it is, the more interesting, intriguing it should be, the more attractive it should be. When something is very simple, who wants to do it? When something is difficult it provokes a challenge in you, it provokes intelligence in you.

It is difficult, certainly difficult for a person who has a legal mind because a legal mind means a cunning mind. It is not necessarily intelligent; in fact, if it is intelligent it will not be cunning. Cunningness is a poor substitute for intelligence. And the legal profession is the most cunning profession in the world.

It is known that Jesus moved with drunkards and gamblers and even a prostitute, but I have not heard that he moved with legal experts. In fact, the Jewish rabbi is nothing but a legal expert because the Jewish religion is more or less law and less of a religion. It is more or less a legal code. It does not have much metaphysics, it does not have great flights; it is very earthly. It tells you in detail what to do and what not to do. Those ten commandments — that may have been the beginning of the legal profession.

You can become a sannyasin. Even if the desire has arisen in you there seems to be a spark of intelligence. Behind all your cunningness there must be a little fire still left.

Devakar, don't be worried. Come into this orange fire — it burns everything; it will burn you too. It consumes everything; it will consume the legal expert too — but only if you are ready to be consumed, if you are ready to drop your cunningness, because that will have to be dropped. Not that I say it is a condition, but as you become a sannyasin and as you move into meditation you will start becoming more and more intelligent and then, naturally, as a by-product, cunningness disappears.

If the legal profession disappears from the world, ninety percent of cunningness will disappear with it. It is the people who know the law who go on creating confusion.

One of my Vice-Chancellors was a great law expert, a world-renowned law expert. He used to tell again and again that once it happened that he was fighting a case for an Indian maharajah in the Privy Council. And he was such a drunkard . . . on the last night he had drunk too much, the hangover was still there, so he forgot whether he was against the maharajah or for the maharajah. So for one hour he spoke *against* the maharajah! The maharajah was perspiring, his assistants were trembling: "What is he doing?" And in the tea break they told him, "What have you done? You have destroyed our client! Now there is no way to save him."

He said, "What has happened?"

"You have been speaking against our own client!"

He said, "Don't be worried, there is still time."

And then when the court started again he said, "You heard me, Your Honor, for one hour. Thank you for your patience, because I was only giving all those arguments that are possible from the opposite side. Now I will defend my client."

And he destroyed his own arguments and won the case!

The legal expert has no dedication to truth, he does not care about truth, he simply cares about whosoever pays the money. He is far worse than a prostitute. The prostitute only sells her body and the legal expert sells his mind. He is ready to be purchased by anybody — whosoever is ready to pay the price. He does not care about what is right and what is wrong.

But if you become a meditator you will start caring about what is right and what is wrong. Not that you will have to, not that it is a commandment, not that it is something like a character that has to be cultivated; it happens naturally that cunningness starts disappearing.

So you have to be alerted. You can become a sannyasin; there is no problem for me — I never ask anybody, "Who are you?" If you want to take sannyas I give you sannyas, unconditionally. Out of my love I give you sannyas, out of my respect for you I give sannyas. I respect each and every individual because to me each and every individual represents God, godliness. Even if the god has fallen very low and has become a legal expert, still the god is a god! Even in your fallen state, Devakar, I respect you, I will give you sannyas. It is for you to decide, because this is risky — risky for you, for your profession.

In the days of the Raj in India, a British soldier was expected to do his duty and very little else. Any display of human weakness by the troops was regarded as letting the side down in front of the natives.

So naturally, the new commanding officer was very worried when an angry crowd of Hindus approached the barracks, complaining that one of their sacred cows had been outraged by an infantryman. They demanded an immediate court martial.

"Don't worry, sir," said an experienced law expert. "Our man is bound to get off. This cow has a very bad reputation — it has already been cited in seven previous cases."

You get the idea?

You will have to drop such legal expertise, you will have to drop such cunning approaches. You will have to become more human. But these are the consequences of meditation; nothing is imposed here.

Just the other day I was reading an article written by a bishop in *The Times* against me. He says: "Beware of this man." He quotes me: "This man says, 'Character is the concern of the stupid. The really intelligent people are only concerned with consciousness.' " He is quoting me to make people beware because this is a dangerous statement. He says: "Rather than publishing articles on this man, *The Times* should publish more articles on Mother Teresa of Calcutta, who teaches character. And character is the only thing, the real thing."

Character is not the real thing at all. But the poor bishop has not been able to understand what I have been saying. He does not understand the consequences of consciousness. Character is a consequence of consciousness. If character comes out of your consciousness then it has a beauty of its own; if it is just imposed from the outside then it is ugly. But that's what Christians are doing all over the world — and Hindus and Mohammedans; they are all in the same boat.

My whole concern is consciousness. I teach you how to be more conscious because I know one thing for certain: that if you are more conscious your character will change of its own accord. A conscious person lives in a totally different way: he is more compassionate.

Mother Teresa of Calcutta is not compassionate — she behaves compassionately but is not compassionate. All her compassion is nothing but a means to reach to heaven. And to reduce compassion to a means is ugly; compassion is an end unto itself.

An ancient Taoist parable says:

A man fell into a well. He started shouting loudly, "Save me! I am drowning!"

A Buddhist monk passed by. He looked in the well and he said, "Be calm, be quiet, don't be disturbed. Life is a flux. It comes, it goes. And remember what Gautam the Buddha has said: It is all dream. Your drowning is a dream, my seeing is a dream. Don't shout. And even if you are saved, what is the point? Sooner or later you will have to die, so why not now? Why postpone it? Die silently, peacefully, so that you are not born again. Get out of the wheel of birth and death!"

The man was aghast. He said, "What nonsense you are talking! You can sermonize later on. First take me out! This is no time to teach me great philosophy!"

But the Buddhist said, "I cannot be distracted by things. The Buddha has said: 'Walk on undistracted.' Good-bye." And he walked on undistracted!

Then a Confucian monk looked in the well, and the man said, "Now please save me. Don't waste time!"

And the Confucian monk said, "Do you know what the Master has said? Confucius has said that each well should have a protective wall around it. Don't be worried. I will create a great movement all over the country so that no well is unprotected like this."

The man said, "But that is not going to save me!"

The Confucian monk said, "It is not a question of individuals. The Master says the question is always of the society, the question is of the future. Think of the future and think of the society. Don't be so selfish!"

And he went into the marketplace and started teaching the people: "Look at this example of what is happening. Our Master has already said that each well should have a protective wall. He is always right, but people have not listened to the Master and they are suffering."

Then a Christian missionary looked into the well and the man said, "It seems my death is certain. Today no layman is coming to the side of the well! Now you will teach me your gospel!"

But the Christian said, "Don't be worried." Out of his bag he pulled a rope, threw the rope in, told the man to tie the rope around his waist and he would pull him out. The man was surprised — no metaphysics, no religion. He was pulled out, he was very thankful. He fell at his feet and he said, "You are the only really religious person! But only one curiosity — how come you were carrying a rope in your bag?"

He said, "We always keep all kinds of arrangements with us. Who knows what opportunity will arise to serve? — because service is religion and it is through serving people that one can reach to heaven. I am not concerned with you," said the missionary, "my concern is with my own place in heaven. Now I have scored! In fact, I am grateful to you. Go on falling in! Help us poor missionaries to serve you. Go on teaching that to your children and don't listen to these Confucian people who say that every well needs a wall to protect it. If every well has a wall, nobody will fall in and then how are we going to save people? And without saving people there is no way to heaven. Go on falling into wells, go on making wells without walls. Teach your children to fall in, because unless we serve you there is no way to God!"

Don't laugh at it — this is the real situation. Just think: if there were no poverty in India, no orphans, no paralyzed people, no people suffering from leprosy, where would Mother Teresa of Calcutta be? Then no Nobel Prize either! These people are needed to create a Mother Teresa. These missionaries will not like a world where all are rich, happy.

Bertrand Russell used to say — and I agree with him absolutely — that much of religion will disappear if the world becomes rich, people are healthy, people live long lives, people's lives are joyous; much of religion will disappear. It is true because much of religion depends on all these things; particularly Christianity depends on all these things.

Now, that bishop in London is saying that Mother Teresa is doing great work. But how will you do great work if poor people are no longer there, if blind people are not there, if lepers are not there? What are you going to do? The missionaries will be at a loss! You have to keep this world in the same misery and mess as it is in. Just think of the poor missionaries, otherwise they will be nowhere.

My concern is certainly with consciousness, not with character. My concern is to make you more aware, alert, and out of that alertness whatsoever happens is good. If out of that alertness service happens it is good, if love happens it is good, if compassion happens it is good, if sharing happens it is good, because out of that awareness evil is impossible.

Devakar, you are welcome. I am not concerned with what you are doing. My whole concern is with your being, not with your doing.

And the last question

Bhagwan,
No! No! I don't get it! Breeches? Roar?
What? Am I just dumb or something?

Prem Katina,

Neither are you dumb nor "something". Either

you are British or you must have been British in your past life!

A seventy-five-year-old British field marshal tells his adjutant to bring his brigade to attention and announces: "Gentlemen, I am proud to tell you that at 08.30 hours, Greenwich Mean Time, my wife gave birth to a seven-and-a-half-pound baby boy! Gentlemen, I thank you!"

Katina, get it?

This very proper Englishman walks into a pet shop. As he closes the door behind him he hears a voice welcoming him, "I know something about you! I know something about you!"

Embarrassed, he looks around and finds that it is but a parrot. Impressed, he asks to buy the bird.

"So sorry, sir," replies the owner, "I cannot sell it. But I can sell you a couple of eggs which after incubation will give you the same breed."

The man buys the eggs, takes them home and puts them in the incubator. After ten days two little ducklings crawl out of the eggshells. Furious, he goes back to the shop to complain. As he enters he hears, "I know something about you! I know something about you!"

9

The first question

Bhagwan,
I have been here now for almost two and a half
years, but I still feel that something in my
life goes basically wrong. Except for short
glimpses, I am unable to find any lasting
meaning in it. Most of the time I'm hanging
in a bottomless, quite frightening, uncomfortable
"nowhere." What is wrong? Please comment.

Prem Gayan,

THE WHOLE PROBLEM is rooted in the desire of attaining a permanent meaning for life. Life is not a problem at all, but we expect things which are against the fundamental law of life and then we are in trouble. Life is constantly changing and it is good that it is constantly changing; that's its beauty, its splendor. If it were permanent, static, it would be not life but death and it would be utterly boring. It would stink because it would be stagnant. And the mind is constantly asking for something permanent. The mind is the desire for the permanent, and life is impermanence.

Hence if you really want to be blissful you have to live the impermanent life as it is, without any expectation, without any imposition on your part. Flow with life. It changes — *you* change with it. Why bother about a permanent meaning? What will you do with a permanent meaning?

And meaning exists only when something functions as a means to some other end. Life is not a means to some other end, it is an end unto itself, hence really it cannot have any meaning. That does not mean it is meaningless, it simply means it is transcendental to meaning or no-meaning. Those words are irrelevant.

What is the meaning of a rose flower? And what is the meaning of a sunset? What is the meaning of love? What is the meaning of beauty? There are no meanings because they are not *means* to anything else. A sunset is simply beautiful just for its own sake; it has no utility, you cannot use it as a commodity. A car has meaning, a machine has meaning, a house has meaning, but what is the meaning of a rose flower? There is no meaning in it, but because there is no meaning in it it has tremendous beauty. A machine, howsoever meaningful, is never beautiful; it can't be — it is a commodity, it is utilitarian; it is not poetry.

Life is poetry, life is a song, life is a dance.

Gayan, your very approach is wrong, that's why you go on missing.

You say: *Except for short glimpses, I am unable to find any lasting meaning in it.*

Just meditate over those short glimpses. Those glimpses must have happened when you were not seeking for meaning, when you were relaxed, when you had forgotten all about meaning, when you were not concerned about meaning. Then suddenly there was joy, there was bliss. The moment you start grabbing, clinging to those beautiful glimpses, those moments, the

205

moment your mind says, "Make it permanent. Now this is the thing that I have been always asking for, now don't let it go," you destroy it, you kill it. The glimpse disappears; it remains only a memory and it goes on fading far away. Soon you will not be able even to believe that it had existed. It will happen again only when you have forgotten again the constant desire for meaning, the constant desire for permanency, the constant desire that things should be according to you.

No, that is not the way of a sannyasin, Gayan. A sannyasin has no expectations from existence; he simply flows with the existence without any resistance. The sannyasin allows existence to have its own course; wherever it leads, the sannyasin is ready to go with it. The sannyasin has no destination, no goal as such. And then these glimpses will be coming more and more.

But you have to meditate on these glimpses — when they happen, how they happen, what makes them happen. And you will find a few essential things: you are relaxed when they happen, you are at rest when they happen, you have no desire when they happen, you are not greedy when they happen, you are not thinking of meaning, significance, value when they happen. There is the secret. Drop all these hindrances forever. Let life exist according to its own harmony; simply be a part in it, just a wave in the ocean. Don't try to dominate the ocean; that very effort is an ego trip.

Meditate over Murphy's maxim:

If you don't care where you are you ain't lost.

And also:

Nothing is ever so bad that it can't get worse.

Rejoice! And why be afraid of the "nowhere"? Everywhere is nowhere. Wherever you are it is nowhere. Existence is infinite, so you will always be in the nowhere. You have to accept it. Buddha calls it *tathata* — suchness. Such is the case: wherever you are it is nowhere, whoever you are you are a nobody.

206

Once these truths are accepted, life starts happening in a totally different way, because in this acceptance the ego dies. The ego can exist only through resistance, through fight, through struggle.

That's what you have been doing, Gayan. But it is nothing special about you, that's how the whole German mind is conditioned.

Gayan is a German — one hundred percent German. Once I wanted to choose her as one of my mediums, but I had to drop that idea at least for the time being for the simple reason that the German conditioning is very deep-rooted in her. She could not flow with my energy — unconsciously, she was not aware. She wanted to be a medium, she was immensely happy that I had called her; she was hoping that she would be chosen. She would have been chosen, but there was deep unconscious resistance. Consciously she was totally in my hands, but unconsciously she was trying to give my energy a certain shape, a certain pattern, a certain flow. Hence I thought it better to wait a little longer.

Gayan, you will have to drop your German conditioning. That conditioning is good if you want to become a soldier, but it is not good if you want to become a sannyasin; they are poles apart — they are just the opposite of each other. The sannyasin has to be utterly restful, relaxed, resistanceless — a hollow bamboo — so he can become a flute for the divine lips, so a song can flow through him.

It will happen, Gayan, it is going to happen. If glimpses are happening then there is no problem. If once in a while a few windows open then doors will also open, and you can escape through those windows into the open sky. But you are too much after becoming perfect. Drop that idea. Imperfection is perfectly good. Don't try to do the impossible. Just being ordinary is immensely beautiful.

But I can see her problems. The fundamental problem is: she is a German. The second problem: she has worked as a fashion model so she has the idea of how to be perfectly beautiful. Those things have gone deep into her. She is a perfectionist, so wherever she has been in these two and a half years she has come into conflict with people. Because this place is not for perfectionists, this place is a crazy place — it is absolutely un-German! And the problem is that I have got so many German sannyasins! And I can understand why the German government is so worried, because I am destroying their young people — I am destroying their conditioning as Germans. Once they have been sannyasins, once they have understood the art of being a sannyasin, no Adolf Hitler can ever dominate them; that is impossible.

Perfectionism is a kind of neurosis; it *is* neurotic — it is a beautiful name for neurosis.

Gayan, drop that idea. Just be ordinary, simple, nobody, and then things will start happening in leaps and bounds.

I am sending her back for a few days to Germany just to see and compare what has happened to her. She will not be able to realize it here; she will be able to realize it only in Germany. There she will be able to see that in these two and half years much water has gone down the Ganges; she is no more the same person. And there she will be able to recognize how people are behaving, how people are being trained to be neurotics. And when she is back I hope she will come with a better understanding, more relaxed, more restful.

I have great hopes about you, Gayan — much *is* possible. You are just on the verge. If you start accepting things as they are and you drop the idea of how they should be, if you drop the "shoulds" and "should-nots," then there is not much trouble. Life starts helping you, caring about you. Life is very caring, very loving; we just never allow it. We are always trying to force it to go *our* way, and that is not possible. Life cannot go our way, *we* have to go life's way.

That's what I mean when I emphasize again and again the philosophy of let-go. Let-go is my only approach towards life and existence.

The second question

Bhagwan,
I just decided to take sannyas because I
wanted to do it anyway (during my five weeks
of being here). Now inner struggle starts
again; I feel under pressure and that it was
not a free decision and did not really come
from my heart.

Helga Szelinsky,

PLEASE DON'T TAKE SANNYAS. Wait. This is not the right time. If it is not really coming from your heart then don't force it upon yourself; it will be something imposed and ugly. Anything imposed becomes ugly, even sannyas. It will be plastic; it will not be real, it will not be alive. There is no need. If it happens spontaneously without any feeling of pressure, only then; otherwise it will create trouble for you, and I am not here to create unnecessary trouble for you. Once you are a sannyasin there are many many *necessary* troubles, so avoid unnecessary troubles as far as possible because there are too many necessary ones.

And never do anything for wrong reasons — because so many people are taking sannyas, because your friends have taken sannyas, "There must be something in it — why so many people are attracted." These are all wrong reasons.

Murphy says: Nothing is ever done for the right reasons.

He is right in almost ninety-nine point nine percent cases: nothing is ever done for the right reasons. People go on doing things for wrong reasons and then they complain that their life is miserable; it is bound to be so. They are responsible for it; nobody else is responsible for it.

Do things always for the right reasons. And the right reasons always come from your heart, not from your head.

Murphy also says: No matter where you go, there you are.

So how is it going to help? You may become a sannyasin, Helga, you may wear orange, but there you are underneath the orange clothes, behind a new name. Everything will be old, just the label will be changed. By changing the label you don't go through a revolution, you are not reborn. And unless you are reborn you cannot be a sannyasin.

Wait. This is not the right time. And never be in a hurry about such important matters. It is a question of life and death — in fact far more important than life and death because it can take you *beyond* life and death. That's the whole alchemy of sannyas: to take you beyond life and death. It is far more important than anything else, so one should not be in a hurry. Don't be impatient.

In these five weeks just be here, meditate, do a few groups, watch sannyasins, then go back home. Don't create this anxiety in your mind: "To be or not to be. . ." otherwise your five weeks will be wasted. You will not be able to participate in anything totally because your constant worry will be: "When am I going to take sannyas?" If you don't take sannyas you will feel you are missing; if you do you will think you have done something which was not coming out of your heart. Either way you will be a loser.

There is a season, a right season, when things happen easily, when you need not do them, when they simply happen; you are only a witness to the fact that they are happening. Just as the snake leaves the old skin one day, slips out of it — it did not make the decision; the time had come. One day the child is born out of the womb; nine months are over. It is not a decision on the child's part that "Now is the time for me to be born." Spring comes, and flowers and flowers . . . the whole earth rejoices.

Sannyas also happens like that. Then there is beauty, then there is grace, and *only* then are you a sannyasin. It is not a question of being recruited, it is not some discipline that has to be forced on you, it is not a question of arguing for or against. When it comes from your heart there is no alternative, there is no either/or; it is not philosophy.

Soren Kierkegaard has written one beautiful book; the name of the book is *Either/Or.* And it is not only the name of the book, his whole life can be called an experiment in either/or. In his whole life he was never decisive — always thinking whether to do it or not to do it.

For years a woman waited for him and he was unable to decide whether to marry her or not to marry her. He pondered and pondered, he consulted encyclopaedias, great treatises on marriage and love, took many notes for and against, weighed it this way and that, but could not come to a conclusion. All the arguments came out almost equal. Much could be said for, much could be said against, and it was so equally balanced — how to decide? Tired, the woman married somebody else.

And this was his whole life: about everything he went on pondering and pondering; he never could do anything. If death had also been a question to be decided by him he would not have died yet; he would be sitting in

Copenhagen and pondering over death. If birth had been a question of a decision on his part he would have never been born; he would have pondered and pondered in the mother's womb, sitting there — to come out or not? His approach, this stupid approach towards life, became so famous that when he used to pass down the streets — only once a month; he had to go to the bank to draw some money. . . . His father, seeing his son and his inability to decide about everything, had deposited some money in his name because it was absolutely certain he would not be able to do anything in his life. A good offer had come for a professorship; he pondered so long that the university decided to appoint somebody else. So he lived in a very poor way, because the money in the bank was limited — that was his only money, and he had to live his whole life on that money. Once every month, the first day of the month, he would go to the bank to withdraw a small sum of money and come back home. Even going to the bank he would ponder whether to go this way or that. He would stand at the crossroads for hours — and not just once, it was an every-month affair, and every month he had to decide again and again. His approach became so famous that urchins used to follow him from his house to the bank and from the bank to the house, calling behind him, "Either/Or, Either/Or, Either/Or!" Copenhagen knew him not by his name, Soren Kierkegaard, his name became Either/Or.

Helga, wait. Next time when you come — if I am still here. . . . Until then, wait. And there is no better time than the present when you want to postpone a thing. And who knows? We may not be made for each other. I am not saying *you* are not made for me, that I cannot say, but I may not be made for you; that much I can say. I may not deserve you! So leave it aside; the very question has to be put aside.

She has also asked another question: "Bhagwan, when

you tell jokes I cannot laugh. I can only listen to serious things." That's enough indication that we don't deserve each other. Certainly I don't deserve you—I take the whole responsibility on myself. Then this place will not fit with you and it will be difficult for me to make the whole lot fit with you and according to you. If you can only listen to serious things . . . listen! The world is full of serious things.

This is a place of laughter and love. We don't believe in serious things, we believe in living non-seriously.

The third question

Bhagwan,
What is Gautam the Buddha's message in short?

Gautami,

ALL THINGS BEING EQUAL, YOU LOSE. All things being in your favor, you still lose. Win or lose, you lose.

The fourth question

Bhagwan,
I am a fool. What should I do?

Muktananda,

THAT'S JUST FAR OUT! Don't do a thing. Please remain as you are. Remember, fools rush in and get the best seats!

The fifth question

Bhagwan,
You said today that all women are essentially
nuns but that no men are monks. But since I
came to live in Poona my sexual energy seems
to have disappeared — I think I'm just terrified
of all the vibrant, alive women here!

Swami Anand Neeraj,

I THINK YOU ARE turning into a nun — miracles happen!
I will have to change your name; just wait a little longer.
If you finally decide that it has really happened and it
was not just a passing phase, you will be known as Ma
Anand Neeraj.

An old man phoned his son-in-law — he had just got
married to his daughter — and asked him, "How are
things going?"

The son-in-law said, "I am sorry to say, sir, but it
seems I am married to a nun."

The old man said, "What do you mean — 'married to a
nun'?"

The young man said, "None in the night, none in the
morning."

The old man laughed and he said, "Now I understand.
Then tonight you come for dinner to my home and see
the Mother Superior."

If, Neeraj, you have turned into a nun, slowly you
will grow into a Mother Superior! Don't be worried.
Growth is all that is needed — this is a growth center.
Just go on growing. Don't be worried about what you
are growing into; growth is the point. If you are growing, all is right.

The sixth question

Bhagwan,
A few questions . . .

Now, I always get puzzled with Dutch names. The spelling says "Joke," but Dutch people are strange, they pronounce it as "Yokay"—they destroy the whole beauty of it! Okay, Yokay. . . .

The first question:
How many Women Libbers does it take to screw in a light bulb?
Five: one to screw it in and four to consider the implications.

Second:
And how many Buddhists does it take to screw in a light bulb?
Two: One to screw it in and one not to screw it in.

Third: And how many Jewish mothers does it take to screw in a light bulb?
None: the Jewish mother says, "So? I will sit in the dark!"

And fourth: And how many sannyasins does it take to change a light bulb?
Only one to screw in the light bulb and ten thousand to celebrate the great occasion!

The seventh question

Bhagwan,
What is being open?

Devena,

BEING OPEN SIMPLY MEANS being without mind. If the

mind is there you are closed. Mind is a wall surrounding you. It is a transparent wall, hence you can see through it and you can go on living behind it without ever becoming aware that you are living in a prison cell. Prisons should be made of glass, then very few people will suffer so much in prisons. They will be able to see the people walking on the road, talking; they will be able to see everything, and they will believe that they are free. If they are not going out and mixing with the people, that is simply their own decision that they don't want to mix with the crowds. They are "aristocrats," they are not ordinary people, they are "special" people. And these walls which cannot be seen will not be thought of as walls, they will look like protection.

That's how the mind is: mind is a transparent wall of glass, very transparent glass — Belgian-made, not Indian, because in India you cannot make transparent glass; it is impossible.

If you have a mind then politically the mind is going to be either communist or socialist or fascist; religiously it is going to be Catholic, Protestant, Christian, Hindu, Mohammedan; philosophically it will belong to a certain school of philosophy. It can't be free. Mind can't have freedom — its very existence is a slavery — and mind keeps you closed. You always look from a certain fixed angle, from a certain fixed obsession; you can't see things as they are. It is impossible for the mind to see things as they are — it is inevitable that it will distort them according to its own *a priori* conclusions.

Just the other day I was telling you I received a letter from an Irish mother written to her daughter who is a sannyasin here, saying that she has been reading my books, she has looked at pictures of me, she felt something — the books are beautiful. The only question she wants to ask is: Is this man a Catholic or not? "If he is a Catholic then everything is okay; if he is not a Catholic, then come back home as soon as possible."

And Irish Mukta has also received a letter from her mother, a totally different letter but in a way the same. Mukta's mother says, "As I have understood, you are in the best of places in the world. The only thing that disturbs me is that it is a religious place; if it were not for the religion, then it would be one hundred percent beautiful." Now, for one the word "religion" is creating trouble; for the other, if it is not Catholic then there is trouble.

People go on inquiring who I am, Hindu, Christian, Mohammedan. And I say I am neither this nor that, I am simply a blissful man who is enjoying life in totality. And I call *this* religion — the only real religiousness.

Devena, dropping the mind is becoming open. Meditation is an effort to dismantle the wall brick by brick. Sannyas is a decision that we will behead ourselves and we will start living as no-minds. We will function from a state of not-knowing, because only then are you innocent and only then are you open. And that's the really scientific attitude, the scientific approach towards life.

At the ultimate peak, science and religion have to meet. If both are seeking truth — and both *are* seeking truth — then at the ultimate peak they are bound to meet. Howsoever different the paths are that they follow, their fundamental, their essential core cannot be different. The essential core of the scientific approach is that you should not approach any fact with any conclusion; you should approach the fact in a state of not-knowing; only then will you be able to encounter it as it is. If you have a certain idea then your idea is going to influence your conclusion; your observation will become prejudiced. And a prejudiced mind can never be scientific; in fact, a prejudiced mind is the only mind there is. Hence I say a mind can never be scientific, nor can a mind be religious.

Science approaches the outer world of facts without any fanatical attitudes and religion approaches the inner world of facts without any fanatical attitudes. The fanatic believes more in his fiction than in the facts; he imposes his fictions on the facts.

A certain Dr. Banerjee came to me; he wanted my help. He said, "I am a scientist." He is the head of a department at Rajasthan University, doing some research work in parapsychology; he is the head of the parapsychology department. He told me that he wanted my help because he was doing some scientific work on the theory of reincarnation: that man is born many times again and again.

I talked with him and I said, "Do you believe in reincarnation?"

He said, "Certainly. I am a Hindu and I believe that it is true. Now I want to prove it scientifically."

I said, "Then your research is unscientific from the very beginning. If you are a Hindu and you believe that it is true without experimenting, without going into the process of experimentation, without gathering facts, and already the belief is there, then you will impose your belief. You will not listen to the facts; you will try to distort the facts according to your theory, according to your *a priori* belief. You are not a scientist at all. Forget that idea that you are a scientist. Who has given you a Ph.D.? And what nonsense are you doing in your parapsychology department? Better call it the teaching of Hindu religion. Why call it parapsychology? Then some Christian will try to prove scientifically that there is no reincarnation, there is only one life. And if it is to be proved democratically, then Christians, Jews and Mohammedans outnumber Hindus and if it is to be decided democratically, by vote, then they will win because how many Hindus are there? Almost half of humanity is Christian, the second great religion is Mohammedanism, then there are Jews — all three together are enough to defeat a small community of

Hindus very easily. If everybody sets out with his belief to find out facts to prove it, then it is not scientific."

He had come to stay for a few days; he escaped immediately, and I have not heard of him anymore since then. He was not interested in inquiring, he did not have an open mind, but he confessed to me that he was a Hindu thinking that I was also a Hindu. He would not have said that to any Christian or to a Mohammedan or to a Jew. He was very embarrassed when I said these things to him. The last thing that he asked me was, "Are you not a Hindu?"

I said, "I am nobody. Why should I be a Hindu? Blood is neither Hindu nor Mohammedan nor Christian, nor are bones Hindu, Mohammedan, Christian. How can consciousness be Hindu, Mohammedan and Christian? I am just my consciousness, I am my bliss. How can bliss be Hindu or Mohammedan?"

Devena, being open means dropping your mind politically, religiously, philosophically; dismantling it brick by brick. It is a painful process, but it is the only way to know the truth and it is the only way to be free from all kinds of superstitions, from all kinds of fanatical beliefs. The idea of the fanatic is: "My religion is true, and don't be misled by the facts!" He does not trust the facts; he believes his dogma. And the more ancient it is the more he believes in it. His idea is: "How could people have believed in it for such a long period? It must be true."

But the Jews are as old as the Hindus and they have always believed that there is only one life, and Hindus have always believed that there are many lives. The religions that were born out of Hinduism — Jainism and Buddhism — both believe in many lives, and the religions that were born out of Judaism — Christianity and Islam — both believe that there is no other life, only one life. Time cannot be decisive, nor can numbers be decisive.

219

Only a scientific approach or a religious approach . . . it is the same to me. I call it science when your inquiry is objective, I call it religious when your inquiry is subjective, but for both inquiries an open consciousness is absolutely required. That is the first, fundamental requirement: a consciousness without any mind — and that can happen only through meditation. Meditation is the only magic that can help you to be free from the mind, can help you to be free from yourself, your past and all the burden of the past.

The eighth question

Bhagwan,
What is the difference between an optimist and a
pessimist?

Suriyo,

Not much. An optimist believes we live in the best of all possible worlds. A pessimist fears this is true.

The ninth question

Bhagwan,
Can I count on you to kill me?

Prem Kavita,

Certainly, but you are not ready yet. I am ready to kill, but you can be killed only at the right moment, not even a single minute before. And you are not yet ready. Your desire is good, but it is only a desire. You will have to deserve it.

Just last night I killed Magga. Now she is crying, not understanding what has happened. She was a medium; suddenly I dropped her. It is ego-shattering. The mediums are bound to feel special; they can start gathering a certain ego in themselves — they can become serious.

I have been looking at your questions, Kavita. All your questions show a certain sarcastic attitude. This is the first question that I have chosen as being worth answering, otherwise I simply throw them in the wastepaper basket. They don't show love, they don't show trust, they don't show surrender. And if I kill you without your love it will be murder. If I kill you with your love it is transformation. You will have to look deep within yourself; somewhere the bridge has not happened yet. You are here, but your questions show that you are still functioning from knowledge.

Kavita is a breath therapist here; that may be the cause of the whole trouble. If you are a therapist here you start feeling a certain ego, a subtle ego. The cleaners, the toilet cleaners are in a far better situation: they cannot carry any ego. And it has been my experience that they come far closer to me than the therapists because the therapist comes with the idea that he "knows." Somewhere deep down he also carries the idea that he is helping Bhagwan's work, that he is very essential to the work, that he is indispensable, that without him there will be a gap; he is needed. The cleaner cannot feel that, hence sometimes the toilet cleaners blossom.

Just three days ago I chose Nandan as a new medium. She has been a cleaner, but I am surprised at her availability, at her total surrender, at her absolute trust. I can flow through her just as the wind can pass through the pine trees — no hindrance, no obstruction.

Kavita, I don't feel that in you yet. *I* am ready to kill — that's my whole function here. A Master is needed only because you cannot kill your own ego; it is a difficult task. It can be done, but it is a very difficult task. It is almost like pulling yourself up by pulling your shoe-strings. It is difficult; some help is needed. Some help can be given, but it can be given only when there is no ego.

Kavita, meditate over it. The day you are ready . . . my sword is always ready! What am I doing the whole day in my room? — polishing my sword so it does not gather rust!

The tenth question

Bhagwan,
You said that there is a Russian here. What
do you think of Russians? Will there be a
Third World War?

Anand Devendra,

Russians are beautiful people but they are victims of a very stupid philosophy, of a very stupid political ideology. The people are beautiful but they are dominated by the most ugly regime ever.

A few of my sannyasins in Russia — of course they are underground sannyasins — have sent me a few jokes. Just the other day I received them. They have been translating jokes, Newsletters, *Sannyas* and circulating them underground. They gather once in a while to listen to a tape, to meditate. And they have been hearing so many jokes about everybody that they must be feeling that I am not paying any attention to them, so they have sent me two beautiful jokes.

First:

A man goes into a food shop in Moscow and asks for two kilos of meat. As usual, the shop-girl answers, "No meat today, Comrade."

"No meat!" he shouts. "No meat! They haven't got any meat!" He runs into the street with both arms raised, shouting at the top of his voice, "No meat! No meat! They haven't got any meat!" Then on he continues down the street shouting at everyone, "They haven't got any meat! No meat!"

He makes such a noise that the police come running. They see him shouting his head off, immediately arrest him and take him off to prison. In his cell he continues to cry out as he shakes the bars, "No meat! They haven't got any meat!"

"We'll have to teach this chap a lesson," says the prison officer. "Take him out into the yard and pretend you're going to shoot him. That'll soon shut him up!"

So the guard marches the man, still shouting, into the yard. They line him up against the wall, load the rifles with empty cartridges, take aim and fire.

There are a few seconds' silence and then suddenly the cry goes up. "No bullets! No bullets! They haven't got any bullets either!"

And the second:

A Swede, a Pole and a Russian met together and naturally their conversation got round to sex.

"Sex in Sweden," said the Swede, "is a group of people getting together in someone's flat and having an orgy."

"Sex in Poland," said the second man, "is a group of people watching a program on TV about people having an orgy in a flat in Sweden."

"What does sex mean in Russia?" they both asked the third man.

"Sex in Russia," said the man sadly, "is a group of people meeting someone from Poland who saw the TV program about the Swedish people having an orgy. . . ."

They are beautiful people but under a rotten regime. They need to be freed — they need to be freed from this violence, this dictatorship that is imposed on them against their will. But the imposers say this is for their own sake. In the beginning the communists used to say that the dictatorship was only a temporary phenomenon; soon it would disappear. Once socialism was established even the state would wither away, so what to say about dictatorship? But now sixty years have passed since the Revolution; just the contrary has happened: the state has become more and more powerful. There seems to be no sign of its ever withering away. It is the first time in the whole history of humanity that a state is so powerful that there is no possibility of any revolution against it. No people have been so crippled and paralyzed. Before there was always at least a possibility of rebelling against a regime. If it was too much you could always throw it away. But now for the first time it has happened: the Russian government is so powerful, so immensely powerful, that the individual is nothing.

And they have learned one thing: how to prevent a revolution from the very beginning, from the very seeds of revolution, so not even freedom of opinion is allowed. You are even afraid to talk to your own wife because, who knows? — she may be an informer. Nobody knows about anybody. You are afraid to talk to your own children because they belong to the Young Communists' League and they inform against their parents. Only in Russia do walls have ears — only in Russia. Everywhere else it is only a proverb, in Russia it is a reality. You cannot even think independently because to think independently you need certain things to be made available. If Marx had been born in Russia he would not have been able to write *Das Kapital* because there is no British Museum where he could have gone and consulted all kinds of books.

My books cannot enter Russia legally. They enter illegally, but not legally. The government watches everything that comes in. For freedom of thought you need some kind of climate; that climate has been destroyed. And every child is conditioned according to the state religion — communism is the state religion.

Russians are beautiful people as *all* people are beautiful. They deserve the love and sympathy and compassion and help of the whole world because there is only one possibility: if the free world helps them from the outside, only then they can be free; otherwise now, scientifically, technologically, the government is so powerful it is impossible to overthrow it, absolutely impossible to throw it. Even to talk about throwing it is enough and you will disappear; you will never be found again, no one will know where you have gone. Anybody who disagrees politically is immediately declared a mental case. According to their definition, according to their belief, only a madman can disagree with communism. How can a sane man disagree with communism? That's what fanaticism is. Even if the person is a Nobel prize-winner it does not matter — if he disagrees about anything he is insane. Now, he is not even declared a political prisoner, he is not thrown in jail, because that has certain respect.

Jesus was crucified; that was respectful. At least they accepted him as a dangerous man. But if Jesus was born in Russia he would not be crucified, remember; they would simply declare him mad. They would give him electric shocks, not crucifixion. They would give him insulin shocks, they would operate on his brain, they would destroy his whole nervous system — they would make him a wreck of a man. They would not kill him; that way they would look very compassionate. They would not crucify him; there is no need to crucify now. He would be put in a mental hospital where he would be given treatment along with the mad people; that would be far more dangerous.

Socrates being treated in a madhouse would be far more disrespectful. At least the Greeks were respectful: they poisoned him — that's okay. If you don't agree with the man and the man is not ready to agree with you, you kill him! It seems perfectly okay. But to make him a madman and then torture him and slowly slowly destroy his whole mechanism of thinking, his whole brain system, to operate on his brain and do damage to his brain, that is ugly. That's what is happening in Russia.

Russians are beautiful people, Devendra, but they are living under a very ugly regime. And it is the responsibility of the whole of humanity to help them to be free of this big prison, these iron walls that surround them.

And you also ask me: *Will there be a Third World War?*

It is impossible. A Third World War is not possible for the simple reason that science has given us so much technology to destroy each other that a Third World War means a total world war. A total world war means that nobody will be the survivor — neither will there be any winner or any loser. For the first time war has lost all its meaning. It is not because of Buddha or Christ that the Third World War is not going to happen; it is because of scientific technology — atom bombs, hydrogen bombs, super-hydrogen bombs, death rays. They have made it impossible. Unless we decide on a global suicide, a Third World War is impossible.

Small conflicts will go on happening because they are needed; they are an economic need. Sometimes in Vietnam, sometimes in Korea, sometimes in Israel, sometimes in Kashmir, sometimes in Afghanistan — small wars, not a Third World War. Small wars have to happen, otherwise where are these big powers going to sell their weapons? And those weapons are accumulating and every day new developments are happening so their old weapons become out of date. Who is going to use them? They cannot use them; they cannot be used by themselves. Poor countries, backward countries, like India, Pakistan, Bangladesh, Afghanistan, Iran, these small countries can be sold out-of-date weapons. So these countries have to be continuously quarreling with each other — small quarrels, lukewarm fights. The super-powers, America and Russia, need these wars to sell their weapons, otherwise their stockpile of weapons will be so great that they themselves will die under the burden. So these small wars are an absolute necessity.

And these backward countries are so foolish that they can't see the point, so somewhere or other a war erupts. One country starts purchasing weapons from America, another country starts purchasing weapons from Russia. Both are in a way in the same business. Those who can see, they can see they are partners — they both need wars to continue somewhere or other. But they should not trigger a Third World War, no, because a Third World War means those two superpowers coming in conflict directly.

If Russia attacks America, then it will take only ten minutes for America to retaliate; or if America attacks Russia, it will take only ten minutes for Russia to re-taliate. There will be only a ten-minute gap, that's all. If you think that is victory, then it is okay. After those ten minutes both are finished. In fact, if these super-powers come in conflict there is every possibility that people who are very primitive and living far away in the forests of South Africa or in the Himalayas, in Tibet, may be the only survivors. They will be the only people who will be benefited. For the first time their backward-ness will pay; for the first time they will be the winners and the winners will be the losers. But that too is a far, far-away, remote possibility because a Third World War will trigger so much fire around the earth that there seems to be no possibility that anybody can survive.

Not only human beings — trees, birds, animals, all will be gone.

Hence I can say it categorically: there is not going to be any Third World War. With the Second World War, world wars were finished. Now there will be only small fights — battles but not wars.

The last question

Bhagwan,
I am leaving for Italy. Would you please tell
me a joke to tell to the Italiano?

Sarjano,

NEVER ASK FOR ONE JOKE. You can ask Laxmi: whenever I order one thing she always orders two — she knows me! So whenever you ask for one joke you have to suffer two.

First:

Two Italian nuns were sitting at the table talking about the beauty of the flowers, plants and vegetables in the garden of their nunnery.

One of the nuns says, "Did you see the big, red, juicy tomatoes in the vegetable garden?"

As she is talking the nun joins both hands into a circle, showing the size of the tomatoes.

"Yes," answers the other nun, "and did you see the size of the cucumbers this year?"

While she is describing them, her hands indicate the size of the long cucumbers.

An elderly nun sitting in the corner of the same room, nearly deaf but not blind yet, asks with an eager voice, "Which Father are you talking about?"

And second:

An explosion once happened in an Italian salami factory and one of the salamis is blown into heaven. An angel flying around heaven bumps into the salami and grabs it with her wing. "This is a funny thing," she says. "I wonder what it is?"

She flies to Joseph and asks him, "Have you ever seen such a thing before?" swinging the salami in front of his nose.

Joseph, staring at the salami, says, "No, I've never seen one before!"

The angel flies away and meets Mary. "Mary, do you know what this is?" she says, swinging the salami in front of her.

"Oh!" exclaims Mary, "You know, if there wasn't that funny net around it I would say it is the Holy Ghost!"

10

The first question

Bhagwan,
What is the goal of meditation?

Prageeta,

THERE IS NO "GOAL OF MEDITATION." Meditation is the dropping of all goals, hence it can't have a goal of its own; that would be against its very nature. Goals exist in the future; meditation is to be in the present. There is no meeting ground between the present and the future — the future exists not — how can the non-existential meet the existential? That is impossible. The future is our creation, it is our imagination. We create it for a certain purpose; the purpose is to avoid the present. We don't want to be in the present, we want to escape from the present. The future gives us an escape. To live in the future is to be an escapist.

Whatsoever the goal — it does not matter what that goal is — it may be God-realization, it may be attainment of *nirvana* — still it is a goal and any goal is against meditation. But our whole mind exists in the future; our mind is against the present. In the present the mind dies. How can the mind exist in the present? If you are utterly now, utterly here, there is no question of mind. You cannot think because thinking needs space and the present has no space in it. It is just like a needle point: it cannot contain anything, not even a single thought.

Hence if you want to live in the mind, either you have to live in the past or in the future; these are the two ways. The old-fashioned, the orthodox, the conventional — the Christians, the Mohammedans, the Hindus — they live in the past, and the so-called revolutionaries, the progressives, the avant-garde, they live in the future. The communists, the socialists, the Fabians, the utopians, all kinds of idealists, they live in the future. On the surface they seem to be very different — the Catholic and the communist seem to be antagonistic — but deep down they are not antagonistic at all. They belong to the same category, they are doing the same work: they both are escaping from the present.

The Hindu lives in the golden age that has passed; his golden age was somewhere far far away in the past, it is only a memory, it has never been there. That past is simply a creation of imaginative people, but it helps them to escape from the present. Hindus call it *Ramrajya* — the kingdom of God. It existed in the past and since then man has been falling down. Hence Hindus cannot agree with Charles Darwin, with the idea of evolution. Hindus have a totally different idea: the idea of involution, not evolution. Man is not progressing, man is regressing. Man is falling every day, man is going downhill. The peaks are left in the past — the golden peaks, the sunlit peaks.

The communist lives in the future; his golden age has still to come. It will come one day, somewhere far away in the future when the state withers away, when the society becomes classless, when there is no exploitation, when there is no need for any government, when people live in equality. That will be the kingdom of God — but that is in the future; that too is never going to happen.

The communist and the Hindu both are doing the same thing, they are partners in the same business: the business is how to escape from the present, how not to live in the present. Hence you will see a strange thing happening: Hindus are against me, Mohammedans are against me, Christians are against me, communists are against me. On one thing they all agree — at least on one thing they all agree. At least I am happy that I give them one point to agree about! But in fact they agree because my insistence is against the past and against the future, my insistence is on being in the present. Hence meditation cannot allow any desire for goals.

I can understand your question, Prageeta, because the mind always asks, "Why are you doing it?" It can't do anything simply, spontaneously — the "why" is always there. You don't know any action in your life which is spontaneous, you don't know any response. All that you do is not action in fact but reaction. You do it because there are reasons for doing it, there are motives for doing it, there are desires behind it. Something is either pushing from behind or pulling from the front. You are never acting out of freedom, you are a slave. Hence you always ask "Why?"

A man was sent by his psychiatrist to the mountains just for a change to rest, to relax, to enjoy nature. The next day his telegram arrived: "I am feeling very happy. Why?"

One cannot accept anything without asking "Why?"

Now one thing about happiness has to be understood: misery may have causes, happiness has no cause. And if it has a cause it is nothing but misery masquerading as happiness. When happiness is true — that's what is meant by bliss — it has no cause, no causality. It is beyond cause and effect; it is beyond the chain of cause and effect. You cannot answer why.

Buddha was asked many times, "Why are you so blissful, so peaceful?" He always said, "Such is the nature of awareness — *tathata.*"

Now his answer has to be deeply pondered over. He says, "There is no 'why' to it — such is the case. The trees are green and the flowers are red, and the man who is awakened is blissful. There is no 'why' to it."

But the people who were asking again and again. . . . I think he must have been asked the same question thousands of times by different people. The people may look different from the outside, but deep down they are all unconscious, so the same question arises again and again out of their unconscious mind: "Why? There must be some reason. Have you discovered some treasure? Have you found some Kohinoor? Have you found some alchemy so that you can transform baser metal into gold? Have you found some secret that can make you immortal? *Why* are you so blissful?"

The people who are asking are saying something about themselves; they are not really asking why Buddha is blissful — they can't understand Buddha — they know only themselves. They know they are miserable and that their misery has a cause, and once in a while when they feel happy that happiness is also caused by something. You win a lottery and you are happy; without the lottery how can you be happy? And Buddha has not won any lottery. In fact he has renounced his palace and kingdom and all the riches. The people must be searching, trying to find out: "There must be something that he has found which he is hiding and not telling us. What is it? Why do you look so happy?"

Prabhu Maya has asked me a question — the same question that Buddhas have always been asked is being asked again and again here too. She asks, "Bhagwan, I have recently been discovering the phoniness behind the smile I sometimes wear. Now I wonder about you — the same face, the same smile every morning, year in, year out. Is it for real?"

I can understand her question because whenever she is smiling she knows it is phony, and I am constantly smiling. Naturally, year in and year out, it must be phony; otherwise there must be some hidden cause for it which is not visible to you. Either it is phony or I have discovered something which I am not telling you, which I am hiding from you.

Even Ananda, Buddha's closest disciple, asked one day when they were walking through a forest. It was autumn and leaves were falling from the trees and the whole forest was full of dry leaves and the wind was blowing those dry leaves about and there was a great sound of dry leaves moving here and there. They were passing through the forest and Ananda asked Buddha, "Bhagwan, one question persists. I have been repressing it, but I cannot repress it anymore. And today we are alone; the other followers have been left behind so nobody will know that I have asked you. I don't want to ask it before others. My question is: Are you telling us all that you have discovered or are you still hiding something? — because what you are telling us does not clarify your bliss, your peace. It seems you are hiding something."

And Buddha laughed and he showed a fist to Ananda and asked, "Ananda, do you see what it is?"

He said, "Yes, I can see it is a fist — your hand is closed."

Buddha said, "A Buddha is never like a fist." He opened his hand and he said, "A Buddha is like an open hand — he hides nothing. There is nothing to hide! I have said everything, I am absolutely open."

Ananda still insisted, "But we cannot explain your constant bliss — and I have been watching you day in, day out. In the day you are blissful, in the night when you go to sleep you are blissful. Your face seems so innocent even in sleep. Even in sleep you look so peaceful, so serene, so tranquil, so calm, as if not a dream is passing within you. You are always a still pool with no ripples. How is it possible? I have also tried, but I can do only a little bit and then I feel tired.

If you are trying you will feel tired.

Prabhu Maya, if you try to wear a smile you will feel tired because wearing a smile means making great effort. You have to practice it like Jimmy Carter . . . then it is not a smile at all; your mouth is simply open, your teeth are simply showing, that's all.

I have heard that his wife has to close his mouth every night because once a rat went in his mouth. She phoned the doctor and the doctor said, "I am coming, but it will take time. Meanwhile you hang cheese in front of his mouth."

When the doctor came he was very surprised: she was hanging up another rat! He said, "What are you doing? I told you to hang cheese in front of his mouth!"

She said, "That's right, but a cat has entered behind the rat, so first the cat has to be taken out!"

Since then she has to close his mouth every night forcibly. It is dangerous! And the White House is an old building — it has many rats. In fact, who lives in the White House except rats? Who is interested in living in the White House? And because rats live there, cats also live there.

Meditation has no goal; it has no desire to attain anything. The dropping of the achieving mind is what meditation is all about. The understanding of desire and the understanding of the constant ambition for goals, for achievement, for ambition brings you to a point, a point of tremendous awareness, when you can see clearly that all goals are false, that you need not go anywhere, that you need not attain anything to be blissful, that to be blissful is your nature. You are missing it because you are running here and there, and in that running, in that hustle and bustle, you go on forgetting yourself.

Stop running here and there and discover yourself. The discovery of yourself is not a goal. How can it be a goal? A goal needs a distance between you and itself. The discovery of yourself is not a goal because you are already it! All that is needed is that you stop running here and there, you sit silently, you relax, you rest. Let the mind become calm and cool. When the mind is no longer running towards the past and towards the future, when all running has disappeared, when there is no mind as such, when you are simply there doing nothing, just being, this is meditation. Suddenly you know who you are. Suddenly you are overflooded with bliss, overwhelmed by light, by eternity. And then your life becomes a natural phenomenon. Then you need not *wear* smiles — a smile becomes natural. Then you need not pretend to be happy.

Only an unhappy person pretends to be happy. A happy person has no idea even that he is happy, he is simply happy. Others may think that he is happy; he has no idea. He is simply just being himself.

Yoka says:

Those who understand always act naturally.

Out of his understanding his actions are natural — his laughter is natural, his smile is natural, his whole life is natural. Your whole life is artificial, arbitrary. You are always trying to do something which is not really there.

You are trying to love. Now, trying to love is to start in a wrong way from the very beginning. You are trying to be happy. How can you be happy? It is not a question of trying. You are making all kinds of efforts to be graceful. Now, grace is not an effort; if there is effort, there is no grace. Grace is an effortless beauty. The really graceful person knows no effort.

Yoka says:

> *Those who understand always act naturally.*
> *Most men live in impermanence, the unreal,*
> *but the man of Zen lives in the real.*

You live in the phony, in the unreal, and when you come across a man of Zen — remember the man of Zen means the man of meditation — then there is a problem for you. Never try to understand the man of Zen according to *your* ideas; they are irrelevant. You can understand the man of Zen only through meditation. Learn the art of meditation, of being here and now — not for peace, not for bliss, not for anything. *Effort without goal . . .* that's what meditation is: effort without goal.

Now, you only know effort when there is goal. Otherwise you will ask, "This is illogical — effort without goal? Then why should we make an effort?" You have been making efforts for goals — what have you attained? It is time to try something else. Enough is enough!

Yoka says:

> *Effort without goal is quite different —*

Quite different from all that you have done up to now.

> *It opens the door of truth which leads to the*
> *garden of Tathagata.*

The word *tathagata* comes from the same word I used just a few moments ago: *tathata*. Buddha says, "I am peaceful because this is my suchness, my *tathata*." Ask him anything and he always says, "This is my nature, my *tathata*." Slowly slowly it became known to his disciples that *tathata* is his most important word, his key word. Hence he is called *Tathagata:* one who lives in suchness, one who lives now and knows no other time, one who lives here and knows no other space.

If you can also be here and now,

> *It opens the door of truth which leads to the garden of Tathagata.*
> *A true student of Zen ignores the branches and the leaves, and aims for the root.*

What is the root of your misery? This goal-oriented mind. What is the root of your misery? This constant escape into goals. What is the root of your misery? Your mind is the root of your misery. But you never cut the root; you go on pruning the branches, you go on pruning the leaves. And remember, the more you prune the leaves and the branches, the thicker will be the foliage; the tree will become stronger.

I have initiated more than one hundred thousand sannyasins and I have been teaching meditation for twenty years to millions of people, but not a single person has come with a root question to ask. They all come with "How to cut this branch?" and "How to cut this leaf?" Somebody says, "I am suffering from anger. What should I do with it?" And somebody says, "I am suffering from too much greed. What should I do about it? How can I drop greed?" Somebody is suffering from jealousy and somebody is suffering from something else — and these are all branches and leaves. Nobody comes and says, "I am suffering from my mind. How should I get rid of it?" And that is the root question.

The day you see the root, things are very easy. Cut the root and the whole thing withers away of its own accord. Anger and greed and sexuality and jealousy and possessiveness — everything disappears.

But you don't want to cut the root. You are living a very paradoxical life: you go on watering the root, you go on training and refining your mind, you go on making your mind more informed, more nourished, and on the other hand you go on desiring that there should be less anger, less ambition, less greed, less ego. "How to be humble?" you ask. And you go on giving water and you go on giving fertilizers to the roots and you go on cutting the leaves. You cut one leaf and three leaves will come in its place. The tree immediately accepts your challenge and instead of one it brings three leaves!

Hence a society that has been against sex becomes morbid, becomes sexually obsessed. It has happened in India; you will not find such a sex-obsessed country anywhere else for the simple reason that they have been cutting the leaf again and again. They are constantly cutting that leaf and the tree goes on growing more leaves. So sexuality has penetrated in such subtle ways that unless you are very alert you will not be able to see how it has penetrated in different ways, how the Indian mind has become more and more sexual than that of anybody else.

Do you know? India was the first country to think about sexual postures. The *Kama Sutra* was written in India — the first treatise on sexology. Sigmund Freud came after five thousand years. And Masters and Johnson, and other researchers into sex, are just breaking ground in the West. And they have not yet the sophistication which Vatsyayana's *Kama Sutra* has — even the French are not as sophisticated. Vatsyayana has discovered almost everything about sex; nothing is left — his treatise is almost complete. And it is a "how to" book; it gives you all the techniques.

Why did India discover the *Kama Sutra?* The country which has been celebrating celibacy for centuries, which has been teaching and preaching celibacy, this country discovers the *Kama Sutra.* This country gives birth to a man like Vatsyayana. And then came Pundit Koka, another Vatsyayana. Now, modern pornography is nothing compared to Koka! Modern pornography is very ordinary. Pundit Koka is a perfect pornographer.

But why were these people born in India? And thousands of temples are devoted to the *shivalinga;* that is a phallic symbol. No other country worships phallic symbols except India. And it is both; it represents man and woman — both. If you go to a Shiva temple observe well. It represents the feminine sexual organ, it represents the masculine sexual organ, and it represents them in a state of meeting, in a state of orgasm. And this is worshipped.

People have completely forgotten what they are worshipping. If you look into Indian scriptures you will be surprised. You will find them so obsessed with sex: on the one hand continuously condemning, and on the other hand continuously, in subtle ways, depicting it. No other country has temples like Khajuraho, Konarak, Puri. Why? Why did this have to happen in India? For the simple reason that if you cut one leaf, three arrive. You cut three and nine leaves arrive. You cut nine — remember it — twenty-seven leaves will arrive. Nature believes in the magic number three. It believes in trinity.

This is not the way to transform a man, this is a way to deform humanity.

So on the surface the Indian tries to show that he is not interested in sex at all and deep down he is boiling with sexuality, he is constantly looking for sexuality. His whole mind is full of sexuality. If we could make windows in the heads of people, then Indian heads would be really worth seeing!

This was bound to happen. Whatsoever you repress, whatsoever you cut, if it is not cut at the roots, it is bound to grow, it is bound to grow in subtle ways. It may start asserting itself in morbid and perverted ways.

Yoka says:

> *A true student of Zen ignores the branches*
> *and the leaves, and aims for the root.*
> *Like the image of the moon reflected in a jade*
> *bowl I know the true beauty of the jewel of*
> *freedom.*
> *For myself and for others.*

There is only one freedom: the freedom from all goals.

Prageeta, don't ask me what the goal of meditation is. Try to understand why you are constantly hankering for goals, and in that very understanding meditation will arise in you, meditation will flower in you.

Meditation is not something that you can enforce, that you can practice; it is something very mysterious, tremendously vast. It comes only when your heart opens its doors to understand everything with no prejudice, with no *a priori* conclusions.

Being here with me, learn to be without goals. My sannyasins have to know perfectly well that we are not working for any goal at all. Our whole point is to live in the present moment so totally that all past and all future disappear. Who cares about that which is already gone? And who cares about that which has not come yet? Enough is the moment unto itself. And that is the way of meditation: enough is the moment unto itself. Living the moment in its totality, in joy, diving deep into it without holding anything back, is bliss. Getting rid of all goals — worldly and other-worldly, material and spiritual — one knows the taste of meditation. It is the taste of absolute freedom.

The second question

Bhagwan,
Why does everyone here understand you in
his own way?

Leeladhar,

IT IS JUST NATURAL — *tathata.* How can it be other-wise? Everybody has to understand me in his own way, because everybody has a mind — and right now the understanding is happening through the mind. When mind disappears then of course everybody will under-stand in *my* way. Then there will be no problem, then there will be no question. Then there will be no need for me to say anything — I will be sitting in silence, you will be sitting in silence, and we will enjoy silence; there will be communion, a heart-to-heart communion.

But right now you have minds and there is no other way for me to communicate with you. And one has to accept this: that when you are communicating with minds you have to accept that they will understand differently, they will understand in their own way.

Each mind is different. And here we have all kinds of minds — this is not a community of people from one certain society.

If only Hindus were here they would understand or misunderstand in the same way. But here are Hindus and Mohammedans and Jainas and Buddhists and Chris-tians and Jews and Zarathustrians — they have all their own religious backgrounds and all kinds of political ideologies. And we have people from all the nations of the world; nearabout forty nations are represented here. How can you expect . . . ? This is not a Catholic church, this is not a Hindu temple, this is a miniature universe! In fact it is a miracle that some understanding is happen-ing, that people are not cutting each other's throats, that people are being very friendly and loving.

These are the people who have been cutting each other's throats for centuries: Hindus killing Mohammedans, Mohammedans killing Hindus. And here you will see the miracle: you will find a man called Krishna Mohammed. You cannot find this anywhere else in the world. Krishna Mohammed?

In fact I am very worried. When I die and I go to the other world then all these people — Krishna and Moses and Mohammed and Mahavira and Buddha — they will jump upon me. They will say, "What have you been doing? Calling a man Krishna Mohammed?" Because I have heard that even in heaven they have compartments: Hindus live in one compartment, the Hindu colony, and Mohammedans live in another compartment, and they don't see each other eye to eye. In fact everybody believes he is in heaven and nobody else is in heaven. God has to maintain that illusion, otherwise they will be creating trouble for God. So big walls surround those sections.

Now God is also going to be in trouble. Where will he put Krishna Mohammed — in the Hindu section or in the Mohammedan section? Our people will be flying all over the place!

It is natural, Leeladhar, that people should understand differently — people have different minds.

Julius: "How many Commandments are there?"
Julia: "Ten."
Julius: "What would happen if you — er — well — you know — if you broke one of them?"
Julia: "So, there'd be nine!"

On Mother's Day her husband presented her with a beautiful skunk coat.

"I can't see how such a beautiful coat comes from such a foul-smelling beast," said the mother.

"I don't ask for thanks, dear," replied the husband, "but I do demand respect."

An Italian calls Alitalia's office and is answered by the office boy.

"Please, sir, is-a that-a the Alitalia office?"

"Yes," answers the boy.

"Can you tell-a me how long-a it takes from Roma to Poona?"

"Just a minute, sir."

"Thank-a-you!" answers the Italian and hangs up.

"Have you ever been bedridden?" the new doctor asked Mrs Longo.

"Sure I have. And I've been screwed lots-a other ways, too," the lady said proudly.

"What do you want for your birthday, son?" the indulgent Italian father asked his kid.

"I want-a watch," the kid said.

Shrugged the father, "If it's all right with your mother, it's okay by me."

During an official ceremony in a European country, the Brazilian ambassador is in a carriage with the Queen of England when suddenly the horse farts noisily.

Very embarrassed, the Queen apologizes, "I'm very sorry, Ambassador."

"It was nothing, Your Majesty, it happens. Mind you, I even thought it was the horse!"

The third question

Bhagwan,
What is courage?

Prem Leela,

THERE IS ONLY ONE COURAGE and that is the courage to go on dying to the past, not to collect it, not to accumulate it, not to cling to it. We all cling to the past, and because we cling to the past we become unavailable to the present. And the mind has reasons, valid reasons, for clinging to the past.

First: mind itself is the past. Just look at your mind — what it is. It is nothing but the past: all that you have read, listened to, experienced, observed, all that *has been*. Mind never *is*; it consists of the past tense. So naturally mind feeds on the past, it clings to the past, because that gives it strength, power, energy, life. But the more the past accumulates around you, the more you become like a mirror covered with layers of dust. And, of course, the past is comfortable, it feels cozy, because you are well-acquainted with it. You know it perfectly well, so you know how to deal with it. You are skillful with it, you are artful with it; your whole intelligence depends on it. To drop it will mean you will have to learn again and again, and that is inconvenient, uncomfortable.

To drop the past will mean you will have to become a child every day, and your ego wants to be an adult not a child. Your ego wants to pile up the past and sit upon it so that it looks higher than others. Without the past you will always remain a child with no knowledge, but full of wonder, of awe.

That is the only courage: to drop the known and to move into the unknown. And it has not to be done only once, it has to be done every moment. It is not a question that once done it is done forever, you have to do it every moment, every day, till the very last moment of your life when you are dying on your bed. Then too you have to continue the process of dying to the past so that you can live each moment with pristine clarity, with no dust on your mirror. When you can reflect the present as it is you know what God is, what godliness is. God is another name for what is, for that which is.

But you are collecting information about God, and that is one of the greatest barriers. Hence I have heard of sinners reaching God, but I have never heard of scholars ever reaching God. Pundits are the most impossible people. The more they know the farther away they are from God. So many scriptures are preventing them. They cannot reach God and God cannot reach them. They are absolutely closed in their knowledge.

Courage means courage to drop knowledge, courage to be innocent again, courage to function from a state of not-knowing. I don't know of any other courage.

When I use the word "courage" I don't mean the courage of a soldier. That is just stupidity, that is not courage. That is just stubbornness, that is not courage. That is just forced, you have to train the soldier so that he becomes dull. It is unintelligence, not intelligence. Hence soldiers become unintelligent people. The more medals they have, you can be certain, the more unintelligent they are. Just count the medals on their chest and you know how foolish they are.

The whole process of the army is to destroy intelligence because an intelligent person will not be able to kill. And an intelligent person will ask a thousand and one questions before killing somebody for no reason at all.

An Indian killing a Pakistani whom he had never met before, whom he had never seen before, with whom there is no enmity, and a Pakistani killing an Indian for no reason at all, who has not done any harm to him. . . .

If they were a little bit intelligent would they be able to do it? Would the Indian or the Pakistani be able to do it without thinking of this man's wife who is waiting at home just as his wife is waiting at home for him, and his small children are waiting just as his small children are waiting for him, and his old mother and his old father who depend on him just as his mother and his father depend on him? Would he be able to do this stupidity of killing or being killed?

If soldiers are allowed to be intelligent, wars will disappear from the earth. Wars can exist only if soldiers are made in such a way, conditioned in such a way that they lose all intelligence. That's why unintelligent training has to be forced on them for years. Now the soldier goes on doing things which make no sense for years.

Early in the morning he gets up, he has to line up and the parade begins. And "left turn," and "right turn," and "about turn," and "go forward," and "go backward." For what? And for hours together.

In the Second World War a philosopher was recruited. When the commanding officer said, "Right turn!" everybody turned right except the philosopher. The commanding officer asked, "Why? Why are you not turning right?"

He said, "Why should I turn? I have no business there; I don't see the need. And I think all these people are fools. You just say 'Right turn' and they have turned. You will have to prove to me what the purpose of it is. Why should I turn right?"

The commanding officer knew that he was a famous philosopher. He said, "This man is not right for the military. This type of person is not needed." Even the other soldiers started thinking, "That's right! Why? We are certainly fools. This man just says, 'Right turn!' and he has no answer for it and we turned right!"

The commanding officer thought, "This man will create trouble. Not only will he be a trouble to me, even the others will start getting ideas from him." He took him out and he said, "This is not for you. You come into the kitchen. I will give you some other job, some simple job which will be good." So he gave him a pile of potatoes and told him, "You just sort them out — bigger ones on one side, smaller ones on the other side."

When he came after one hour the philosopher was sitting silently, just in zazen — sitting silently, doing nothing. He had not even touched a single potato. The commanding officer said, "Can't you even do that?"

He said, "I can do it but there is a great problem. Yes, there are a few potatoes which are big and a few which are small, but a few are in between. First it has to be settled where those in between ones go. Unless everything is clear I never take any step. What about the middle-class potatoes?"

He had to be freed. This man was not for the army. In fact no intelligent man is for the army. Parading six hours per day, turning right, turning left, being ordered to do stupid things and following those orders . . . then one day the commanding officer says, "Shoot!" and they just function like machines. Just as they were turning left and right they shoot, without a single thought of what they are doing — destroying life.

A sannyasin needs a totally different kind of courage. This is not courage, this is simply dullness, stupidity — thickness of the head and nothing else. Their intelligence has been completely destroyed, they have been conditioned to be robots. That's why all army races prove to be very unintelligent.

In India the Punjabis, particularly the Sikhs, the Sardars, they are the most warlike people, and the most unintelligent people too. Very courageous, because where an intelligent person will think twice, they will rush in; they will not bother. You just order and they will go into the fire. This type of courage has been taught to humanity for centuries. This is a wrong type of courage. When I use the word "courage" I am using it with a totally different connotation, a different meaning.

Leela, courage to me means courage to be intelligent against this unintelligent crowd that surrounds you.

Courage means fearlessness. The society will try in every way to force you according to its ideas. It is better to suffer than to compromise, because through suffering your soul will be born. Through compromise you may save your skin but your soul will be lost.

Courage means to be an individual; not to be a sheep but to be a lion. Courage means the capacity to assert: "I am myself, and my life is *my* life, and I am going to live it in *my* way. I am not here to live according to others, and I won't allow anybody to dictate to me how I should live, what I should do. I will live according to my light whatsoever the cost, even if I go astray." It is better to go to hell by your own decision rather than to go to heaven by somebody else's order, because then heaven will be just slavery.

Courage means the courage to be free. Courage means freedom. And if you reduce it to the essential core it is in fact dying to the past. If you die to the past you die to the tradition you are born in, you die to the religion you are born in, you die to the society you are born in, you die to the whole past, you die to history and time, and you are born anew — a new human being who belongs to no race, to no country, to no religion, but who belongs to God; a religious person but not a Christian, not a Hindu, not a Mohammedan.

The fourth question

Bhagwan,
What is your English — British or American?

Sanjeeva,

I⊤ IS CERTAINLY NOT BRITISH. To be British is not easy. One has to be born British at least seven times. It takes a very long time to be British. And it is not American either because I am not a tourist. You know I don't even leave my room — what kind of American can I be?

And why should my English be British or American? My English is *my* English — Rajneesh English! And this is a democratic country and the constitution declares freedom of speech as one of the fundamental rights. I speak my own language. Why should I speak American or English? In fact, English is too uptight, it is too tense, and American has become too lousy — just the opposite; it is a reaction.

"Mine American-born daughter she's telling me: 'Yeah, Popsi-wopsi, I gotcha, but you'll hafta lay some heavy bread on me so's I kin strut new threads at the establishment bust-out, ya dig?'

"So I am digging for maybe a half-hour to learn she needs money she should have a new dress by the school dance. . . . And she is criticizing *mine* dialect!" her father was saying to me.

Now it is very difficult for me to understand. . . .

"Yeah, Popsi-wopsi, I gotcha, but you'll hafta lay some heavy bread on me so's I kin strut new threads at the establishment bust-out, ya dig?"

I don't dig it at all! And why should I dig? I have never done such a job in my whole life.

So I simply speak whatsoever way comes to me, whatsoever way comes spontaneously to me. You will have to be a little patient with me.

The fifth question

Bhagwan,
Have you forgotten us poor Australians completely?

Shahida,

I HAVE NOT FORGOTTEN. I am collecting jokes about the Australians. Everybody is welcome to send me jokes about Australians. I have only one.

A man walked into a London pub and ordered twelve pints of bitter. He put them on a tray, took them outside to a car and passed them through the window. Later he brought back the empty glasses, bought another round and passed them into the car.

Curious, the bartender went outside with the next round, and looking into the car, saw twelve midgets carousing and drinking beer.

"Who are they?" he asked.

"Oh," said the man, "they're just Australians with all the bullshit knocked out of them!"

The sixth question

Bhagwan,
You always talk about Masters, and all of them
are men. Does that mean that a woman can't become
a Master?

Ananda Maite,

NO, THAT DOES NOT MEAN that a woman cannot become a Master; many women have become Masters. But then there is a problem. The problem is: unless a man becomes a Master he is not allowed to speak by the wife. And he has not been a Master for thousands of lives, so when he becomes a Master he starts speaking. And when a woman becomes a Master she becomes silent — she is tired. For thousands of lives she has been speaking and speaking and speaking, she has done enough speaking, so she becomes silent.

Now it is very difficult — how to know about silent Masters? Unless you speak nobody will know about you. If Buddha had not spoken, if there had not been any *Dhammapada*, then I would not have talked on his sutras.

A man takes revenge when he becomes a Master. And, do you see? Whenever there is a Master more women gather to hear him than men. In fact the proportion is: in four, three are women, one is a man. That was the proportion with Buddha's disciples, that was the proportion with Mahavira's disciples. So he really takes revenge — so many women! And he remembers all those wives. Many of them may have been his wives in past lives. Wives, mothers, daughters, sisters — they have all tortured him. Now he says to himself, "Now it is my turn! Nobody can prevent me now!"

But women, by the time they become Masters, have run out of gas.

The seventh question

Bhagwan,
Please, before I leave say something to me
without words.

Prem Patipada,

Okay. . . .
Dig it? Get it?
It is not difficult for me, it will be difficult for you. But a little more. . . .

The eighth question

Bhagwan,
How do they catch a lion in Russia?

Prem Amir,

PLEASE DON'T ASK such difficult questions!
They arrest a cat and torture him until he admits he is a lion.

The ninth question

Bhagwan,
What is the secret of success?

Dharmendra,

YOU ARE ASKING ME — a man who is an utter failure?
The secret of success is sincerity. Once you can fake that you've got it made.

The tenth question

Bhagwan,
What is the right Catholic Christian way to
prevent population explosion in the world?

Pragyan,

YOU SHOULD GO TO THE VATICAN and ask the Polack. I'm not a Catholic, I'm not a Pope. You create trouble for me. But I can suggest. . . . This is only a piece of advice:

Sow your wild oats on Saturday night, then on Sunday pray for crop failure!

And the last question

Bhagwan,
What is a blow job?

Muktananda,

YOU FOOL! Now this question is just the right question from you. I always knew you would ask something really great. The moment I saw you I immediately realized that here is a great fool, hence the name Muktananda — although I didn't explain it to you that way. I give beautiful explanations just to be polite. Truth can be said only later on when you are ready.

For example, you know our great guard, Sant. Somebody has asked me, "Why, Bhagwan, have you given him the name Sant?" In Hindi *sant* means saint, the English word "saint" comes from *sant.* But in Hindi we also have one beautiful expression: *ant sant. Ant sant* means "nonsense." So when I saw Sant for the first time, I said, "Here comes *ant sant!*" But *ant* I had to drop because that would have been too much just in the beginning. So I called him Sant. But now it can be said. There is no trouble.

Muktananda, I immediately saw the fool in you. But even I was not so sure that you would be a perfect fool. Otherwise I would have called you Paramahansa Muktananda. *Paramahansa* means perfect. Now you deserve to be called Paramahansa Muktananda.

Now, what kind of question is this?

"Drinks on the house," the Italian said to the bartender. "I feel great — just had my first blow job."

"What was it like?" the barkeep asked.

"Okay, I guess," the wop said. "But it did taste kind-a funny."

A brave young Irish Revolutionary comes to London

to blow up a bus and burns his mouth on the exhaust-pipe.

An Italian dwarf was very famous among his friends for the size of his prick. A sex-starved American female tourist heard about him and visited his home to offer him twenty dollars to see his massive member.

Luigino agreed and pulled down his zipper to display his pride and joy.

The American lady was awe-struck at the sight and asked hesitantly, "Is it all right if I kiss it?"

"Please, Missus," said the dwarf, "no more blow jobs! Ten years ago I was seven feet tall with a tiny prick. Just look at what all these blow jobs have done to me!"

Muktananda, never ask me such dangerous questions. You are expected to ask spiritual questions, esoteric questions, supramental questions — and you are asking such questions which no Buddha had to answer before. And I don't think anybody else in future will have to answer them because I will finish them all!

11

The first question

Bhagwan,
What is the meaning of existence?

Pravino,

MEANING IS A HUMAN INVENTION. There is no meaning in existence itself, it is beyond meaning. It is not meaningless either because a thing can be meaningless only if it is possible for it to have meaning. Meaning and meaninglessness are two sides of the same coin. As far as existence is concerned meaning is totally irrelevant, so is meaninglessness.

For centuries man has been imposing meaning on existence because it needs guts to live joyously without meaning. It needs real intelligence to live in ecstasy without any meaning at all. The crowds don't have that much intelligence, they need some excuse. Howsoever false the excuse is it does not matter — even a false excuse is good enough for them to live for. But they are absolutely in need of a meaning. It is man's need that imposes meaning on existence. The more immature a man is the more his need for meaning. As he becomes mature the need becomes less.

When man really comes of age there is no need for meaning at all. One simply lives, for no other reason; one lives for life's sake. Then existence is not a means to something else, it is beautiful as it is; it is not fulfilling any purpose. In fact, it is because it is not fulfilling any purpose that it is so beautiful, so utterly beautiful. It has no utility, it is not full of commodities, it is full of poetry. What meaning does a poem have, what purpose? What meaning does a rose flower have, what purpose? What is the meaning of a night full of stars? And what is the meaning of love? What is the meaning of all that you are surrounded by? There is no meaning in it. And if you are in need of meaning, then you will project. Then existence becomes just a screen and you project your meaning on it.

For centuries humanity has done that and because of it now we are suffering tremendously. Now man has become more mature; he is not as childish as he was before and he can see that all those projections are nothing but projections. All the meanings are collapsing and now a great chaos is created by the collapsing meanings which we have believed in for thousands of years. A great meaninglessness is felt all over the world.

All modern thinkers from Soren Kierkegaard to Martin Heidegger are concerned with one single question and that question is the question of meaning. And all are convinced that there is no meaning in life. But then why live? Naturally, inevitably, the second question arises: If there is no meaning then why live? Then why not commit suicide?

Marcel used to say that the only significant philosophical question is suicide. Why go on living when there is no meaning? It is sheer cowardice to live when there is no meaning. And Marcel has some relevance in the context of the whole human history of thought, philosophy, religion. All the values are disappearing and man wants anything to cling to. Because the old gods have failed, man is inventing new gods.

It is difficult now to believe in the Christian trinity: God the Father, Christ the Son and the Holy Ghost. It is almost impossible for any contemporary person to believe in this nonsense. But when this belief disappears a vacuum is felt; you start missing something. You cannot continue in the old belief and you cannot tolerate the emptiness that is left behind. Then something has to be substituted — anything will do. And then there are many substitutes.

Communists have provided their own unholy trinity: Karl Marx, Friedrich Engels and Lenin. You see the point? The Christian trinity was all male, the communist trinity is also all male. There was no woman in the Christian trinity, there is no woman in the communist trinity. It is a replica, exactly the same. Many theologians have tried to bring Christ's mother Mary into the trinity from the back door, but they have all failed. For centuries, again and again, the effort has been made, but it has not succeeded. And the same has happened with the communist trinity. Stalin tried to become one of the parts, but the magic number of three cannot be disturbed. So while he was alive he imposed himself, he became one; the trinity was no more a trinity, it started consisting of four persons. The moment he died the fourth was dropped. Even his grave was removed from the close proximity of Lenin's grave; they could not even tolerate his dead body there.

Mao Tse Tung tried in China to enter into the trinity; the day he died he was removed.

When old gods fail a great vacuum is felt. It is not accidental that in this century Adolf Hitler, Joseph Stalin, Mao Tse Tung and people like them became so powerful. Their power was not their own, their power existed in the vacuum that was left in the human heart because of the old values disappearing. And man has lived for so long with a certain meaning in life that he has become incapable of living without meaning. Either commit suicide or invent a new meaning.

My own approach is totally different. There is no need to commit suicide; that is sheer stupidity. There is no need to invent any new meaning; that is falling back, that is regressive, that is again becoming immature. It is a great opportunity that is knocking on your doors. Humanity as a whole has come to a certain point of growth from which a quantum leap is possible. Man can start living without any meaning and still live beautifully, still with tremendous joy.

That was one of the greatest contributions of Gautam the Buddha. He has not been understood yet, but now his time has come. He came a little too early — twenty-five centuries before his time — but he speaks like a contemporary. Jesus speaks the old language, the language which children can understand. And so is the case with many others — with Moses, with Mohammed. But Buddha speaks the language of maturity. He says there is no meaning in life and there is no need for any meaning. Drop the hankering and don't try to fill this vacuum. This vacuum is good, it is healthy. Abide in this emptiness, rejoice in this emptiness! Don't go on stuffing it with unnecessary things. It has a purity — this emptiness which is being felt now by many more people than it was ever felt before. Only once in a while has a man like Buddha felt that all ideals are false, imaginary inventions — toys to play with, to keep children engaged so they don't create mischief.

Temples, churches, mosques, *gurudwaras*, these are places to keep children engaged so they don't create any trouble, so they don't create any mischief. These are sedatives so that you go on sleeping; these are sleeping pills, tranquilizers which help you to remain non-violent, to remain non-destructive, to remain peacefully sleepy; otherwise there is danger. You cannot be trusted, you cannot be allowed freedom.

These are your bondages. These are prisons which you think of as temples; they are not temples. And the gods you worship are not gods; they are just play-things to keep you occupied, to keep you afraid, to keep you frightened, to keep you greedy. They don't transform you; their whole function is to serve the status quo, to serve the vested interests of the society.

Buddha says: The inner emptiness is so beautiful, don't stuff it with junk, leave it as it is. And that's what meditation is all about, that's what Zen is. It means living out of emptiness, asking nothing from life, living moment to moment for no other reason, just enjoying being alive. It is more than you can ask for! What more meaning do you need? Is breathing not enough? Is this chirping of the birds not enough? Is the green and the red and the gold of the trees not enough? Is this vast existence with all its splendor not enough? You want some meaning?

Yoka says:

> *The moon rises above the river.*
> *On the bank the wind plays softly in the pines*
> *all night long, pure and calm.*
> *What is the meaning of that serenity?*
> *Look on the Buddha's precepts of nature.*
> *Winter and autumn mists,*
> *dew, clouds, spring mists*
> *are the true robe which covers our body.*

> *What is the meaning of that serenity?*

There is no meaning at all, but let me remind you again, I am *not* saying life is meaningless. You are so much obsessed with meaning that the moment I say there is no meaning, immediately you conclude the opposite. Immediately something inside you says, "So there is no meaning in life, that means life is meaningless?" I am not saying life is meaningless, I am simply saying meaning is absolutely irrelevant. Life is more than meaning, far more. Machines have meaning, flowers don't have meaning; meaning means utility. A car has meaning because it serves a certain purpose. A railway train has meaning, an airplane has meaning; they are utilitarian. But what is the meaning of a beautiful sunset and the clouds turning all the colors of the rainbow? What is the meaning of it? What is the meaning of a rainbow?

Can't you see things just as they are? Can't you just be a mirror without projecting any meaning? If you can be just a mirror, there is no meaning and no meaninglessness. You rise above both, you rise above duality, and then there is great serenity.

> *The moon rises above the river.*
> *On the bank the wind plays softly in the pines*
> *all night long, pure and calm.*
> *What is the meaning of that serenity?*

And realize it this very moment! Don't think about it. If you think, you have already gone astray. A single thought and you are as far away from the truth as you can be. Just see it! I am not preaching a certain ideology to you, I am not imparting any information, I am not concerned with any creed, I am simply sharing my vision. Just for a moment, look through my eyes. For a moment, feel through my heart. Let your heartbeats be rhythmic with my heartbeats. That is *satsang*. That is communion with the Master. For a moment, breathe with me. For a moment disappear, for a moment don't think, for a moment forget that you are. Then only will you be able to understand. Seeing is understanding; it is not a question of thinking.

And once you are freed from meaning *and* meaninglessness you are freed from all the prisons of beliefs,
ideologies, scriptures — Hindu, Mohammedan, Christian, Jaina. You are suddenly out of all the prisons; for
the first time you are under the sky. When you are
utterly empty, just as the sky is outside you, infinite, so
there is a sky within you as infinite as the outer one.
And when you are not asking for any meaning, both
these skies meet, merge into oneness. That experience is
God. God is not a person, that *experience* is God.

The second question

Bhagwan,
It is impossible to find jokes about Aussies:
they are so lukewarm, so boring, so nice, they
never offend anyone. There is no character to
poke fun at. Have you noticed?

Prabhu Maya,

IN A CERTAIN WAY YOU ARE RIGHT: they *are* lukewarm
and they are nice. And certainly lukewarm people are
boring; to be interesting you need a certain intensity.
Nice people are boring. You can have nice people
around only for a little while, you cannot live with nice
people for long: they will kill you with boredom. They
don't have any spice in them, they don't have any salt,
they don't have any taste at all — they are tasteless. In
that sense you are right. But that is enough to create
many jokes. In fact, that is a perfectly beautiful jumping
board, Prabhu Maya!

An Englishman decided that he wanted to become
Irish. After much research he discovered that the only

way to become truly Irish was to have half his brain removed. He managed to find a surgeon who would operate, but during the operation the doctor made a dreadful mistake and removed his entire brain.

When the man woke up, the doctor said, "I'm very sorry, I've made a mistake. Instead of taking half your brain, I removed it all!"

To which the patient replied, "No worries, cobber!"

He had become an Australian!

A young Australian got married.

"Look, son," said his father. "When you are alone tonight with your bride, take her clothes off, take your clothes off, put your hand on her belly and say, 'I love you, darling!' "

"Yes, pa," said the young man.

When the feast was over he took his eager bride to the room, dimmed the lights, stripped off all her clothes, sat naked by her side, laid his hand on her stomach and said, "I love you, darling!"

"Ah, lower, lower!" groaned the girl, patting his hand.

"Mm," says the Aussie (lower), "I love you, I love you!"

The third question

Bhagwan,
Please talk about surrender and obedience.

Mahasatva,

On the surface they appear alike, but they are polar opposites. One who is surrendered need not be obedient; obedience is needed only if there is no surrender. You will be a little puzzled because you have been told

and taught and conditioned that obedience and surrender are synonymous. Obedience means you are not
surrendered, so you are forced to be obedient; there is
ego inside you which you are repressing, hence obedience is needed. In the army obedience is needed, obedience has to be enforced. Those who are obedient have to
be rewarded and those who are not obedient have to be
punished. Slowly slowly everybody becomes obedient.

This is just a conditioned reflex. This is what they do
with rats in psychology labs, this is how they train the
rats. Psychologists don't think there is any difference
between rats and man, and about ninety-nine point nine
percent of people they are right, there is not much
difference.

Only once in a while a Socrates, a Zarathustra, a Lao
Tzu, a Buddha may not fit their idea, but they never
come across such people. And even if they do come
across a Buddha they will not be able to persuade
Buddha to come to their lab so that they can experiment
on him. They can get hold of rats, they can get hold of
monkeys, they can purchase ordinary human beings
who are ready to be experimented upon if they are paid
well. And anything can be taught to you.

For example, now Skinner and company propose that
there is no need to tell people that smoking is bad or
dangerous to their health, there is no need to tell them
that it is a sin, immoral; all that is needed is to give them
a few electric shocks. Whenever the urge to smoke arises
in them, the moment they take out a cigarette from the
packet, give them an electric shock so that a shiver goes
down their spine. Soon just the idea of smoking a cigarette will be enough — there will be no need to give them
electric shocks — they will get the shock; the cigarette
will drop from their hands. Slowly slowly even the urge
will disappear.

They say, "We can condition a man in whatsoever
way you want. There is no need to follow these very

long, old, rotten tracks of moral preaching and teaching which still have no effect. Nobody is afraid of them." Who is afraid of hell now? Maybe in the beginning it was like an electric shock, but now people have become accustomed to it, they have become adjusted to the shock, now hell is not a shock at all. If somebody says to you, "Don't smoke cigarettes — you will go to hell!" it is no shock to you. But five thousand years ago it was enough to give you a shock. The idea was the same: make people frightened.

Modern technology makes it easier; they have found short cuts. And they think that there is no difference between rats and man because rats learn the same way. Punish them and they will stop doing a certain thing, reward them and they will start doing it again and again. That is the way to create obedience. That's how it is created in the army, that's how it is created in the scouts, that's how it is created in the police. That's how it is imposed on the whole society.

Surrender is a totally different phenomenon. Surrender means you are in deep love and a great trust has arisen in you — such trust that there is no question of repressing yourself.

You are sannyasins here. I have nothing to reward you with; in fact, you have to go through all kinds of difficulties here. You come from far better, far more advanced countries, you have had beautiful homes, you have lived more comfortably, with all the luxuries, with all the gadgets that science has made available. You would have never thought that you would have to suffer this nightmare in Poona — this heat, mosquitoes, rats, cockroaches. In the West many things have disappeared, but here you have to live in very primitive conditions. You have to live almost two thousand years back.

I am not offering you any reward, I am not promising you any paradise either, because I say drop the very idea of the future, live in the moment. And to live in the moment *and* in Poona . . . it is arduous, it is difficult.

Then why are you here? I don't promise you anything at all. You are here just out of sheer love — you have fallen in love with me. It is not a question of obedience. You are not drilled to be obedient, you are not conditioned in any way to be obedient.

Just the other day Prem Zareen asked a question: "Bhagwan, you say, 'I give freedom to my sannyasins.' Is this applicable to sannyas, too?"

She means: is she free to drop sannyas? Yes, Zareen, I give you total freedom. Total means *total*, without any exception.

If you have taken sannyas out of love, then there is no question of dropping it. If sannyas has really happened, then how can you drop it? It is not something that you have put upon yourself, it is something that has *grown* in you. Just as you cannot drop your heart, how can you drop your sannyas? If it is your heart you cannot drop it. From my side yes, absolutely yes. I give you total freedom — there is no question about it — you are free to drop sannyas. It was your freedom to be a sannyasin, it is your freedom *not* to be a sannyasin. But the whole question hangs on something very deep: if sannyas has happened out of a love affair then it is impossible to drop it even though the freedom is available. But if you have taken sannyas for some other, ulterior motives then of course it can be dropped. And then it is better to drop it because it has not happened in the first place. Why carry an unnecessary burden?

In short, if sannyas has happened you cannot drop it; if you can drop it, it had not happened in the very first place and then you *must* drop it. Not only do I give you freedom to drop it, I will *help* you to drop it because I am not in favor of you being burdened by anything that is not growing in you.

You are already too burdened, Zareen. A thousand and one things have been imposed upon you. I will be the last person to make your life more of a burden.

Sannyas is not like an arranged marriage, it is a love affair. In a love affair there is no question of divorce because we are never married, so the question of divorce does not arise at all. And if love is authentic, if love *is* really there, it is forever, there is no end to it. It begins but it never ends. Hence I can give you total freedom because I am not imposing any obedience on you. Where obedience is imposed freedom cannot be given, because if you give freedom then obedience will disappear.

Here trust is happening, surrender is happening, love is happening. From your side, trust, surrender; from my side, freedom. From the disciple's side, surrender, and from the Master's side, freedom. Where this freedom and surrender meet there is communion, there is *satsang*. It is not a question of obedience.

When I say something to you and you do it, you do it out of your love, not because it is an order and you have to do it. There is no question of forcing yourself to do it. In obedience you are doing it even against yourself, even in spite of yourself. In surrender the ego is no longer there to resist; the ego is absent.

When I move my hand, what is happening? Is the hand obeying me or is the hand totally surrendered to me? The hand is totally surrendered to me; there is no question of obeying me. The hand no longer exists as a separate entity.

Zareen, in sannyas the disciple disappears, becomes part of the Master. He becomes his hands, his eyes.

Ramakrishna was dying. He had cancer of the throat, and in his last days it became impossible for him even to drink water.

Vivekananda said to him, "Bhagwan, can't you ask

God to do you just a little favor? If you simply ask God that at least you should be allowed to eat and drink it is bound to happen. It is becoming too great a suffering for your body—and not only for your body but for us all. We cannot eat because we know *you* cannot eat. It has become impossible for us to drink because we know you cannot drink. How can we drink? So if you don't care about yourself, okay, but think of us—we are also suffering. Just for our sake close your eyes and say to God, 'Do me just a small favor.' "

Ramakrishna closed his eyes, opened them and started laughing. He said, "You fool! If I listen to your advice God will laugh at me. I asked him. . . ." That was his way. He had not asked—there is nobody to ask—that was his way. He would not hurt Vivekananda. He closed his eyes, he may have even moved his lips to show Vivekananda that he was praying to God. And then he opened his eyes and he said, "God laughed at me and he said, 'Ramakrishna, you are listening to these fools? You follow their advice? Are they your disciples or are you their disciple? Who is who? You have eaten with this throat for so many years—can't you now eat and drink with the throats of your disciples?' " And Ramakrishna said, "Vivekananda, his argument appeals to me. So stop torturing yourself, suffering, because now that I have lost my throat, I have to depend on your throats. Eat as much as you can—a little more than usual, because a part of it has to go to me. Drink a little more than usual because there will be my share, too. So eat, drink and rejoice, because God has said, 'Ramakrishna, you can eat through your disciples' bodies. Why depend on this body? And this body is gone and rotten!' "

There is a certain invisible unity, an organic unity, between the Master and the disciple.

Zareen, one is free, absolutely free with me. If one

wants to drop sannyas one should not think twice, one should simply drop it and forget all about it. If it can be dropped it should be dropped; if it cannot be dropped, only then is it worthwhile. I give you total freedom. But if surrender is there, there is not going to be any difference; in fact, total freedom will make your surrender easier. When there is somebody to impose something upon you, a natural resistance arises. It is very natural. If I am here to impose something upon you and to make you obedient, then you will resist; then it is just human. But I am not imposing anything.

That is the beauty of this commune. That is something unique that is not happening anywhere else in the world. Everywhere obedience is being imposed in subtle ways or not even in such subtle ways, either directly or indirectly: "Do this, don't do that." People are being treated like slaves, with no respect.

I respect you. I love you far more than you can ever love me, I respect you far more than you can ever respect me, because whatsoever you can do will be limited and whatsoever I can do will be unlimited.

Your so-called gurus and your pseudo Masters all depend on your obedience; they force it upon you. And you are willing for the simple reason that when somebody is there to impose something upon you he becomes a father figure for you. He takes the responsibility — you need not feel responsible for yourself. You need to depend on somebody and you have to pay the price for that. Then they go on ordering you about as if you were small children.

A little boy went to the school for the first time and the teacher asked, "What is your name?"

He said, "Johnny Don't."

The teacher said, "I have never heard such a name before — Johnny Don't?"

He said, "That's my name. Whatsoever I do, my mother shouts, 'Johnny, don't!' my father shouts, 'Johnny, don't!' Wherever I go somebody or other immediately says, 'Johnny, don't!' So I assume that this is my name. This *must* be my name."

And because from the very beginning your father, your mother, your parents, your teachers, your priests are all teaching you, "Do this, don't do that," they all create a certain obedience in you. You become addicted to obedience; it is a drug.

So when you come to me you would like. . . . People go on asking me — I never answer their questions — they go on asking me, "Give us detailed instructions what we should do and what we should not. We want clear instructions from you." I give you clarity not clear instructions, because my instructions may be right today and tomorrow they may not be right. My instructions may be a hindrance to your growth tomorrow because nobody knows about tomorrow; it is unpredictable. So I give you clarity so that you can find your own way of life today and tomorrow and the day after tomorrow. Wherever you are, if you have clarity, you will be able to find your way.

I give you total freedom. I share my light with you, I share my joy with you, I share my freedom with you. I don't want to become in any way a father figure for you. Always remember me only as a friend.

You ask me, Mahasatva: *Please talk about surrender and obedience.*

Surrender happens through love, trust, egolessness; surrender means surrendering the ego. Obedience is a cultivation of the ego, of pruning the ego here and there, of bringing it into a certain shape, into a certain form so that it can co-exist with the society, so that it can co-exist with the already established order of things. Obedience is in the service of the past, surrender is not in the service of anybody else.

Surrender is simply becoming free of your ego. And the moment you are free of the ego, your life starts growing wings. Ego is heavy; it is like a rock hanging around your neck. It goes on keeping you tethered to the earth, it gravitates towards the earth. Once the ego is dropped, suddenly you start rising upwards: your life becomes a tremendous upward movement, you are uplifted. Surrender makes you weightless; it allows you to go against gravitation. Another law of life starts functioning: the law of grace.

There are two laws. Science knows one law: the law of gravitation, that everything falls downwards. Religion knows another law: that everything rises upwards if you are ready to drop the ego.

It is said about a Hassid mystic, Zusya — who could have been a Zen Master, who could have been a Sufi. . . . In fact, enlightened people don't belong to any tradition. They are born somewhere — one has to be born somewhere, you cannot be born everywhere. . . . So it was a coincidence that he was born a Jew in the Hassidic tradition. But he was a strange Hassid. Hassids are strange, but he was the strangest; he was very unpredictable.

I at least come here and tell you a joke so that you can laugh. He was far more strange: he would simply come here and start laughing! Not even a joke! Hassids love beautiful jokes and stories.

So once he was asked, "Zusya, what kind of Hassid are you? At least tell some jokes, some stories. You simply come and start laughing!"

He said, "I am saving all my jokes for God because I don't have anything else. I don't know how to pray, I don't know any scriptures; I am saving some beautiful jokes for him. And when Zusya dies you will see!"

And it actually happened. When he died there was great thunder and people said, "He has arrived, and God is laughing!"

Zusya was staying in a house, in a disciple's house. The family was a little worried about the man because his ways were strange—he might do anything. In the middle of the night he might start laughing, he might wake up the neighbors, he might create a scene. So they put him in the basement and locked the door for the night so that at least they could rest and the neighbors could rest.

In the middle of the night suddenly they heard laughter from the terrace! They could not believe it! They rushed out and Zusya was rolling about on the roof, laughing! They said, "Zusya, what is the matter?"

He said, "That's why I am laughing! I was sleeping in the basement; suddenly I started rising upwards!"

But he was simply making it clear that there is another law which does not believe in locks and does not believe in falling downwards. His actual words were, "Suddenly I found myself rising upwards."

That is the law of grace: surrender, and suddenly you are in a totally different law; your gestalt changes, you start rising upwards. And there is great laughter in you and the whole existence laughs with you.

There is no question of obedience here. "Obedience" is an ugly word.

The fourth question

Bhagwan,
Please tell a British lady a British lady
joke for those of us learning to laugh at
ourselves!

Diane Ramsey,

Half way through her world cruise the English lady attended the ship's ball, became slightly intoxicated by champagne and ended up sleeping with a good-looking Italian steward. But the very next day when the steward approached her on the quarter-deck, the English lady cut him dead.

"Hey, contessa mia," said the steward, "donna you remember the good times we had last-a night?"

The English lady looked up briefly from her game of bridge. "In the circles in which I move, young man," she said crisply, "sleeping with someone does not constitute an introduction!"

The fifth question

Bhagwan,
I am always worried about what others are thinking
about me. What should I do?

Gayatri,

There is no need to do anything, because I know about those others — they are constantly worried about what you are thinking about them!

The sixth question

Bhagwan,
Is it true that the meek shall inherit the earth?

Rudresh,

Yes, because the rest of us will escape to the stars!

The seventh question

Bhagwan,
Who are the most noisy while making love?

Amir,

Two skeletons on a tin roof!

The eighth question

Bhagwan,
Gurdjieff had a beautiful waterpipe and did
not hate cigarettes either. All his life Baal
Shem had a clay pipe in his mouth. Does smoking
really have to drop? And if so, how come the
only temple in the ashram is the smoking temple?

Anando,

My whole effort here is to transform the mundane
into the sacred. It is an alchemical school: we change
base metals into gold. That's why the smoking place is
called a temple; that is the only temple we have.

I am not against smoking. I don't smoke myself because now there is so much smoke in the air that one
need not bother carrying a clay pipe or a waterpipe in
one's hand; just ordinary air is enough — it is so polluted.

In fact, ecologists say that it is a wonder how man is

surviving because just fifty years ago scientists used to think that if air became as polluted as it has become today in New York, in Bombay, in Calcutta, in London, then people will die. But man has a tremendous capacity to adjust to *any* situation. Where so many cars are moving and trains are moving and planes are moving and there are factories and so much smoke, there is no need to carry a private pipe anymore; you simply breathe air and you are smoking!

I am a lazy person; Gurdjieff was not a lazy person, that's why he used to carry his beautiful waterpipe. And in Baal Shem's days the air was not so polluted. If you wanted some smoke to go in your lungs you had to make private arrangements! Now it is universal.

And I am not against it because at the most it can kill you a little earlier. So what? If you don't live eighty years and only live seventy-eight, does it matter? In fact, the world is so overcrowded that everybody will be happy that you are gone. Do you know how much we celebrate when somebody goes? We don't celebrate anything like that! A little space is created.

So, Anando, you can smoke as much as you want. "Health is merely the slowest possible rate at which one can die."

You can go a little quicker! And in these days of speed when everything is going faster and faster, this is old-fashioned just to go on dying in a healthy way, to go on lingering and lingering. Health is the longest route! But finally, you have to reach the grave, and when shortcuts are available the wise people always choose the shortcuts. So don't be worried.

In the new commune we are going to make many temples and we are really going to make them beautiful temples, because when somebody is in such a hurry we should make every arrangement that we can, we should give him all the help that we can. We will make beautiful temples, well-decorated, comfortable, luxurious, so you can rest and smoke to your heart's content.

If you are living in an unconscious way it makes no difference whether you live to seventy, eighty, ninety, a hundred; it does not matter. Living consciously even for a single moment is enough.

My whole effort here is to help you to become conscious. Even if for a single moment in your whole life you become absolutely conscious you will not be coming back. You are well-gone. Then you are really gone into the universal source.

That is one of the names of Buddha: Sugata. *Sugata* means well-gone — one who has *really* gone and will not be coming back.

And if you are conscious then it is up to you to decide whether you would like to live a little longer or little less; nobody else should decide it for you. And how can anybody else decide?

Morarji Desai's government was trying to impose prohibition on the whole of the country — and eighty percent of his cabinet ministers were drunkards! And he himself was worse than all of them — he was drinking his own urine! I would rather drink wine. If one has to choose between wine and urine, wine seems to be far more aesthetic — and it is far more vegetarian, too! Urine seems to be an animal food. And just think of the whole passage it comes along, the long journey it takes . . . now the second step after that is not very far away!

When Indira became Prime Minister I was wondering why she was not moving into the Prime Minister's house; she took two months to move in. I inquired, "What is the matter?" And I was informed that she was changing all the tiles in the bathrooms because . . . who knows what he was doing inside the bathroom? And the whole house was being almost renovated. Everything had to be cleaned, all the utensils had to be removed.

Who knows what he was doing? And in his bathrooms all that was found were different kinds of enemas. Two months it took to change the whole house — it must have been stinking!

I am not against smoking or even against drinking. Once in a while it is really beautiful to drink. There is no need to be so superhuman — be human!

That's what I love more in Jesus than I love in Mahavira or Buddha. Buddha and Mahavira are too abstract, almost inhuman; Jesus is very human. He drinks and he eats and he loves feasting. And late in the night they eat and drink and they gossip.

The new commune is not going to be a commune of ascetics — ascetics are pathological people. My sannyasins are not ascetics, my sannyasins love life. Of course, when you live consciously it is up to *you* to decide. If you want to drink a little beer once in a while there is nothing wrong with it, but the decision comes through your own awareness. If you don't want to drink there is no need.

In fact, I don't drink for the simple reason that just soda water gives me enough intoxication, so there is no need to mix it with whiskey. Why waste whiskey? I keep it for others. Whenever Paritosh celebrates his birthday I send him a bottle of whiskey or brandy. Whenever somebody brings brandy I keep it because Paritosh will need it soon, his birthday will be coming! For me, just soda is enough.

The last question

Bhagwan,
Please, just one joke more about the blow job
phenomenon.

Mᴜᴋᴛᴀɴᴀɴᴅᴀ . . . sorry, Paramahansa Muktananda . . . I mean, you son of a bitch! Are you mad or
something? Why are you obsessed with this great phenomenon? But if you want, it is okay!

George Stearman was a legendary businessman, a
great success in America. He began as an IBM salesman
of typewriters and within ten years his sales and executive leadership was so outstanding that he became sales
director for all office products and small computers for a
nine-state area from Texas to California. When Xerox
expanded into computers he was lured away to their
corporate headquarters outside New York and within
ten years of record achievement he was national sales
director for Xerox. With a position on the executive
committee all he lacked before the presidency was a seat
on the board of directors.

He had a beautiful wife and three children in college
and a house in Darien, Connecticut, that looked like
Mount Vernon. Then, on Christmas Eve, when the
other chief executives had all gone off to the Bahamas,
Florida or Aspen for the holidays, George went into the
office to get his year-end pay check with the expected
large bonus. When he opened his pay check, instead
of a big bonus he had a check for severence pay. He
was fired.

George felt totally destroyed but made it home after a
few martinis. When he opened the door, there was a
note on the Christmas tree that said: "George, I've had
it. I want a divorce. The children and I are gone!"

Blindly he went back to the city, got himself thor-
oughly drunk, took the elevator to the top of the Empire
State Building and was about to jump off when he felt a
small tug on his pants leg. He looked back — there stood
Santa Claus.

George said, "Santa, get lost! Get away! I've lost

everything! My job is on the rocks and my wife and children have left me!"

Santa replied, "Wait, George, I'll give you two wishes if you give me one."

"Okay," said George, "I want my wife and kids."

"No problem," said Santa, "in two days they will be back."

"Great!" exclaimed George. "What about my job?"

"Well," said Santa, "there has been a power play. You just wait until New Year and you will be the director of Xerox."

"Wow!" said George, "That's great! And what can I do for you?"

"Well," said Santa, unzipping his fly, "my wish is for you to give me a blow job."

"What!" screamed George. "I'm forty-five years old and I've never done a thing like that!"

"Well," said Santa, "a deal is a deal!"

After George had finished, Santa zipped up his fly. Looking up George saw tears streaming down Santa's face. "What's wrong?" he asked.

Santa looked down at George and said, "It is rather touching to find a forty-year-old man still believing in Santa Claus!"

12

The first question

Bhagwan,
The Buddha said, "If you want to see, see at
once. Don't let the mind enter into it."
Can you tell us more about "seeing"?

Anand Deepesh,

SEEING IS A STATE OF NO-MIND, a state of no-thought, a state of pure awareness, when you simply reflect that which is without any interference, any judgment, any like, any dislike; when you don't say a thing about it, you just function like a mirror.

That's why Buddha says, "If you want to see, see at once," because if you start thinking you have already missed. Seeing at once means don't bring the mind in. Mind brings time, mind brings future, mind brings past.

Mind starts comparing whether it is right or wrong. It compares with the old prejudices — with the Gita, with the Koran, with the Bible, with all your conditionings — or it starts projecting itself into the future, into the world of desires: "If I believe in this what am I going to attain? What will be the achievement?" The moment the mind comes in it brings the whole world of the past and the future. Suddenly you are in a turmoil. Memories are there, desires are there, and that which was said to you is lost in the turmoil, in the noise.

Buddha says: See it right now! Not even a single moment's thinking.

Thinking means missing.

Hence this has been Buddha's constant practice: whenever a new seeker came to him asking questions, inquiring about truth, God, after-life, he would always say, "Wait, don't be in a hurry. Just sit by my side for at least two years not asking anything. If you really want to be answered, then forget all your questions for two years. If you don't want to be answered, then I am ready to answer right now. But you are not ready to listen. Your very question is coming out of an inner insanity. There are a thousand and one questions inside asking for attention. While I am answering your question you will be preparing a new question to be asked; you won't be listening to me. So if you really want to be answered, wait for two years. Sit silently by my side not asking, simply watching what is happening here.

"Much will transpire in these two years: you will see many people flowering. You will see all kinds of people coming to me: the curious ones who come empty-handed and go empty-handed, the real seekers who come empty-handed but never go empty-handed — they stay, they remain with me till they are fulfilled. You will see the slow ones who take a very long long time, a gradual process, and you will see the quick ones, the intelligent ones who understand immediately. Simply watch. Walk with me from one village to another village, sit with me under this tree and that tree, imbibe my spirit, feel my silence, look into my eyes, watch the way I walk, watch the way I sit. Simply watch for two years and forget all your questions, don't formulate any questions, and after two years, if you can fulfil this condition, you will be allowed to ask and I will answer you. And I promise you that whatsoever the question is it will be solved, whatsoever your thirst is it will be quenched."

One great philosopher, Maulingaputta, had come, and he was asking great philosophical questions, of course. Buddha listened—he was very famous, he was well-known all over the country. He had not come alone, he had come with five hundred of his own disciples. They were sitting behind him. Buddha listened patiently. For one hour he was asking this question and that—very complicated questions, complex questions, subtle questions. Then he said, "I have asked so many questions, but you have not answered."

Buddha said, "My way of answering is that you will have to wait for two years with me. These are the questions you have asked of many people. Have you asked them or not before asking me?"

Maulingaputta said, "That's true. I have asked Mahavira and he immediately answered. I have asked Sanjay Vilethiputta"—he was another famous teacher of those days—"and he immediately answered. I have asked Ajit Keshkambli"—he was a very skeptical philosopher—"and he was very much interested in my questions. And I have asked so many others. We have been traveling all over the country."

Buddha said, "You have asked so many people and they have all answered, but have you got the answers? If you have got the answers, then why waste my time?"

Maulingaputta said, "They have answered, but I have

not got the answers yet. My questions remain the same, untouched. Their answers have not satisfied me."

Then Buddha said, "I can also answer right now as they have answered — it will not satisfy you either. Now you have to decide. If you really are interested then risk two years' time and sit silently by my side."

Maulingaputta waited for two years, but before he said, "Yes, I am ready to wait," one of Buddha's great disciples, Manjushri, started laughing. Maulingaputta said, "Why is this man laughing like mad?"

Buddha said, "He is not mad — he is my first disciple who has become enlightened. And I know why he is laughing — you can ask him yourself."

Maulingaputta asked Manjushri, "Why are you laughing?"

He said, "I am laughing because this Gautam Buddha is tricky! He tricked me the same way. Listening to what he is saying to you I remembered my own journey to him. Twenty years have passed; suddenly I remembered — I had completely forgotten — that these were my questions too. It is as if history is repeating itself. And it is strange that I came with five hundred disciples of my own just as you have come, and I asked Buddha and the same reply was given to me: 'Wait for two years.' I waited for two years, and I am laughing! I would like to say this to you as a warning: if you want to ask this man, ask right now, because after two years you will not ask and he will not answer."

Buddha said, "I will be ready to answer, but if *you* yourself refuse to ask, what can I do? My promise will stand — I am a man of my word."

And the story happened the same way that Manjushri had predicted. Two years passed. Maulingaputta had completely forgotten, because who remembers time when one is with a man like Buddha?

You remember time only when you are miserable;

when you are blissful, time is forgotten. Time depends. . . . If you are very miserable then one hour appears as if many days have passed. If you are blissful, then many days appear as if just a few moments have passed. And if you are totally blissful then time stops, then time disappears, evaporates; then there is no time anymore. Then you simply live beyond time.

Two years passed. Maulingaputta had forgotten, but Buddha reminded him. Suddenly one day he said, "Maulingaputta, two years have passed. It is time now that you should ask your questions. And I am ready to answer."

And Maulingaputta laughed. Buddha said, "You are laughing like mad! What has happened? Do you remember Manjushri's laughter that day?"

Maulingaputta said, "My questions have fallen. I have nothing to ask. I have become utterly silent. You have not answered and yet you have answered."

This is the true answer. The real Master kills your questions in such a subtle way that you never become aware of it; without any bloodshed he goes on destroying your questions. Slowly slowly, by and by, you become aware of the absurdity of all your questions. Slowly slowly you become aware of the utter mystery of life. Life is not a problem and it cannot be reduced to questions and there is no answer for it. It is a mystery, unanswerable, insoluble. You have to live it, you have to taste it, you have to experience it. And it is experienced in silence.

Hence meditation contains all the answers because meditation is the art of getting beyond the mind. Once the mind has gone with all its chattering, you are able to see, seeing happens. And seeing is transformation. When you can see that which is, your whole life is transformed. You cannot live now against existence; it is impossible. You start living in harmony with existence.

Knowing, seeing, how can you go against the ultimate law of life? Nobody is so foolish. You go against it because you are not aware of it. When you are aware of it you simply become a harmonious part of it; you fall into the organic unity of existence, you disappear as an ego — the dewdrop disappears into the ocean and becomes the ocean. And that is fulfilment, and that is contentment, and that is the ultimate bliss, *nirvana*.

The second question

Bhagwan,
I have four specialties: I sleep very deeply
in your discourse, I eat lots of chocolate and
ice cream, I am a German girl and I am fooling
around with an Indian swami. Can I get enlightened?

Prem Gayano,

SLEEP IS VERY HELPFUL. Enlightenment is very close to sleep. Patanjali has exactly defined *samadhi* as sleep, with only one little difference: that it is *conscious* sleep. The body sleeps, the mind sleeps, but something far more deep in you remains awake — at the very center of your being, a flame of awareness. So deep sleep is nothing to be worried about. That is very good. And these discourses are meant for that! Just keep a little alert deep inside. If you don't listen to my discourse, that is not to be worried about; just remain a little alert inside. And if my discourse can help you to fall into a deep sleep, at least something is happening, you are on the right track. Just a little deeper. . . .

And if you eat lots of chocolate and ice cream it's perfectly good because you may not be coming again, so be finished with it. Eat as much chocolate and ice cream as you want because on the farther shore there is no ice cream, no chocolate — and I am telling you from my experience! Do you know how miserable I feel? Now I repent — why didn't I eat chocolate and ice cream and all kinds of things? But when I was as asleep as you are, Deeksha was not around!

And there is no need to be worried that you are a German girl. If you had been a California girl, then there would be trouble. Germans are one-pointed people; they go like arrows, direct to the point, they don't go zig-zag. That is not their way. Once they have decided something then they follow it to the very end — whatsoever happens. They don't look here and there, they don't look backwards. That's why I have such a soft spot for German people. That's perfectly okay. Just Californians are in a difficulty.

A Californian bumper sticker: WARNING: I BRAKE FOR HALLUCINATIONS.

As far as enlightenment is concerned one has to beware only of hallucinations, because one can hallucinate that one has become enlightened. Many Californians *are* hallucinating. Now there are as many enlightened people in California as there have ever been anywhere in the world. In the whole history of humanity there have not been so many enlightened people as you will find everywhere in California. Almost in every house you will find enlightened people! Anybody can hallucinate. So I am perfectly happy that you are a German girl.

The only problem is that you are fooling around with an Indian swami. I have to ask you two questions, Gayano. Is by any chance this Indian swami called Paramahansa Muktananda? Then avoid this fellow! And he is trying to hide his name, remember it. He is not telling people his name. Now everybody is inquiring about him, "Who is this Paramahansa Muktananda?" Fooling around is okay, but avoid this fellow because with him there is no possibility of enlightenment at all. I have known people who have become enlightened and just by being with this man they have become unenlightened again!

How will you recognize him? He goes on laughing like Jimmy Carter! So you have to watch that. And now, because I am saying it, he may try to hide even that, so you can watch him in the night when he sleeps because then he completely forgets, naturally. He has the face, the same diplomatic face, the same stupid face as Jimmy Carter.

Mrs Carter went for a checkup at the dentist's.
"How is the mouth?" asked the dentist.
"Ah, he is away playing golf this weekend," she replied.

Otherwise everything is going well, Gayano. If you can be aware of this Paramahansa Muktananda, then all is perfectly okay with you. I can guarantee your enlightenment.

The third question

Bhagwan,
I took sannyas out of the wrong reasons, not out
of the heart. I had thought, "As I'm fucked up
anyway, I might as well try sannyas."
But the very day after darshan everything changed.
Now I feel you in my heart stronger and stronger.
Wearing the mala is no longer a sacrifice but a
grace and a pleasure. Even some old problems
just disappeared. How could the wrong moment
prove to be the right one?

Uli,

Y‌OU ARE NOT AWARE of your own heart, that's all. You were thinking that it was not coming out of your heart — it must have come out of your heart, otherwise what has happened would have been impossible. Many people are not aware of their heart for the simple reason that our whole society, culture, education, condition us to bypass the heart; they want us to reach the head as quickly as possible. They try to find a shortcut, and the heart is left on the side. Your energies become completely oblivious of the fact that there is a heart beating inside you. And the physiologists go on saying to you that your heart is nothing but a part of your physiology. Yes, they are right. The heart has two aspects: its outer aspect is part of physiology, its inner aspect is part of your spirituality. The physiologists are concerned only with the outer aspect, but the inner goes on working. Even though you are not aware of it it works continuously in you; it goes on influencing your life in many ways.

That's why many times you feel something has happened which you never wanted to happen. You fall in love with a woman; your mind says, "It is simply madness. What am I doing?" It seems so irrational — it does not appeal to your mind and your reason. Still, something deeper than the mind is pulling you; you cannot resist it. You fall in love in spite of all your rationality, your mind, your scientific training, your thinking. And the mind goes on saying, "What foolishness you are doing! This is not right! You should not do it." It can find a thousand and one excuses not to do it. But something far more powerful, far more intrinsic, far deeper is working, and the mind feels almost impotent. Then mind is very clever — it never accepts its defeat — it says, "Okay, let's try."

That's what happened with you. Your mind says to you, "As I'm fucked up anyway I might as well try sannyas." Something deep was stirred, but the mind won't accept it because it does not want to accept that there is anything deeper than it. It won't accept its defeat.

I have heard about Mulla Nasruddin. He was going on his donkey very fast; the donkey was almost running. And the people asked, "Nasruddin, where are you going?" He was passing through the marketplace.

He said, "Don't ask me, ask the donkey!"

They said, "This is strange!"

Nasruddin said, "There is nothing strange. This donkey is so stubborn that whenever I try to direct him he gives me such a fight — he won't go that way. So when I am alone on the road I beat him and I take him to the place where I want to go, but in a marketplace people gather and a crowd starts laughing at me: 'Your own donkey and you are not the master of it!' And the more he sees the crowd the more stubborn he becomes. So I have learned one lesson: that when passing through the marketplace I simply go wherever he is going. Outside the town I will see to the fool, but in the marketplace I allow him to lead me. That at least gives a false impression to the whole town that I am the master!"

That's the way of the mind.

Mulla Nasruddin was telling his son, "Sit silently, don't make noise!"

But the son was not listening. The more he was telling him to sit silently, not to make noise and to obey his father, the more rebellious the child was being.

Finally Nasruddin said, "Okay, now disobey me and let me see how you can disobey *this* order! Disobey me — this is my order! And now let me see how you can disobey me."

This is the strategy of the mind; the mind knows. First it tries to overpower the heart; if it cannot, then it says to itself, "Let us try — what is wrong with it? We have tried so many things."

But, Uli, something deep down of which you are not clearly aware was pulling you into sannyas. It is a magnetic force. Certainly you are in it in spite of your mind, but not in spite of your heart, otherwise what has happened would not have happened at all.

You say: *But the very day after darshan everything changed.*

That shows that the heart bloomed, flowered. For the first time something of the heart has been heard. For the first time you have given it a chance. For the first time you have listened to love rather than logic. For the first time you have been a little poetic rather than just a thinker. For the first time you have put aside all your arithmetic and you have taken a jump into something mysterious, incalculable. For the first time you have not been calculative.

You say: *Now I feel you in my heart stronger and stronger.*

The seed must have been there, but you cannot see the seed. When it starts sprouting, then you can see it. When leaves start coming out of the soil, then it becomes visible. But without the seed the leaves cannot come. Now you are seeing the leaves; retrospectively they are proof enough that there must have been a seed. You were unaware of it; now those leaves are making you aware of it.

Wearing the mala is no longer a sacrifice but a grace and a pleasure.

Not only leaves but buds and small flowers are on the way.

Even some old problems just disappeared.

That's the miracle of the heart: the heart simply helps to get rid of those problems that the mind cannot solve. The mind goes on and on moving in circles. The heart simply takes a jump out of those circles and suddenly has transcended those problems which have always tortured you. Suddenly you see that they are irrelevant, that there is no need to solve them, that there is no need even to bother about them, that they are not your concern, they don't belong to you — as if a person has come out of sleep and the problems that he was facing in his dreams evaporate, are suddenly no longer relevant. That's what has happened, Uli.

Now you say: *Even some old problems just disappeared. How could the wrong moment prove to be the right one?*

It simply proves it was not the wrong moment; it was the right moment, but you were just not aware of it. Now you are aware of it. Now move consciously deeper into it. If unconsciously so much has happened, if just by groping in the dark so much has happened, then if you start moving consciously, immense is the possibility of your growth, great is the hope. Greater flowers are waiting. The spring has come, you have seen the first blossoms; now soon all the trees will be blossoming. Your whole being will become a fragrance.

But drop that idea that you have moved out of a wrong decision; it was not wrong. Your mind was thinking that it was wrong, but your heart knew far better. The heart always knows better than the mind.

The fourth question

Bhagwan,
What do you say to a mind which goes on thinking
in four different languages? (Persian, English,
French, German.)

Shraddes,

Whether you speak one language or one dozen languages makes no difference — it is the same mind. All those languages will be speaking the same mind. If a madman speaks Persian, do you think it will be different than when he speaks English or French or German? A madman is a madman; in any language he will be mad.

An enlightened person is an enlightened person; in any language he will be enlightened. Whether he speaks or not he remains the same. Of course, four languages will make it a little more complicated, but the basic problem is the same. Your mind is one, your mind's disease is one. You can express that disease in four languages, that's all; but only the expression will be different, the root can't be different.

When Johnny Fuckerfaster went to school one day, the teacher decided to review the alphabet. She told her students, "I'll name a letter of the alphabet and you tell me a word that begins with that letter. We'll start with A."

Johnny Fuckerfaster raised his hand shouting, "I know, I know!"

The teacher knew Johnny had a dirty mind and thought to herself, "He'll say 'asshole' and embarrass the class." So she called on another student who answered, "Apple." The teacher called out the letter "B" and again Johnny raised his hand furiously and yelled, "Please, me, call on me, I know!" The teacher imagined he would say "bastard," so she asked another child for the answer.

He replied, "Boy." The teacher continued through the alphabet until she got to the letter "R." By this time Johnny was jumping up and down in his seat and making such a commotion she could no longer avoid him. "What dirty word could he possibly make with 'R'?" she thought. None came to mind so she called on Johnny.

"Rat . . ." he said. The teacher breathed an enormous sigh of relief, then smiled and said, "Very good, Johnny!"

Then Johnny added, ". . . and it had a fucking tail that long and took a shit on the floor!"

You can't avoid your mind; it will find its way. Any language will do — four languages or forty languages. Yes, it is a little more complicated, Shraddes, but mind is capable, so capable that one staggers to think of its potential.

The people who understand, who have worked on the inner mechanism of mind, say that a single human mind can contain all the libraries of the world; its capacity is almost infinite. But if you are a fool, even if you know all that is written, even if you become a walking Encyclopaedia Britannica, it won't make much difference; you will remain a fool. Of course, your foolishness will now be a little more decorated foolishness. That's what scholars are: decorated fools with great degrees, certificates, diplomas. They can pretend that they know — and they can pretend more logically than anybody else because they are well-informed — but deep down there is just the same darkness, the same unconsciousness.

You say: *What do you say to a mind which goes on thinking in four different languages?*

It is the same — thinking is the same, the disease is the same. And the remedy is not different: meditation can help you to get rid of one language, it can help you to get rid of four languages or four hundred languages. Meditation gets you into a space where mind is left behind with all its knowledge. Suddenly you start functioning from a state of not-knowing, from innocence. And that innocence is beautiful and that innocence is fragrant. That innocence is the essential religion.

The fifth question

Bhagwan,
Why am I so much afraid of death?

Chinmayo,

ONE IS AFRAID OF DEATH because one is unaware of what life is. If you know what life is, the fear of death disappears of its own accord. The question is not of death at all, the question is of life. Because we don't know what life is, hence we are afraid that it is going to end one day. We have not even *lived*. How can you live without knowing what it is? You have neither lived nor loved; you have simply been dragging, vegetating. And you know that one thing is certain: death is coming closer every day, every moment, hence the fear. The fear is natural because death will close the door forever. And without ever knowing what life was you will be taken away. You were given an opportunity, a great opportunity, and you missed it.

You go on postponing for tomorrow. You say, "Tomorrow I am going to live." But simultaneously, side by side, there is a fear: you know, "Tomorrow, who knows? Tomorrow maybe death will come, then what?" And you have postponed life for tomorrow and there is no more tomorrow — then what? Then fear arises. And you don't know how to live right now. Nobody tells you how to live right now.

The preachers, the politicians, the parents, they all tell you about the tomorrows. When you are a child they tell you, "When you are a young man then you will know what life is." When you are a young man they say, "You are young fools — youth is foolishness. When you are old, then you will understand." And when you are old they say, "You are finished. Now there is nothing left. You are like a used cartridge." This is a strange world!

In my childhood, as it happens in every child's life, I used to ask all the elders available thousands of questions. It almost became a torture for them because my questions were embarrassing to them. So the easiest way was: "You are too young. Wait."

One of my father's friends was known in the whole town as a sage. With my father I used to go to him and I used to torture him the most. And he would always say, "Wait. You are too young and your questions are too complicated. When you are a little more grown-up, then you will be able to understand."

I asked him, "You please give me in writing what year I will be grown up. Then I will ask you these questions. Because this is a tricky thing: whenever I ask — I have been asking for at least five years — you always say the same thing: 'When you grow up. . . .' You can go on saying this to me again and again! You just write it down on paper and sign it."

I saw his hand was shaking. I said, "Why is your hand shaking? Why are you afraid? If you know at what age a person becomes able to understand, write it. And if you say at twenty I will ask at twenty-one — I will give you one year more!"

So he wrote, "Twenty-one years."

So I said, "Okay, I will come only after I am twenty-two."

He must have thought, "At least the problem is solved

for the time being. Who knows? After he is twenty-two. . .?" I must have been at that time nearabout fourteen.

When I became exactly twenty-two I arrived, and I arrived with a crowd — I had gathered many people. I said, "You come with me," And I had his signed letter. I said, "This is your letter. Now answer!"

He said, "You are such a nuisance! Why have you gathered all these people?"

I said, "Just to witness that you have been cheating me. And not only you have been cheating me, this has been going on all over the world. Every elderly person is cheating young people, telling them 'Tomorrow' — and the tomorrow never comes. Now I am twenty-two years old and you have written twenty-one. I have given you one year more just in case I am not intelligent enough and I take a little longer time to grow up. But now I am not going to leave, I will be here. I want all my questions to be answered."

He said, "To tell you the truth, I don't know anything. And please don't ask me again. Forgive me. You are right — I have been lying to you."

"Why did you lie to a child?" I asked him. "How could you lie to a child who was asking out of such innocence, who trusted you? — and you deceived him! You don't know whether God exists or not and you were telling me that God exists and that I would be able to understand later on. And I knew that very moment that even *you* didn't understand. You don't know anything about God, you are just repeating like a parrot."

But this is the situation: teachers don't know, professors don't know, priests don't know. Without knowing, they go on pretending that they know. And the whole strategy consists of a single trick: go on postponing. "You will also know when the time is ripe." Of course it is never ripe — you never grow up. And by the time you are old enough you have to save your own face, so you start saying the same things to your children.

If you love your children, if you love your younger brothers, sisters, never tell lies to them. And your whole religion consists of lies! Be truthful, tell them, "I don't know and I am searching." Don't postpone it for tomorrow.

Our whole life is a postponement, hence the fear of death: "I have not known yet and death is coming."

It is not you alone, Chinmayo, who is afraid of death.

You ask: *Why am I so much afraid of death?*

Everybody is afraid of death for the simple reason that we have not tasted of life yet. The man who knows what life is is never afraid of death; he welcomes death. Whenever death comes he hugs death, he embraces death, he welcomes death, he receives death as a guest. To the man who has not known what life is, death is an enemy; and to the man who knows what life is, death is the ultimate crescendo of life.

But everybody is afraid of death; that too is contagious. Your parents are afraid of death, your neighbors are afraid of death. Small children start getting infected by this constant fear all around. Everybody is afraid of death. People don't even want to talk about death.

There have been only two taboos in the world: sex and death. It is very strange why sex and death have been the two taboos not to be talked about, to be avoided. They are deeply connected. Sex represents life because all life arises out of sex, and death represents the end. And both have been taboo — don't talk about sex and don't talk about death.

And there have been only two types of cultures in the world. One category consists of the cultures for whom sex is taboo. They can talk about death, in fact they talk too much about death. For example, in India, listen to the mahatmas, to the saints, and you will find it. Nobody talks about sex, everybody talks about death — to frighten you, to create fear in you, because out of fear you can be enslaved, out of fear you can be forced to be religious, out of fear you can be forced to bow down to some stupid idea of God, to some stupid idol of God. People are worshipping anything!

Just put a stone in front of your house, paint it red, and just wait on the side and see. Within an hour somebody is going to pass and will bow down to it, thinking it is Hanumanji. Somebody else will come and will put two flowers there and somebody else will follow with a coconut. And this is the beginning of a temple! Soon you will find that a temple has arisen there.

People are so afraid, they are ready to bow down to any nonsense, to any stupidity.

We call religious people "God-fearing." In fact, a religious person is never God-fearing; he is God-loving, certainly, but never God-fearing. Fear has no place in a religious man's life — love and only love. And where love exists, fear disappears; and where fear exists, love has no possibility to grow.

In a society like India, death is not taboo. Indian scriptures are full of very detailed descriptions of death. They describe with gusto how ugly death is. They describe your body in such ugly, disgusting ways that you will be surprised at these people — why are they so interested, so obsessed with all that is disgusting and nauseating? — for the simple reason that they want you to become so afraid of life, so antagonistic to life, so negative to life. . . . They destroy your love for life, your affirmation of life by talking about death, by making death as big as possible and as dark as possible, by depicting death in all the ugliest colors.

And then there are societies. . . . For example, Christianity for centuries has been a society, a culture against sex; sex is the taboo. "Don't talk about sex." Hence the idea — a sheer nonsense idea — that Jesus is born of a virgin mother. They have to create this fiction because how can Jesus, a man of such purity, come out of sexuality? Such purity coming out of such impurity? Impossible, illogical! A lotus coming out of mud? Impossible! But, in fact, all lotuses come out of mud.

Jesus is born as naturally as you are born — he is not a freak! He is not abnormal. And this whole nonsense about the Holy Ghost, that the Holy Ghost makes Mary pregnant. . . . Now ghosts are making love!

Hamid guards near my room. Just outside the curtain he stands there with a big staff. One day I asked, "Hamid, have you seen the Holy Ghost or not?"

He said, "Holy Ghost?"

"Yes," I said, "some day he will come, so be alert — because if the Holy Ghost does not come to visit me, then where will he go?"

And one day Rajen was standing there and I told him, "Keep your staff in your hand, otherwise the Holy Ghost may use the staff against you! Rather than this staff being a protection, he will hit your head with your own staff!"

Since then he has left his staff somewhere; I don't see his staff anymore. Maybe afraid. . . . Sometimes you are not so attentive, and keeping your staff in your hand the whole time . . . sometimes one has to relax too. Even guards have to go to sleep! And the Holy Ghost comes and finds the staff and hits him on the head! And if the Holy Ghost can make a woman pregnant, what can he not do? He can do anything — he can even make a man pregnant! Anything is possible; with the Holy Ghost nothing is impossible.

Sex is a taboo for Christianity: "Don't talk about sex!"

Now, after Sigmund Freud, the first taboo is broken; sex is no more a taboo. We have shifted to another taboo; now death has become the taboo. Now don't talk about death. It seems as if man needs some taboo or other. The Victorian society was a society rooted in the taboo of sex. Now the modern society, Western society, is rooted in the taboo of death. Don't talk about death at all, forget all about death as if it does not happen — at least it does not happen to you, at least it has not happened to you up to now, so why bother about it? Forget all about it.

When a man dies in the West now, there are experts to decorate the man. He may never have looked so beautiful as he looks after death — painted and his cheeks so red as if he had just come from a three months vacation in Florida! And so healthy, as if he had just been exercising and were now doing *shravasan* — the death posture — not really dead. The pretension has to be created that he is not dead. And even on the gravestone it is written: "He is not dead, he is only asleep."

And in all the languages we say . . . whenever somebody dies nobody says that he is simply dead. We say, "He has gone to God. He has become beloved of God. God has chosen him and called him. He has gone to the other world. He has become heavenly."

One man was saying to the other, his friend, "My wife is just divine."

And the other said, "But my wife is still alive!"

You talk about people's divinity, etcetera, when they are dead.

There was a great conflict between Voltaire and Rousseau; their whole lives they were quarreling. Voltaire died; somebody informed Rousseau that Voltaire had died. He said, "Really? He was a great man — provided that he is really dead!" If he is not dead then he will withdraw his words. Alive, they are enemies; dead, "He was a great man." So he makes a condition: provided that he is really dead, he was a great man.

Once a man dies, nobody speaks against him, nobody says anything against him. He becomes suddenly a saint, suddenly great. His place will never be filled again, his place will always remain empty. The world will always miss him; he was so essential. And nobody had taken any notice while he was alive. These are tricks — tricks to keep death away, to shut the doors, to forget all about death.

A real humanity will not have any taboos: no taboo about sex, no taboo about death. Life should be lived in its totality, and death is part of life. One should live totally and one should die totally.

And that's my message to my sannyasins, Chinmayo.

You ask: *Why am I so much afraid of death?*

Because you are not yet living totally. Live totally and the fear of death will disappear. And you are not alone; everybody is in the same boat.

It was a typical British Men's Club: pipe smoke hanging in the air, thick leather chairs, carved oak panels.

The old retired colonel was recounting his daring exploits in Africa. "Nearly lost me life to a black-maned lion once!"

"Oh, really, sir?" said a young officer, feigning interest. "Do tell about it."

"Well, fella me lad, there I was striding through the thickest part of the Congo jungle with my faithful gun-bearer, Umbogo, when across a small clearing I saw the biggest lion you have ever seen. Cool as a cucumber sandwich, I took my trusty rifle from Umbogo, took aim, and pulled the trigger. 'Click' — the damn thing was a dud. Unperturbed, I handed back the dud and took a second rifle. 'Click' — another dud. By this time Umbogo had gone and I thought I had better get going, too. I ran as fast as I could, but in no time the beast was close behind. I could feel his breath down the back of my neck and I knew he was about to pounce; but just as he was about to, he slipped. This gave me my chance and I ran as fast as I could. But he was soon there again — breath down the back of my neck, about to pounce, and again he slipped. This happened three times, and the third time I managed to get into the jolly old Land Rover and get away."

"How amazing, sir," said the young officer. "I am sure that if that had been me I would have messed my pants."

"Messed your pants?!" bellowed the old colonel. "What do you think the lion was slipping on?"

The sixth question

Bhagwan,
What do you do for exercise?

Anand Prachi,

I JUST TELL a few really good jokes to myself and then laugh loudly and roll on the ground. I know no other better exercise! You can ask Vivek — once in a while she catches me rolling on the ground!

Just the other day I was telling these jokes to myself:

Richard Nixon was suspicious of some of the politicians surrounding him, thinking there was a conspiracy developing against him.

So he gathered together his closest aides and they went to a small village somewhere in the Alps to investigate the problem.

On the second morning Nixon opened the blinds to his bedroom window, and there in the snow someone had pissed: "Nixon is an asshole." Disturbed by this, Nixon set his smartest forensic scientists to work to find the culprit.

After forty-eight hours they reported back to him. "We have bad news," they said. "We've analyzed the urine and found that it came from Henry Kissinger."

"Oh no!" said Nixon.

"But there is even worse news to come, sir. We've also discovered it is Mrs Nixon's handwriting!"

Richard Nixon, Henry Kissinger, a catholic priest and a hippie were riding in a small airplane when the landing gear fell off.

The panic-stricken pilot rushed out of the cockpit. "I'm sorry, boys, this plane's not going to make it. There are only four parachutes and as I'm the captain I get one."

He grabbed a parachute and jumped out.

Richard Nixon stood up and said, "I'm the President; the nation needs me — sorry, gentlemen. . . ." He grabbed a parachute and jumped.

Henry Kissinger jumped up shouting, "I'm the smartest man in the world! The world cannot afford such a sacrifice!" He grabbed a parachute and jumped out.

The priest spoke next: "My son, you are still young — you take the last one!"

"Don't worry, father," the hippie said. "There is a parachute for each of us — 'the smartest man in the world' just grabbed my backpack and jumped with it!"

The last question

Bhagwan,
Are there really any coincidences?

Prem Doug,

MAN, WHILE HE IS UNCONSCIOUS, lives only in co-incidences; his life consists of only coincidences and nothing else. The unconscious life is an accidental life.

Only the conscious man goes beyond the accidental and enters into the intrinsic. The conscious man transcends coincidences. Without being totally conscious you are a victim of all kinds of unknown forces that surround you. You don't know why things are happening to you, why you have done this and why not that, why you have chosen this and why not that.

When I passed my matriculation and went to university I wanted to fill in my form, but I had no fountain pen with me. So I asked the next student who was filling in his form, "Will you be kind enough to give me your fountain pen so that I can fill in my form?"

He was very happy and willing. He said, "First you fill in your form."

I filled in my form. I said, "Why did you want me to fill in my form first?"

He said, "Because I cannot decide what subjects to take." He looked at my form and whatsoever subjects I had taken he filled in the same subjects.

I said, "Are you mad or something?"

He said, "It does not matter. It is all the same to me. Whether I read philosophy or politics or economics is all the same to me. I had to copy somebody's form; you are as good as anybody." He said, "In fact, I have been passing all my examinations by copying other people's answers. I don't know how I have passed the matriculation."

Now this man is now a professor of philosophy. What will you call it? Just a coincidence, accidental. I might have been just a few minutes late that day and he would have never been a professor of philosophy. I may have had a fountain pen; he would have never been a professor of philosophy. He may have copied from somebody else; then he would have been a professor of politics or economics or who knows what.

One Jewish novelist writes: "My father was traveling in a train; the train was late. It arrived in the middle of the night somewhere in Russia." He was hungry and cold; it was a cold Russian night, snow was falling. He rushed to find out whether he could get some coffee or something hot to drink.

The woman who owned the restaurant was just closing. He pleaded, he said, "Just five minutes. Give me two cups of coffee — I am tired and I am hungry. And if you can give me something to eat I will be grateful."

The woman opened the door again — she was just going to lock up — poured coffee, gave him something to eat. And of course they started talking, and the woman asked from where he was coming — the usual conversation with a stranger — "And where are you going to stay?" And the woman said, "It is good that you arrived right in time because now the taxis have all left — the train was so late. And we were not hoping — from this train nobody ever comes. So please come in my car and I will drive you wherever you want."

The man said, "I don't know where to go. You tell me some good hotel."

The woman said, "Hotels there are but no good hotel. And they will all be closed. It will be better if you come with me and rest at my place. In the morning you can find the hotel."

And the man, of course, very gratefully agreed. And this is how the story begins. They fall in love . . . and then you can develop the whole story yourself.

Now this Jewish novelist says: "If the train had not been late I would not have been born at all. If the train was a little more late I would have missed again, I would not have been born. If the woman had been a little hardhearted and had refused to open the restaurant again, I would not have been born at all. If the woman had left my father at some hotel, the story would have ended then and there. But he stayed with the woman; the woman was a widow. In the morning she invited him for breakfast, and one thing led to another.

This is how ordinary life is.

Prem Doug, unconscious man lives in coincidences; he is accidental.

Vidhana has written to me: "Bhagwan, I would like you to know that sometimes meditation can be very dangerous. I was doing a visualization technique: imagining I was a tree. I was imagining what kind of roots I had, what color and texture I was, which kind of leaves I had, and there I was swaying in the breeze . . . when suddenly a dog came trotting along and pissed on my leg."

Now Vidhana thinks the dog knows that he is visualizing, that he is thinking he is a tree. The dog must have been as mad as you are, otherwise dogs don't get so easily deceived — very difficult to deceive dogs!

It is said when Columbus saw, after three months, the leaves, green leaves floating in the ocean, he was tremendously happy. But his biographers say that was nothing, you should have seen his dog! He was jumping! For three months. . . . Think of the dog, poor dog — no tree. That is celibacy! If the dog were an Indian he would have been a mahatma!

A black man, an Arab and a Jew are walking together in the desert. Suddenly a horrible witch appears in front of them, riding a dragon. As they beg for their lives, the witch softens.

"Okay," she says, "if the length of your pricks, added together, measures exactly one meter, I'll spare your lives."

The black man takes his prick out — seventy-five centimeters. The Arab measures his prick — twenty-four and a half centimeters. With trembling hands, the Jew takes off his trousers and what a relief — exactly half a centimeter. As they happily part from the witch, the black brags, "Ah, you are lucky you had a black with you — seventy-five centimeters!"

"Nonsense," says the Arab. "It was my prick, the gift of Allah, that saved us!"

"That's what you think!" says the Jew. "What would have happened if she hadn't turned me on?"

13

The first question

Bhagwan,
How can I become a light unto myself?

Shraddho Yannis,

THESE WERE THE LAST WORDS of Gautam the Buddha,
his parting message to his disciples: "Be a light unto
yourself." But when he says, "Be a light unto yourself,"
he does not mean become a light unto yourself. There is
a great difference between being and becoming.

Becoming is a process, being is a discovery. The seed
only appears to become the tree, that is an appearance.
The seed already had the tree within itself, it was its
very being. The seed does not become the flowers. The
flowers were there unmanifest, now they are manifest. It
is not a question of becoming, otherwise a pebble could
become a flower. But that doesn't happen. A rock cannot become a rose; that doesn't happen because the rock
has no potential for being a rose. The seed simply discovers itself through dying into the soil: dropping its
outer shell, it becomes revealed in its inner reality.

Man is a light in the seed. You are already Buddhas. It

is not that you have to become Buddhas, it is not a question of learning, of achieving, it is only a question of recognition — it is a question of going within yourself and seeing what is there. It is self-discovery.

Yannis, you are not to become a light unto yourself, it is already the case. But you don't go in, your whole journey is outward. We are being brought up in such a way that we all become extroverts. Our eyes become focused on the outside, we are always seeking and searching for some goal "there," far away. The farther the goal, the more challenging it appears to the ego. The more difficult it is, the more attractive it appears. The ego exists through challenges; it wants to prove itself. It is not interested in the simple, it is not interested in the ordinary, it is not interested in the natural, it is interested in something which is neither natural, nor simple, nor ordinary. Its desire is for the extraordinary. And the reality is very ordinary, it is very simple.

The reality is not there but here, not then but now, not outside but in the innermost sanctum of your being. You have just to close your eyes and look in.

In the beginning it is difficult because the eyes only know how to look out. They have become so accustomed to looking out that when you close them, then too they continue to look out — they start dreaming, they start fantasizing. Those dreams are nothing but reflections of the outside. So it is only in appearance that you seem to be with closed eyes, your eyes are still open to the outside world, you are not in. In fact, every meditator comes across this strange phenomenon: that whenever you close your eyes your mind becomes more restless, your mind becomes more insane. It starts chattering in a crazy way: relevant, irrelevant thoughts crisscross your being. It is never so when you are looking outside. And naturally you become tired, naturally you think it is better to remain occupied in something, in some work, rather than sit silently with closed eyes, because nothing seems to happen except a long long procession of thoughts, desires, memories. And they go on coming, unending.

But this is only in the beginning. Just a little patience, just a little awaiting. . . . If you go on looking, watching these thoughts silently, with no judgment, with no antagonism, with no desire even to stop them — as if you have no concern with them — unconcerned. . . . Just as one watches the traffic on the road, or one watches the clouds in the sky, or one watches a river flow by, you simply watch your thoughts. You are not those thoughts, you are the watcher, remembering that "I am the watcher, not the watched." You cannot be the watched, you cannot be the object of your own subjectivity. You are your subjectivity, you are the witness, you are consciousness. Remembering it. . . . It takes a little time, slowly slowly the old habit dies. It dies hard but it dies, certainly. And the day the traffic stops, suddenly you are full of light. You have always been full of light, just those thoughts were not allowing you to see that which you are.

When all objects have disappeared, there is nothing else to see, you recognize yourself for the first time. You realize yourself for the first time.

It is not becoming, it is a discovery of being. The outer shell of the thoughts of the mind is dropped, and you have discovered your flowers, you have discovered your fragrance. This fragrance is freedom.

Hence, Yannis, don't ask, "How can I become a light unto myself?" You are already a light unto yourself, you are just not aware of it. You have forgotten about it — you have to discover it. And the how of discovery is simple, very simple: a simple process of watching your thoughts.

To help this process you can start watching other things too, because the process of watching is the same. What you are watching is not significant. Watch anything and you are learning watchfulness. Listen to the birds, it is the same. One day you will be able to listen to your own thoughts. The birds are a little farther away, your thoughts are a little closer. In the fall watch the dry leaves falling from the trees. Anything will do that helps you to be watchful. Walking, watch your own walking.

Buddha used to say to his disciples: Take each step watchfully. He used to say: Watch your breath. And that is one of the most significant practices for watching because the breath is there continuously available for twenty-four hours a day wherever you are. The birds may be singing one day, they may not be singing some other day, but breathing is always there. Sitting, walking, lying down, it is always there. Go on watching the breath coming in, the breath going out.

Not that watching the breath is the point, the point is learning how to watch. Go to the river and watch the river. Sit in the marketplace and watch people passing by. Watch anything, just remember that you are a watcher. Don't become judgmental, don't be a judge. Once you start judging you have forgotten that you are a watcher, you have become involved, you have taken sides, you have chosen: "I am in favor of this thought and I am against that thought." Once you choose, you become identified. Watchfulness is the method of destroying all identification.

Hence Gurdjieff called his process the process of non-identification. It is the same, his word is different.

Don't identify yourself with anything, and slowly slowly one learns the ultimate art of watchfulness. That's what meditation is all about. Through meditation one discovers one's own light. That light you can call your soul, your self, your God — whatsoever word you choose — or you can remain just silent because it has no name. It is a nameless experience, tremendously beautiful, ecstatic, utterly silent, but it gives you the taste of eternity, of timelessness, of something beyond death.

The second question

Bhagwan,
Will surrender happen only when I am ready
to die for you?

Veet Marc,

I AM NOT TELLING YOU TO DIE FOR ME. I am telling you just the opposite: to *live* for me. The surrender will happen only when you start *living* for me. I am not a worshipper of death, I am a worshipper of life. I am not here to teach you some kind of martyrhood. Enough of it! For thousands of years stupid people have been sacrificed by the cunning ones. Somebody was dying for Christianity, somebody was dying for Mohammedanism, somebody was dying for Hinduism. Everybody was dying — as if death were the goal! — and nobody was being taught how to live.

Live for God, because God is life. And, of course, God is also death, but death is beautiful only when it comes out of a fulfilled life, when it is an ultimate flowering of life. When death is a sacrifice it is ugly. Then you are dying for some cause, for some purpose, for some vested interest. Then some cunning politician, some cunning priest is using you as a means to his own ends. Of course he makes promises to you, otherwise how are you going to sacrifice your life? He promises you everything — after death. Now nobody knows what happens after death so it is very easy to promise something after death.

I promise you everything *before* death, not after death. That is the way of the cunning people — promising you something after death. You sacrifice now and the rewards will be given after your death. Now nobody knows what happens after death. Mohammedans say if you die in a *jihad*, in a religious war, you may be a sinner but you will directly go to heaven because you are dying for religion. The same is the attitude of the Christians and the same is the attitude of all the religions.

And who would not like to go to heaven? All the heavenly pleasures . . . and they are eternal and this life is momentary, this life is going to finish anyway sooner or later. And what is there to be so worried about in this life? It is ugly, it is painful, it is suffering, it is misery. These same people have made this life so miserable that anybody would like to die.

I have heard:

A British politician was talking to Adolf Hitler just before the Second World War started. He had gone to persuade him not to enter into this foolish war: "It is not going to help anybody, it will be destructive to the whole world."

But Adolf Hitler was adamant. In fact he thought that the coming of this diplomat simply showed the weakness of the English people. He made it a point to prove to this diplomat that "We *are* going to fight. And it will be better and in your favor if you surrender easily, otherwise you will be unnecessarily massacred, killed and destroyed."

He showed him all the scientific developments that they had made, that they were going to use in war. Of course they were the most superior power of those days; they had the most developed technology, particularly war technology. And then, finally, to prove that "Not only are there machines which are far bigger and better than you have, we also have men who are ready to die," to make the point absolutely clear, he came out of his room with the diplomat.

They were on the fourth story of a building. Three guards were there.

He ordered the first guard to jump out of the window. The man simply jumped! The British diplomat was aghast; he could not believe his eyes. The man did not even think twice! When Adolf Hitler said, "Jump!" he jumped. There was no question of asking why. He could not believe his eyes.

And then he said to the second, "Jump!" and the second man jumped. By that time the English diplomat became aware what was happening — two lives lost. He looked from the window; their bodies were just in pieces, in fragments, spread all over the road.

Adolf Hitler saw that he was impressed, tremendously impressed. In fact he was in such shock; he could not believe such an inhuman act. To strike while the iron was hot he ordered the third man to jump.

By this time the diplomat was alert. He jumped immediately, took hold of the arm of the third man and said, "Are you mad or what? Why are you jumping? Why are you so eager to die? Don't you want to live?"

The man looked at him with anger and said, "Do you call this life? Is it life? Is it worth living? Death is far better! Life is so miserable — death is a relief. Let go of my hand and let me jump!"

Since life is so miserable — and Adolf Hitler had made life miserable — everybody was ready to die. First make people's lives miserable, don't let them enjoy life, destroy all the roots of enjoyment, teach them all kinds of inhibitions, tell them that sex is sin, love is sin, teach them that to drink, to eat, to be merry — these are the goals of ugly materialists. Tell them to be self-destructive, prepare them for a kind of masochistic lifestyle in which they become ascetics and they become experts at torturing themselves; and then naturally they would like to get rid of this life as soon as possible. Then it is very easy to persuade them; in fact there is no need to persuade, they are already ready, just waiting for the opportunity. And whenever such a great opportunity arises to die in a religious war, when heaven is so close and so easily available, who would like to miss it? Everybody is ready to die!

No, that is not my idea of religion, Marc.

Do you know? Marc means a warrior, a soldier. Mythologically it means the god of war. I have changed his name, but by changing his name it is not so easy to change him. I have given him the name Veet Marc. Veet Marc means go beyond war, go beyond fighting, go beyond the very idea of fight.

But he asks: *Will surrender happen only when I am ready to die for you?*

Veet Marc, I don't want anybody to die for me — I am not a sadist. I want you to *live* for me. I want you to blossom and flower for me. I want you to eat, drink and be merry for me. I want you to celebrate for me. I want you to live your life as totally, as fully as possible. Yes, death will come, but when it comes out of a fulfilled life it has a beauty of its own. It is not death then, not at all; it is the door to the divine. But you need not die. Your work is to live; that is your *sadhana.*

That's my whole teaching: live, because that's the only way to show gratitude towards God. He has given you life and you want to die. No reason is worth dying for. Find out every excuse to live and live to the utmost, live to the maximum; don't live in a minimum way.

That's how people are living. People are living only a very minor percent of their total, just a small percent of their potential — not more than seven percent. Even your greatest geniuses live not more than fifteen percent of their potential, while you can live a hundred percent. Only once in a while a Buddha, a Krishna, a Christ lives a hundred percent.

If you can live a hundred percent, if you can burn your life's torch at both ends together, simultaneously, then you are surrendered to me. Surrender to life is surrender to me. I don't stand against life, I simply represent life, love, laughter.

Of course, this is far more difficult; that I know. Dying is so simple, it is so easy; living is difficult, arduous. Dying does not need much intelligence. Any fool can be a soldier — in fact only fools can be soldiers — and anybody can commit suicide. What intelligence is needed? Any idiot can do it. Just jump from any mountain, into any river, into any ocean. Or now even better and simpler processes are available: just take a few sleeping pills and die silently. There is no need to make much fuss, because even jumping from the mountain peak you may hesitate, you will have to take a decision. Just swallowing some pills is not that big a problem; you can easily do it. You can inject poison.

Dying is not of any value. To live is to really accept a great challenge, moment to moment. One has to live with a thousand and one problems, through a thousand and one problems and yet one has to keep one's cool.

That's the way of a sannyasin. A sannyasin is not a soldier, so you are not expected to be martyrs, you are expected to be lovers of life. And the more you love life the closer you are to God because it is his gift. Destroying his gift is ugly, is irreligious, is a sin.

Veet Marc, learn to live for me. I am giving you a bigger task, I know. And it is a lifelong process; death can happen in a single moment. Unless you are really unfortunate death can happen in a single moment.

Mulla Nasruddin wanted to commit suicide. Being a man of a very calculative nature he made all the arrangements possible so that in case one arrangement failed, another would work. He went to the top of a small hillock with a rope, with kerosene, with a matchbox, with a pistol. He found a beautiful place — the branch of a tree which hung out just above the river from the top of the hill. He made arrangements to hang himself on the tree. There was every possibility that just the rope would do and he would die, but if something were to go wrong he had other arrangements, alternatives.

So he hangs himself. Before hanging himself he pours kerosene on his body, hangs himself, sets fire to his clothes. But who knows? So as a final precaution he shoots himself also. The bullet hits the rope, he falls into the river, the river puts the fire out.

Next day I met him in the marketplace and said, "Nasruddin, what happened?"

He said, "It was just luck!" He told the whole story and I said, "This is really something! You had made so many arrangements?"

He said, "Yes, I had made so many arrangements. If I had not known how to swim I would have died!" But he knew how to swim, so he is still alive!

Unless something like this happens — which is very rare — unless the whole existence conspires against you, you can kill yourself very easily. But living is a long process. It will need guts, not stupidity; it will need intelligence.

The more intelligent you are the deeper will be the quality of your life, the higher will be the value of your life. The more meditative you are the more you will be able to know what life really is. It is nothing but God in a manifest form. To destroy this for any reason whatsoever is wrong, is a sin. So remember it.

You are not here to die for me, you are here to learn how to live. Let death come as an ultimate reward of living. And if you have lived rightly you will be able to live through death too, you will be able to *live* death too. And that is the most beautiful experience because it is through living one's death that one transcends death and becomes one with the eternal.

The third question

Bhagwan,
I still don't accept myself. Why not?

Anand Leena,

Iᴛ ɪꜱ ʙᴇᴄᴀᴜꜱᴇ ʏᴏᴜ ᴀʀᴇ ᴄᴏɴᴅɪᴛɪᴏɴᴇᴅ to be perfectionists, and perfection is such an ideal that everybody falls
short of it. Then condemnation, self-condemnation
arises. These are the tricks that have been played upon
you — beware of these tricks. It is time that man should
be mature enough to know that imperfection is the way
of life. Everything is imperfect, and it is beautiful that
things are imperfect. If everything was perfect and
everyone was perfect, life would be so dull and boring
that it would be impossible to tolerate it even for a
single moment.

I perfectly agree with Bertrand Russell. He used to say
that he did not want to go to heaven — jokingly, humor-
ously, because in fact he never believed that there is any
heaven or hell. But he used to say, "Even if there is
heaven I would prefer hell because in hell you will find
good company."

In heaven you are bound to be bored, utterly bored.
Just think — living with saints for eternity! Mahatma
Gandhi sitting on one side and so many saints, Jaina,
Hindu, Mohammedan, Christian, Buddhist, and to only
live with them! They don't even know how to play
poker, they don't even drink beer! Beer? They will not
even be ready to drink Coca-Cola, because there is
cocaine in it! And smoking of course is not possible in
heaven because cigarettes contain nicotine. In fact, life
will be so impossible with these saints. And they will
never laugh — laughter is for imperfect human beings.

Christians say Jesus never laughed. If the Christians
are right, then Jesus must have been absolutely wrong.

But I know that they are not right. Jesus must have laughed, must have — his whole life says so. He enjoyed the small things of life; he even enjoyed drinking wine. Now I don't think your saints will allow him into heaven; they will call him a drunkard and throw him out. And he lived with drunkards and gamblers and prostitutes. Your saints will be very angry. The rabbis who crucified Jesus may be allowed into heaven, but not Jesus. He is too human, too alive, too imperfect.

Bertrand Russell is right that in heaven you are not going to find good company. You will see sad faces, long faces, everybody almost dead. And what will these people be doing there? No gossiping — you cannot even sermonize because to whom will you sermonize? They are all sermonizers! You cannot find disciples in heaven — they are all Masters! And Jainas say no woman has ever entered heaven. Now you see the utter boredom? Just these ugly, half-starving saints and not even a single woman! It will be like a desert without any oasis.

Have you seen? If a dozen men are sitting in a room, it is full of a certain vibe. And let one beautiful woman enter and the vibration immediately changes. The desert is no longer a desert; an oasis has come in. They all become alive, their kundalinis start rising! Those who had fallen asleep wake up. Buddhas go on saying, "Wake up!" and they won't listen. But just let Sophia Loren enter and immediately all the saints are alive, awake, fully awake!

But Jainas say no woman can enter into heaven. If a woman is religious and spiritual she will be born in her next life as a man and then she can go to heaven, but only from a man's body, never from a woman's body. As if souls were also male and female! As if bodies also went to heaven! What kind of stupidity is this? But the fear. . . . A woman can create a disturbance and, naturally, if for centuries no woman has entered into heaven and suddenly one woman enters, there will be a great commotion, there will be a great disturbance, chaos, and a great fight will break out. And all the saints will be at each others' throats — a *jihad*, a religious war for the woman! Everybody will be ready to die!

You have been told to be perfectionists. That's why, Leena, this problem arises. It is not only your problem, it is everybody's problem.

But remember a few things. First: All evil is potential vitality in need of transformation.

Even evil is to be accepted because evil is potential vitality in need of transformation. Anger is potential vitality — accept it. I am not saying that you should remain angry; it is through acceptance that you can transform anger into compassion. It is the same energy that becomes compassion. I am not saying remain sexual for your whole life, but it is the energy of sex that becomes love and it is the energy of love that becomes prayer. Go on transforming it. But if you reject it from the very beginning, how are you going to transform it? If you condemn it you create a barrier between yourself and your own energy; now no transformation is possible. You become antagonistic, you become split. You are divided, constantly in conflict with yourself. Your life becomes a sheer wastage.

And I know that you commit many mistakes, but to err is human. It is nothing to be worried about, nothing to make so much fuss about. It is how one learns, it is how one by and by becomes mature. The man who never commits any mistake never grows either. It is by going astray that one learns.

Hence, Leena, learn to forgive yourself again and again and again and again, because life is a constant growth. You will have to forgive yourself thousands of times. And if *you* cannot forgive yourself, who is going to forgive you? But you have been taught wrong values, wrong ideals and they are heavy on your head. Don't be worried about small things — enjoy them. Everyone lies, cheats, pretends — yes, you too, and most certainly I myself. So don't be worried at all.

Even Buddhas have to create false devices. I have to trick you into things which you will not enter into in any other way. I have to create devices. All devices are false; they have to be false because your illnesses are false.

For example, you are suffering from ego; now I say, "Surrender." In the first place the ego is a false entity, there is no ego at all. You are simply dreaming, you are making it up. But what to do? You have made it so big a thing that I tell you, "Please, surrender it to me." Rather than telling you that it doesn't exist — you won't understand right now — it is better to tell you, "Give it to me, surrender it." And you feel good that you can at least do something with your ego — you can surrender. It appeals to your logic.

It is like homeopathy: the illness is false, the medicine is false — just sugar pills, nothing to be worried about. Whenever you are suffering from false diseases — and remember, out of one hundred, almost seventy-five percent are false — rather than torture my doctors in the Medical Center, go to Narendra Bodhisattva. He is the homeopath, although he has not been able to cure his own headache! He has suffered from headaches his whole life. And he will not be able to cure himself — that is the difficulty — because he knows that all those pills are just sugar pills, but he helps others. He has helped many people, he has cured many people's headaches, and he feels puzzled, "What is the matter? Why can't I cure my own headache?"

That's the difficulty with false medicines: if you know, they are useless. But others you can cure easily. That's why there are so many "pathies." Except for allopathy, all "pathies" are more or less psychological. But they have a great appeal for the simple reason that if you go to the allopath and your illness is false he will say, "It is all in your mind." That does not feel good: "All in my mind?" You don't like that idea at all. You immediately start looking for some ayurvedic physician. And they are clever people — they have to be very clever. You start searching for some homeopath, some naturopath, and there are hundreds of "pathies" available. And all "pathies" work, they all help, so as far as help is concerned they are all helpful.

If you go to the ayurvedic physician he will never say that it is in your mind, never. He will talk much about your disease, he will analyze the disease. He may even go to your past lives, he may look at your hand, he may read the lines, he may even ask you to bring your birth chart. Now this man seems to know what he is doing, and that foolish allopath doctor, he was simply saying, "It is in your head." Now he is puffing up your ego. He is telling you your disease is really very dangerous and it needs a long treatment and a very careful treatment and you need a real genius of a physician — and you have come to the right person now. And he will be able to help you. He will give you all kinds of things which are really of no value, no medicinal value. But if you start believing in him. . . . If you go to the homeopath he will ask your whole life history — three hours he will give to you.

Now people who suffer from false diseases also suffer from talking about their diseases; they like very much to talk about their diseases. They magnify their diseases, they make them as big as possible. They have nothing else to brag about, but they have big diseases, great diseases. And the homeopath buttresses your ego.

I used to know a very famous homeopath doctor, a certain Dr Mukerji. He was a famous homeopath in all of India. For three days he would simply talk about your past diseases — from your very childhood when you were three years of age, as far back as you can remember, and he would write down everything. And you are just suffering from a headache! And he would go back to the age of three because he would say that a history begins there. "No disease is a separate phenomenon, it is a continuity." And it seems logical: "Everything is connected with everything else, nothing is discontinuous. Everything relates to everything else so unless we go to the roots. . . ." He would say, "I don't touch the leaves, I go to the roots."

Once I took my father to him. My father was very interested in homeopathy, so much so that when he started talking about his childhood he started talking about the childhood of his grandfather; he always started from there.

Dr Mukerji looked a little worried. I laughed. I said, "Now you have the right patient! Now you will know — three days won't do!"

My father always used to start from his grandfather's illnesses, then his father's illnesses, then his illnesses. It took almost ten days!

Dr Mukerji met me one day in the garden. He said, "I am tired! You please take your father to some other doctor — he is a very dangerous person. I have never come across such a person, but I cannot say anything to him because he is following the homeopathic principle exactly. And if one man's life diseases are connected, then certainly the son's diseases are connected with the father's diseases and the father's with the grandfather's."

I said, "You should be happy that he does not know anything about his other ancestors, that he knows only up to his grandfather! Otherwise it would have taken years for him to come first to his own illness!" And what was his illness? He was suffering for two, three days from a stomach upset. And I knew what the reason was: he always used to suffer whenever he would eat cucumbers. That was the simple reason — cucumbers, nothing else! No need to go to the father and the grandfather.

And I told Mukerji, "Now you know your homeopathic principle can be dangerous. You are a homeopathic doctor and he is a homeopathic patient — be patient! Listen silently to him. That's why I have brought him to you — he will put you right! His problem is very simple, not connected at all with any disease; he has just eaten cucumbers and they always give him stomach ache. It is as simple as that!"

Homeopathy helps you because it accepts your illnesses very seriously and that's what you want really, that's exactly what your desire is: you want attention, and a doctor listening to you silently. . . .

That's the whole secret of psychoanalysis, particularly Freudian psychoanalysis: it helps the patient without doing anything; the psychotherapist just goes on listening. The patient goes on talking for months, for years even, and the doctor has to be very patient and just listen. Whether he listens or not, that is not the point; he has to pretend at least that he is listening very attentively, and *that* helps.

The Buddhas have devised many false methods. In fact, all methods are bound to be false because your spiritual illnesses are all false, because your spiritual being can never be ill; it is just your belief. And your belief has to be destroyed by something which can appeal to you in the mind in which you are right now.

Leena, don't be worried.

You say: *I still don't accept myself.*

Why? What you have done? A few mistakes here and there. Maybe you lied once to somebody, maybe you deceived somebody. So what? This whole life is a drama

and we are all actors. And a little bit of cheating is perfectly okay — it makes life a little juicy, it gives life a little
spice! Otherwise everybody telling just the truth. . . .

That happens to a few foolish people who go through
Encounter and Gestalt — this happens. They start telling
the truth to anybody! Stupid people are stupid people —
they won't understand anything.

They write to me: "Bhagwan, now I am in trouble. I
have been through Encounter and I have learned that
one has to be authentic and one has to be true. So I told
my wife that many times I feel like going with some
woman. Now there is great trouble — my life has become
a nightmare. We are continuously quarreling. Before
this Encounter everything was going smoothly. Now the
Encounter is finished, Teertha is gone, but with my wife
the Encounter continues! And now there seems to be no
end to it. What should I do now?"

You need not be so foolish. In an Encounter group be
authentic — even if you have to lie, lie and be authentic!
If you don't know how to be authentic, pretend to be
authentic, enjoy being authentic. But don't carry this
nonsense everywhere and don't create troubles for
yourself.

Just think: if even for twenty-four hours everybody
on the earth decides to tell the exact truth, there will be
no world — finished! Just think in your mind: twenty-
four hours . . . everybody telling the exact truth and
nothing else . . . nobody will be a friend to you; you
will not find two friends in the whole world. Every
couple will be divorced. Children will leave their parents, parents will leave their children. All will be finished! No customers will come to any shop. The world
will come to a stop immediately — *nirvana* for the whole
world in a single blow!

This world needs a few lies too. It makes life smooth,
it helps. Lies are like lubricants.

Leena, start accepting yourself as you are. And watch, be alert. Of course, ninety percent of it will be transformed — and the ten percent will become more skillful!

The fourth question

Bhagwan,
How many British ladies are here?

Yatra,

FORTUNATELY, NOT MANY — only three. One is Prem Lisa, but she is new, very new, and I hope she will melt. She gets very much offended; whenever I say anything — lovingly — against the British, she gets offended.

Just the other day she wrote to me, "Bhagwan, of course the Australians are such nice people. They were originally chosen by some of the best English judges!"

Judges are never very nice people. Socrates was condemned by very nice Greek judges, sentenced to death. Jesus was also condemned by very nice judges — the highest rabbis and the greatest Roman magistrates and the governor — highly cultured people, well-educated. And Jesus himself was uncultured, uneducated, just a carpenter's son; he belonged to the proletariat. Pontius Pilate certainly belonged to the highest strata of society, but do you think that just because Pilate belonged to the highest strata of society, was one of the best Roman governors, he was right and Jesus was wrong? that Socrates was wrong and the judges, who were certainly the best judges of those days in Athens. . . . And no city has ever seen such culture, such sophistication as Athens has seen. But who was right?

If you ask *my* preference, I am always for the poor

criminals and sinners rather than for the saints and for the judges.

Yes, it is true that the first people to reach Australia were criminals, but so was the case with America. The first people to reach America were criminals, sinners, because sinners and criminals are more courageous people, adventurous. They were not bourgeois. The bourgeoisie is never courageous and judges are always in the service of the vested interests.

And who knows really what is right and what is wrong?

Once Lao Tzu was made a magistrate. Knowing that he was one of the wisest men in the country, the Chinese emperor appointed him a magistrate. He wanted to escape, he wanted to be forgotten, but the emperor was very insistent. He said, "No. You are the wisest man, you should be my greatest magistrate."

He said, "Okay." The first case came to court: a thief had been caught red-handed. And Lao Tzu gave him six months jail and also gave six months jail to the rich man from whom he had stolen.

The rich man said, "Are you in your senses? Six months jail for me too? For what?"

Lao Tzu said, "In fact I am being very lenient with you — you should get one year's jail. You have accumulated the whole wealth of the town — you are the original criminal. This man comes only second. If you had not accumulated all the wealth there would have been no need for him to steal. You have created the need to steal. In fact, *you* are the culprit!"

The rich man went to the emperor. He said, "What nonsense is this? Have you ever heard of this before? Is there any precedent?"

And the king was also worried because if this rich man was a criminal, then what about the emperor? He immediately relieved Lao Tzu from his duties. He said, "You may be a wise man, but you are not needed. You are not able to be a judge. A judge has to follow the rules."

Lao Tzu said, "I am following the ultimate law."

The king said, "There is no question of ultimate law. The law that I have decided, that has to be followed."

Lao Tzu said, "Your law is all nonsense. I follow the Tao. You are also one of the criminals."

Now who were those judges? Whom were they serving? Whom were they representing? They were representing the vested interests.

But Lisa got angry. She is a British lady here. Even in the discourse she sits wearing dark sunglasses. I cannot even see her expression, her eyes — impossible. That's very British-like! Now there is no need for sunglasses here. It is already too dark really; to see is difficult. People are writing to me, "Bhagwan, we cannot see you. Should we start wearing glasses?" And Lisa is wearing dark sunglasses — it is impossible to see her eyes. That is very diplomatic and very British. But she will melt — she has fallen into my trap, now there is no exit. It will take time. It is a difficult thing for a British lady to melt and become a sannyasin. It is such a change, such a transformation.

And the second British lady is Somendra! The second British lady is not in the form of a lady, but I don't look at the form, I look at the formless. This is the first time that he is laughing; otherwise I go on telling jokes and he goes on looking at the floor!

And the third British lady is not yet a sannyasin so I cannot tell you her name, but she has been here for seven months just thinking whether to take sannyas or not — to be or not to be. Seems to be very Shakespearian! Seven months . . . and I don't think that even seven years will be enough! I cannot tell you her name because unless somebody becomes a sannyasin I remain very polite, very British with the non-sannyasin, very mannerly. I talk about the climate and the weather, etcetera, I don't talk about true matters. Once you are a sannyasin then I start showing my true colors. So I am waiting. But she is also taking such a long time, even my patience is coming to a point . . . even I have started doubting whether I can wait anymore. Should I drop the very idea?

Several thousand football fans turned up to watch the match between the elephants and the insects. For the first half, the insect team came out onto the field with only ten members and the match was a slaughterhouse. By the time the whistle blew for half-time, the elephants were winning by ten goals to nil.

When the second half of the game was resumed, the eleventh member of the insect team — a centipede — took the field and the entire match changed completely. The centipede whipped through the elephant defence time and time again. When the final whistle blew, the insects had won by three hundred and ninety-nine goals to ten. As the players marched off the field, the elephant captain strolled up to the insect captain.

"How come you didn't bring your star player on in the first half?" he asked.

"Ah, well," explained the insect captain, "it takes him so long to get his boots on!"

So I am waiting. This lady seems to be a centipede, a British centipede! She is just getting ready, getting ready, getting ready. . . . She goes on writing to me, "What to do? Should I take sannyas or not?" And I cannot say to her, "Take," because this is such a risky thing, I don't want to take the responsibility. If a Britisher comes on his own, it is okay. Because it is not an easy job — even after sannyas it is going to be a difficult thing.

If it takes seven months even to decide whether to take sannyas or not, how many years will it take to be *really* one with me, to be in tune with me, to understand the humor, the laughter, the joy, the bliss, the music, the poetry that prevails here?

The fifth question

Bhagwan,
Do you use your mind when you speak in discourse?

Prashant,

WHAT DISCOURSE? You call this discourse? And what mind? One can easily see that whatsoever I utter is absolutely mindless. I am a madman. What mind?

One madman came to the house of another madman and knocked at the door. The man opened the window from above and shouted down, "I'm not at home!"

The madman below looked up and said, "Well, then I'm glad I didn't come!"

And the last question

Bhagwan,
Will you please tell a few jokes about the Portuguese?
We poor Portuguese sannyasins feel completely
ignored by you.

Dhyano,

FROM TODAY it will not be so.

Late one night, Manuel, staggering home drunk,

passed through a cemetery, stumbled and fell on the ground.

Just in front of his nose he saw a hand sticking out of a grave and a voice cried, "Help me! Help me! Let me out — I'm alive!"

The Portuguese shakily covering the hand with earth, replied, "No, you're not alive — just badly buried!"

A bunch of Portuguese rogues enter a bank.

"Hands up, everybody!" shouts Joachim, the chief. "This is a holdup! Manuel, lock everybody in the toilets. Antonio, bring the manager here!"

The manager is brought trembling to Joachim who asks him for the key of the safe.

"Please, for God's sake, don't kill me! I have left the key at home!" cries the manager.

"Don't worry, man," replies Joachim. "It's only the rehearsal today — tomorrow is the real thing!"

A Portuguese enters a hospital and says, "Doctor, I want to have my testicles removed."

Shocked, the doctor asks, "Have you really given this decision your full consideration?"

"Yes, doctor, I've really decided. I want my testicles removed."

So the doctor operates on him.

Weeks later, fully recovered, Manuel visits his friend who asks him, "So, Manuel, did you follow my advice? Have you had your tonsils removed?"

"Oh, my God!" cries Manuel. "Was it 'tonsils'?"

A Portuguese was on his first flight — Rio to Lisbon.

As the plane was ready to take off, the voice of the pilot came through the speakers: "Ladies and gentlemen, welcome aboard our Jumbo Boeing 747. Our plane is equipped with the most modern and sophisticated equipment for your comfort and security. We have three hundred and eighty passengers aboard, a crew of twenty-five people and thirty tons of cargo. We have two super-equipped kitchens that can provide five hundred meals, two bars, twelve toilets, a gambling hall, two cinemas with two hundred seats, a TV for each passenger, and on the upper floor a disco with an orchestra of twenty musicians.

"Now, please, fasten your belts, extinguish your cigarettes and say your prayers — we are trying to take off with all this junk!"

Manuel and Joaquim were hunting in the Amazon jungle when suddenly a wild animal appeared. Scared, they started to run away, but the animal followed them. Finally Manuel climbed a tree while Joaquim started running around the tree.

From the top of the tree, Manuel shouted, "Aie, Joaquim, the beast is almost on you!"

"Don't worry, Manuel," replied Joaquim, "I'm two rounds ahead of him!"

14

The first question

Bhagwan,
Is it not necessary to desire, to long and to
seek truth and avoid the untrue, to seek
truth and renounce the false?

Divyananda,

THERE IS NO WAY TO SEEK TRUTH because truth is not far away. Truth is not "there" somewhere so that you have to go to it, so that you have to reach to it; truth is not to be sought because truth is the very being of the seeker. How can you seek the seeker? How can you know the knower? That is impossible. You cannot encounter yourself. *You* are the truth.

Hence all seeking is futile, but one learns only through seeking. One learns this tremendously important fact, that all seeking is useless, only through seeking; there is no other way to learn it. You seek and you fail, you seek again and you fail; slowly slowly it becomes clear to you that seeking itself is the cause of missing it. Then seeking drops of its own accord. And when there is no longing, no desire, when you are utterly silent, when the very mind of the achiever has disappeared, you are surprised that what you have been seeking all along has always been with you.

Yoka says:

> *It is not necessary to look for truth or avoid illusion.*

Why? — because to *look* for it is to begin in a wrong direction and to avoid illusion is foolish because illusion means that which is not. How can you avoid that which is not and how can you seek that which is? That which is *is,* and that which is not *is not.*

Yoka also says:

> *We know that both are comprised in empti-ness, that they have no form and bounds.*
> *Non-form is neither empty nor non-empty.*
> *It is the true reality of Buddha.*

One has simply to become utterly empty. And when I say "utterly empty" I mean one has not to be just empty; "utterly empty" means empty of everything and also empty of emptiness. Otherwise the mind is so cunning it can now cling to a new idea of emptiness.

A disciple of Yoka was coming again and again to him, bringing his experiences that were happening in his deep meditation, and Yoka was hitting him. Whatso-ever he said he would be hit, irrespective of what he was saying. He was bringing beautiful experiences: the rising of the kundalini, a great experience of light, a beautiful inner fragrance, the sound of one hand clapping — whatsoever he had heard that people had achieved through meditation he was bringing — but he was being hit again and again.

One day he came with absolute trust: "Now the Master is going to accept my experience, to recognize it — the time has come," because that day he was going to say, "I have achieved emptiness." That is the ultimate. What more can there be? What can there be beyond emptiness? He was very happy that for the first time he was not going to be hit — but even before he had spoken, the Master hit him.

He said, "This is too much! I have not even uttered a single word!"

Yoka said, "It doesn't matter what you say, it does not matter whether you say it or not — I know. I knew the moment you entered in the room that you were again here with some foolish idea."

He said, "But sir, you should have listened. This is not a foolish idea, this is the experience of all the Buddhas!"

So Yoka said, "Yes, so you say. It seems you are hankering for another hit!"

And the disciple said, "Sir, I have experienced emptiness!"

Yoka laughed, hit him and said, "Throw it away! It is all nonsense!"

The disciple said, "How can I throw emptiness? I can throw everything else!" That was the first time that he argued with the Master; obviously, his argument seems to be logical. You can throw the experience of light because you are the experiencer. You can throw the experience of energy — you are the experiencer. Any experience can be thrown, but how can you throw the experience of emptiness? There is nothing to throw!

The disciple said, "How can I throw emptiness?"

Then the Master hit him hard and said, "Then carry it out — but do something. Either throw it or carry it out."

And the disciple said, "What are you asking me? I cannot carry it out because it is just empty, and I cannot throw it either."

335

The Master said, "Now you are clinging to the idea of emptiness. This is not emptiness — this is not true emptiness. Now you are full of the idea of emptiness. Once it was light, once it was energy, once it was fragrance, now it is emptiness. It is nothing but labels changing. And unless you throw this too you will not be truly empty. A truly empty person is neither empty nor nonempty. There is nothing to experience, not even emptiness. And in that state of silence when there is nothing to experience — no object, no content, but only consciousness, only the observer and nothing to observe, only the seer and nothing to see — one attains truth."

Yoka says:

> *Our spirit is like a clear mirror*
> *Thus it reflects the universe harmoniously*
> *Our spirit and the universe are one.*

Once you are utterly empty you are a mirror. You are not only aware of your inner truth, you become aware of the truth of the whole existence. And they are not two; they are two aspects of the same phenomenon, two sides of the same coin — the outer and the inner.

> *All manner of troubles arise if we abandon*
> *existence to obtain emptiness; that too is*
> *sickness.*

Listen to these tremendously significant words of Yoka. Yoka is one of the great Zen Masters. He says:

> *All manner of troubles arise if we abandon*
> *existence to obtain emptiness; that too is*
> *sickness.*
> *It is like throwing oneself into the fire to es-*
> *cape drowning.*

Don't abandon existence. Don't abandon the ordinary existence in any effort for some illusory truth, for some

336

illusory longing for God. Leave that for the fools. The intelligent person simply lives moment to moment with no desire to seek anything, with no expectation of finding anything. He simply lives moment to moment, joyously. His life is very ordinary; he has no desire to be extraordinary. He has no desire to be a Buddha, hence he is a Buddha. He has no desire to be extraordinary, hence he is extraordinary. Because every ordinary person has the desire to be extraordinary; only extraordinary people don't have that desire.

> *If we try to grasp truth or if we wish to escape*
> *error and illusion, we practice discrimination,*
> *an artificial and erroneous attitude.*

Once you say, "This is truth and that is untruth," you have started discriminating — and to discriminate is the disease of the mind. That is the function of the mind: to discriminate. "This is right, that is wrong. This is true, that is false. This is worldly, that is spiritual. This is materialist, that is religious." Once you start discriminating there is no end to it and you are in the grip of the mind. Drop discriminating and you are out of the grip of the mind. To be out of the grip of the mind is to be free, is to know what freedom is.

> *Most men forget spirit treasure,*
> *They have to recourse to dualist thinking and*
> *abandon the true nature of spirit.*
> *To pass the barrier of Zen by means of zazen,*
> *we should finish with reason, knowledge,*
> *illusion.*
> *Then we shall attain to supreme wisdom and*
> *enter into the palace of* nirvana.

Nirvana is not somewhere else; it is your inner space. Just get out of the clutches of the mind. Your mind is like an octopus: if somehow you get free of one of the legs of the octopus, there are other legs. There are gross legs and there are subtle legs, and by the time you start getting free of the other legs you are getting entangled into other legs. It goes on and on in circles.

The man who escapes from the world, what is he saying? In the East for thousands of years people have been renouncing the world because they say it is illusion. If you truly understand that it is illusion, then what is there to renounce?

These fools even come to me and they ask, "What kind of sannyas are you teaching people? Sannyas means renunciation. They should leave the world, but they live in the world. Not only do they live in the world, they live more deeply and totally in the world than other worldly people! What kind of sannyas is this?" They think I am teaching a wrong kind of sannyas.

I am teaching the ultimate sannyas, not a wrong kind but for the first time the right kind. The wrong kind has prevailed for a long time, for centuries. See the stupidity of the whole thing: you call something illusory and then you escape from it. If it is illusory there is no need to escape. It should be so simple! If it is real then why escape? If it is real then how can you escape?

Nobody renounces their dreams. Or do you renounce them every morning when you wake up — "I renounce all my dreams. I renounce all the treasures that I had in my dreams. I renounce the kingdom of my dreams"? You don't renounce them, otherwise people would laugh at you — you have gone mad! Dreams are dreams.

And these so-called spiritual people have been telling the world that the world is a dream — renounce it. What nerve — to call it a dream and in the same breath to say, "Renounce it"! Either it is not a dream or it is a dream — make sure what it is. And either way you cannot renounce it. If it is a dream there is no point in renouncing; if it is a reality, how can you renounce reality? — because reality is synonymous with God.

Hence I teach: Rejoice! There is no need to renounce anything — there is nothing to be renounced. Rejoice, and rejoice more totally! Rejoice in a multi-dimensional way. Dance, sing, be blissful. Let laughter be your life, let love be your life. That is the only true way to know what is.

The second question

Bhagwan,
Much of my Catholic mind has been tense with
struggle for power, approval, love, sex. Medi-
tation stirs up frustration. What is "just
looking"?

Prem Nisang,

Mind, any kind of mind — Catholic or communist, Jew or Jaina — is the same. Mind is a disease, and every mind creates a prison around you. There are different kinds of prisons; their architecture is different, they are made of different material. Some are made of stones, some are made of bricks, some are made of wood, and so on and so forth, but it does not matter — the material is not important — you are imprisoned. A Catholic mind has different concepts, a Hindu mind is rooted in a different ideology, but every mind needs an ideology. Even the atheist lives in a prison although he does not believe in God. He thinks he is a disbeliever — he is not. His disbelief is his belief. He fanatically disbelieves, in the same fanatical way that believers believe, sometimes even more fanatically because the people who believe in God remember God only once in a while, maybe on Sundays — it is a Sunday religion — but the atheist continuously argues against God; he remembers God continuously.

There is a very beautiful story in Indian scriptures:

When Narda, a devotee, a great devotee, was dying, God appeared to him. Such things used to happen in the past; they don't happen anymore. And God asked him what he would like, if he had any desire to be fulfilled in the next life.

He said, "Yes, I want to be born an atheist."

Even God was puzzled. Remember, such things used to happen in the past; now they no longer happen. God said, "What? You want to be an atheist? Such a great devotee, such a believer, such a religious man who has been singing and singing my name?"

Narda said, "Yes, because although I am a devotee, I continuously go on forgetting you, but I have seen atheists who never forget you. That's why I want to be an atheist next time: so that I can remember you continuously. I don't want to forget you even for a single moment. Now you are only one of the items of my mind, but for the atheist you seem to be his whole heart — although he denies you, he remembers you. So just give me one blessing: that I should be born an atheist so that I can talk about you continuously."

This story is beautiful. It says in a very symbolic way that the atheist and the theist are not in different boats.

The communist goes on arguing against God. Now he has no business with God, nothing to do with God. How was Karl Marx concerned with God? God does not come into it as far as economics is concerned; he is not an economic theory or anything. But Marx was obsessed, continuously obsessed: again and again he came to deny God, as if God were haunting him.

These are all fanatics; believers, non-believers, Hindus, Mohammedans, Christians — all are fanatics. And the fanatic never looks at the facts, that's why he is a fanatic. The creed of the fanatic is: "We are right and don't be distracted by the facts — whatsoever the facts say they are bound to be wrong." The fanatic's creed is: "We have already concluded what is true; now the facts have to fit with our creed, not vice versa."

And all these so-called ideologies have created very crippled people, Nisang. Of course the Catholic mind is one of the most crippled and paralyzed minds in the world, because it is repressive — and whenever you repress something you become ugly. Whatsoever is repressed remains there. Not only does it remain there, it becomes every day more and more powerful; it accumulates energy. If you express it, it evaporates.

For example, a man who gets angry in an ordinary way, just as everybody else does — if you insult him, he gets angry — is not a dangerous person because he will never accumulate so much anger that he can prove dangerous. But a man who goes on repressing his anger is sitting on a volcano; any day the volcano can erupt — either he is going to commit suicide or murder — less than that won't do.

It is because of repressive religions that so much pornography exists in the world. Pornography exists because of the priests, not because of the *Playboys*. In fact, the *Playboys* are only by-products of the priests. So much pornography exists simply because so much sex has been repressed; it wants to find some way, some outlet. And once you repress sex it starts finding perverted ways. It can become a political trip — it is sexuality, nothing else, repressed sexuality.

That's why in all the armies of the world, sex is repressed. And American soldiers have been continuously in difficulty for the simple reason that it is the first time that any army has been allowed some sexual outlet. American soldiers cannot win; their defeat is certain. Whatsoever they do, wherever they go, they will be defeated for the simple reason that American soldiers are a new phenomenon in the world — they are not sexually repressive. They can't win against the Russians — they could not even win against the Vietnamese. The poor Vietnamese defeated one of the greatest world powers that has ever existed in the whole history of man for the simple reason that if sex is repressed then a man is very dangerous, really dangerous — he is boiling within. He wants to hit hard, he wants to be violent.

And the person who is sexually satisfied is not really interested in killing. In fact, all the surveys of American armies show that at least thirty percent of the soldiers did not use their weapons in the war; thirty percent is a big percentage. And if thirty percent of soldiers are not using their weapons at all, they simply go every day to the front and come back without killing anybody, how are they going to win? They are not interested in killing, there is no desire to kill.

Killing arises only if sex is repressed very much. It is a strange fact that whenever a society has been affluent, rich, sexually free, it was destroyed by poor, backward, repressive societies. That was the fate of Greek civilization, that was the fate of Roman civilization, that was the fate of Hindu civilization, and that is going to be the fate of American civilization. It is very strange that the further evolved a society is the more it is vulnerable to being destroyed easily by the less evolved, because the less evolved are more repressive — they are more foolish, they are more stupid; they still go on listening to the priests.

Now Ayatollah .Khomeini-type people cannot have any influence in an advanced, cultured country, but they have tremendous power in Iran. The *mullas* of Iran are the most powerful people there. And the Ayatollah is just a madman! But that madman has become powerful. Now he is doing all kinds of things. People are being killed; people are continuously being killed, butchered, in the name of Islamic justice — as if justice can also be Islamic, Christian and Hindu.

Just a few days ago Pakistan decided that women will not be able to participate in any sports with men because that is against Islam. The woman has to be completely covered. Now you cannot play hockey if you are completely covered in a black veil with only two holes for your eyes to see out of. A very strange kind of hockey will have to be evolved! And then they run, and running, their bodies sway and their breasts jump; that is against Islam! So in Pakistan they cannot participate anymore — this is the twentieth century! — they can only play with women players and the spectators also can only be women. And even then they have to use clothes which cover their bodies — they have to use Punjabi clothes, chalwah and kurta, so their whole body is covered. They cannot play tennis in half-pants because their legs will show and that is against Islam.

These are the foolish people, but these foolish people are dangerous people. They can defeat anybody because they will repress sexuality so much, so much energy will be repressed, that it will be ready to explode. Any excuse will be enough. These are the people who are responsible for all the rapes in the world.

This is the experience of my woman sannyasins in India. They love me so much, that's why they are here and suffering so much. It is really a sacrifice to be here because wherever they go they will be watched by the so-called cultured, religious Hindus with such greedy eyes, as if these people are just there to tear them apart. And whenever they have any chance they hit them, they push them, they do anything ugly that they can do. Women have been molested, raped. And these are the great Hindus, the great religious people, the great spiritual people of the world! But it is natural; I don't see any contradiction. This is repression — any chance and it surfaces.

343

Two nuns were walking from the nunnery towards town to do some shopping. To save time they decided to take a short-cut across a dimly-lit, deserted wood. While they were in the wood, both of the nuns got raped.

"Oh no! How are we going to explain to the Mother Superior that we both got raped twice?"

"Just a minute," retorted the other nun, "we only got raped once!"

"Yes, I know, but we're going back that way, aren't we?"

There are rapists and there are women who are waiting for these rapists.

Nisang, you ask me: *Much of my Catholic mind has been tense. . . .*

It can't be otherwise. You will have to drop it, root and all. You cannot save anything of it. Don't try to save anything of it because it is all contaminated.

You say: It is *tense with struggle for power. . . .*

It is bound to be. If sex is repressed it starts moving into other dimensions. It becomes a great lust for power. If sex is repressed you start asking for approval; that is a poor substitute for love, for appreciation. And now that you are here you are becoming aware that there is a great need for love, but you are afraid — your Catholic mind is against love. The Catholic mind says, "Love only God." Now how can you love God? That is sheer nonsense. You have to love human beings; that is the only way to love God. Love unconditionally, love without any demands. But you have to love the people that surround you — these are God's available forms; you cannot love the formless. "Love God," they say, "and avoid man." Now they are teaching nuns, "Love Christ"; nuns are called "brides of Christ." What nonsense! The poor man was never married and now so many nuns are married to the poor man! Brides of Christ! And then of course they start imagining, projecting, and then their mind starts playing tricks on them.

If you look into the history of monasteries and nunneries in the Middle Ages you will be surprised. Thousands of cases are on record that nuns were raped by the devil and his disciples; not only that, nuns even used to become falsely pregnant. What imagination! When a woman imagines, she can imagine far-out things. Men are not that capable of imagining, but women can really imagine things. Women confessed in the courts. And what were these courts doing? These courts consisted of bishops, archbishops, popes. These courts were inquiring about details; in fact they were enjoying as much as possible the details of how the devil made love to the nuns. If you go into the details you will find them more pornographic, more obscene than anything ever written. And they had to confess and they confessed strange things: that the devil came in the night and made love to them, and they were absolutely unable, incapable . . . they could not do anything else. What could they do when the devil came and took possession of them?

All kinds of sexual perversions arose out of the monasteries. Sex would never have become perverted if it were not for the monasteries and nunneries. And the whole world is dominated by some kind of repression or other.

Nisang, you have to drop this whole mind.

You say: *Meditation stirs up frustration.*

It will stir up frustration. It is nothing to do with meditation; meditation simply brings your reality to you and that encounter is frustrating. Seeing the ugliness of your own mind you feel frustrated. But don't be worried. Meditation is bringing up all that is repressed in you; you will have to pass through it. If you know what is there it can be dropped; if you don't know, how can you drop it? Before something can be dropped it has to be known, well understood. In fact, to understand it perfectly is the only way to drop it.

And the day you drop your mind *in toto* you are freed from the priests. Priests are the most cunning people in the world and most foolish too, because only foolish people are cunning. Intelligent people are never cunning; they need not be cunning — intelligence is enough. When you are not intelligent you have to be cunning as a substitute; you have to learn the ways of cunningness.

But remember, all these priests — Catholic or Protestant, Hindu or Mohammedan — all these ayatollahs and all these mullas and all these pundits *are* stupid people but they have dominated humanity and they have reduced the whole of humanity to a big mass of stupidity. Get out of it!

Meditation is bound to stir up all this that has been done to you for centuries, but that cannot be avoided. If you want to avoid it you will remain the same. You will have to go through this pain of seeing all these ugly things that are in you. But better to see and go through it to reach your innermost core so that you can find your own intrinsic intelligence, so that you can find your own lost consciousness.

Once freed from the priests you are free from stupidity. Then you are neither Catholic nor Christian nor Hindu nor Mohammedan; then you are simply a human being, and then great beauty arises in you.

A Catholic priest went into a pet shop to buy a parrot. He was shown an especially fine one which he liked the look of, but he was puzzled by the two strings which were tied to its feet.

"What are they for?" he asked the pet shop manager.
"Ah well, father," came the reply, "that's a very un-

usual feature of this particular parrot. You see, he is a trained parrot, father — used to be in a circus. If you pull the string on his left foot he says 'Hello!' and if you pull the string on his right foot he says 'Goodbye!' "

"And what happens if I pull both the strings at the same time?"

"I fall off me perch, you fool!" screeched the parrot.

Even parrots are far more intelligent than your priests, than your politicians, than the people who have been dominating you.

Nisang, get rid of them.

Meditation is a process of getting rid of the whole past, of getting rid of all diseases, of getting rid of all the pus that has gathered in you. It is painful, but it is cleansing, and there is no other way to cleanse you.

The third question

Bhagwan,
I know that you have left one British lady out
of your account. Why?

Vivek,

Yes, I TOO AM AWARE that I have left one person out of the account and I think everybody else is also aware of it. That person is "Proper" Sagar. But I had to leave him out — he is too proper! He is a category in himself; he cannot be put with others. Moreover, he is really a gentleman.

Somendra I can count with ladies — he is an energy phenomenon, a Holy Ghost type! Now nobody knows who the Holy Ghost is, male or female; you can put him here or there. So Somendra can be counted anywhere. But Sagar is too proper a British gentleman, that's why I left him out. And, moreover, I thought there was no need to tell you his name — everybody knows anyway. Secondly: even if I had counted him he would have missed the joke!

Mulla Nasruddin was brought to court. He was accused of telling a joke to his wife. When she heard the joke, said the police report, she exploded into laughter and laughed so hard that she died.

"I don't believe it," said the judge, who was a proper Englishman. "Tell the joke!"

Mulla tried to refuse, but the Englishman insisted. "Tell the joke! I order you!"

So he told the joke and everybody exploded into laughter, and one by one they all died laughing — except the Englishman, who died one week later!

The fourth question

Bhagwan,
I believe that you are one of the greatest men
who has ever lived. Am I right?

Gitananda,

YOU ARE ABSOLUTELY WRONG — there are no great men. If you have a hero, look again: you have diminished yourself in some way.

This is the truth! This is it! There are no hidden meanings.

I am just an ordinary man — as you are, as everybody else is. The difference is not that I am great and you are not great, the difference is that I am awake and you are asleep. But that does not make you small, that does not make me great either. Nobody is great. This whole nonsense has to be dropped.

Don't start looking on me as a hero. I am still alive! You can do whatsoever you want to do when I am dead because then I cannot prevent you, but right now I won't allow such things!

The fifth question

Bhagwan,
Did Gautam the Buddha and Jesus the Christ have any idea that you would be here one day on earth?

Yogesh,

I SUSPECT SO! Gautam the Buddha used to say that after twenty-five centuries there would arise one awakened man whose name would be Maitreya; *maitreya* means the friend. Now for twenty-five centuries it has been thought that this would be the name of the awakened person, but my own interpretation is that Buddha is not talking about the name, he is talking about the quality of the person. He is saying that he will be the first Master who will be the friend, who will not pretend to be the Master, who will simply say, "I am your friend."

And that's what I am saying to you: I am your friend. Hence I say I suspect he may have had some idea.

But Jesus certainly had a very clear-cut idea about me, because there is an ancient story. . . . You may not have heard it because it has been whispered from Master to disciple in deep privacy, and it has been kept private up to now. For the first time I am telling you!

It was the Last Supper and Jesus was talking to his disciples: "You, Peter, will be the founder of my church. You, Andrew, will spread my gospel to the four corners of the earth. You, John, will go forth and heal the sick and feed the poor. You, Thomas, will write a gospel for Bhagwan Shree Rajneesh to speak about two thousand years from now. And you, Judas, will pay the bill, as no one else has money!"

The sixth question

Dear-a Bhagwan-a,
I dig-a it a lot-a.
It was-a far out-a.
Can you-a lay-a some-a more-a on us-a?
You are out-a sight-a!
Like-a thank you a lot-a!
P.S.-a: You see-a, I am-a American-Italiano —
a real mess-a!

Prem Patipada,

I KNOW, because just the other day somebody was talking about you.

A swami was saying to another swami, "Boy, she is a high explosive girl!"
"High explosive girl?"
"Yes, dangerous when dropped!"

Italian plus American — it is the most dangerous combination.

"That wasn't your daughter screaming," the Italian told the horny broad's father when he came down to the living room with a loaded shotgun. "That was me!"

You get it? Let me repeat it: "That wasn't your daughter screaming," the Italian told the horny broad's father when he came down to the living room with a loaded shotgun, "That was me!"

An Englishman sits down beside a beautiful blonde Italian girl in a pub. After a few drinks she says to the Englishman, "Amore, I love you."

"I love you, too," he replies hesitatingly and a little embarrassed.

"I love you three," says the Italian girl.

A week before the wedding the young Italian girl came to her mother in tears. "I'm so afraid about getting married," she said. "I'm afraid I won't be able to please my sweetheart."

Her mother, who wanted to make the girl's trials easier, undertook to explain to her the secrets of married life. With some hesitation she began to explain to the girl what she would have to go through.

"Oh, that doesn't bother me, mother," said the daughter. "I can screw all right, but I can't cook!"

Roberto and his over-developed wife were sitting in the stands waiting for the football game to begin. A friend walked over, said, "Hello, Roberto," gave his wife's breasts a little squeeze, and walked away.

A few minutes later another guy walked over, said, "Hello, Roberto," fondled the wife's breasts, and walked on. This strange sequence of events went on for some time.

Finally a man sitting next to Roberto spoke up: "Listen, pal, it's none of my business, but isn't it a little odd? At least twelve guys came by, said hello to you, and then grabbed your wife by the breasts. What's the story?"

Roberto looked at him and moaned, "What-a can-a I do? If-a I leave-a her-a at home, she-a sleeps with-a everybody-a!"

Streetcorner hood: "You want a little action, honey?"

Italian girl: "How dare you speak to a strange girl like that? A strange girl who lives at 22 Mulberry Street, telephone, Algonquin 55857."

Patipada, will it do, or you want some more-a?

It is good. I am happy that you are enjoying both worlds together, the Italian and the American; you are doubly blessed.

Patipada is really a beautiful woman, very courageous; she wants, and also knows how, to live dangerously. And they are always to my liking — the people who want, and are ready, to live dangerously. Patipada is almost a crazy girl, but if a woman is a real woman she is a little crazy! If she is not a little crazy she is cold, she is half-dead.

That's why I am joking so much about English ladies — they are half-dead. Italian women are so alive! For centuries Italy has been fortunate in a way. Since the days of the Roman Empire, Italy is the only country which has never been very repressive. The Romans were never phony spiritual people, never; never for a single period did they become so-called holy people. They were very earthly people and that has remained in the Italian blood even now. Even the Catholic Church has not been able to corrupt them very much, although the Vatican is there. But the Italians are incorruptible — they corrupt the Pope!

I like that quality of earthiness, that smell of earth that makes people alive.

I have chosen a few of the Italians as my mediums. Now many ugly women, flat-chested women, go on writing letters to me. It has now reached epidemic proportions: "Bhagwan, it seems we can never be your mediums — we are ugly and flat-chested!"

Don't be worried. You will have your reward in the other world. You can't have both worlds. To be a medium a woman at least has to look like a woman! The day I start choosing flat-chested women, then why not choose men? What is wrong with them? Just a little bit of difference — a difference of little tits and bits! So please stop writing such letters to me. I may be enlightened but I am not so enlightened — I still have some aesthetic sense! When I choose a woman I choose a woman! At least she should look like a woman! And I have to see those mediums every day. . . . And I am finished with all my karmas so I am not ready to suffer anymore — enough is enough! I have suffered a lot in my past lives — I have suffered many flat-chested women.

But you should be happy that I will try in every possible way that you become enlightened in this life so that you need not come again and torture people. I will send you to the farther shore — let the saints suffer! So in that way you are fortunate. My mediums may have to come back — some other enlightened person may need them — but you, rest assured, this is your last life. I am going to finish you! So you be happy on that account. And you will be immensely rewarded in the other world.

That's why Jesus goes on saying. . . . Look at his Beatitudes. He never said, "Blessed are the rich," he said, "Blessed are the poor." Why? — because the poor need consolation. He never said, "Blessed are the successful," he said, "Blessed are the meek." Those meek people, poor people, they need some consolation — they will inherit the kingdom of God.

And I say to you: Blessed are the flat-chested for theirs is the kingdom of God . . . but please, leave the earth alone!

The seventh question

Bhagwan,
What is reincarnation?

Sangeet,

I will tell you a small story that will explain my attitude towards reincarnation.

Suramallo explains to the rabbi the theory of reincarnation: "Let's say, your holiness, that you die tomorrow. A flower blooms on your grave after a few days. A cow comes and eats the flower. The next morning the cow has a good shit. I go for a walk, see the shit and say, "Ah, your holiness, you haven't changed a bit!' "

The eighth question

Bhagwan,
How about some good Jewish jokes? I love to
laugh at myself!

Anand Sudharka,

Two jewish businessmen were relaxing in Harlem one afternoon when one said to the other, "We forgot to lock the safe."
"What does it matter?" asked his partner. "We're both here, ain't we?"

A group of Jewish friends discuss if it would have been better not to have been born.
"Of course it would," says one of them, "but how many of us have such luck?"

It is a little subtle. It will take seven days for you.

Two Jews were walking in a concentration camp. One of them asked, "Hey, Moshe, do you know what time it is?"

"Why?" answered the second. "Do you have to go somewhere?"

A Scotsman, an Englishman and a Jew went to an expensive place to eat, somewhere in London.

The Scotsman was heard to say at the end of the evening, "It's okay, lads, I'll pay tonight."

The next day the newspaper headlines read: "Jewish Ventriloquist Found Dead Outside Restaurant."

And the last:

A man riding in a train is reading a novel; sitting by his side is a young woman.

"Hey, Jew!" says the woman. "What time is it?"

The man is shocked, but plays it cool and does not answer.

A minute later she asks again, "Hey, Jew! What time is it?"

No answer. So she asks five more times.

Finally the man gets angry and says, "Myna watch is in myna pocket. You just take a look and see what time it is."

"How can I see inside your pockets?" she asks.

"How did you discover that I was a Jew?" he replies.

The ninth question

Bhagwan,
I have been here in the East for eight years
now and I keep falling more and more lazy. Why?

Anand Premda,

NOTHING TO WORRY ABOUT — you are just catching the local disease!

And the last question

Bhagwan,
Why am I afraid to ask my real questions?

Avinash,

Everybody is afraid of asking the real questions. That's why people ask metaphysical questions, philosophical questions — questions about God, the creation, after-life, reincarnation — because these questions are not in any way related to you; you remain outside.

To ask a real question is dangerous because when you ask a real question you have to encounter me directly and you have to face the consequences. I am not a predictable man; one never knows what I am going to say. One never knows whether I am going to hit you or to pat you; you can never be sure. And then to ask a real question needs the courage to open your heart, to show your wounds, to show where it hurts. Nobody wants to show their wounds, nobody wants to show their tears — and everybody is full of tears and full of wounds, and everybody is pretending that he is happy.

You ask anybody, "How are you?" and he says, "Beautiful! Perfectly okay!" and nobody is okay and nobody is in a beautiful state. But people have to keep face.

Now asking me a question before three thousand people means exposing yourself. It is standing naked, spiritually naked. It is easy to stand naked physically — that is nothing much, one can drop the clothes very easily — but to stand spiritually naked needs tremendous courage. One has to be a dare-devil because it is like dropping your skin, showing your skeleton, it is like showing all your ugliness; and nobody wants to be exposed.

We are all covering our faces with masks — beautiful masks. The original face has never been shown to anybody; you yourself have forgotten what your original face is. In fact, when you look for the real questions, first you will come across unreal questions, a thousand and one unreal questions. Unless you are very persistent and go on digging and go on throwing the unreal questions. . . . When the mind says, "Ask who created the world," if you are a real seeker you will say, "What nonsense! What does it matter? Anybody will do. The whole point is that the world *is* there. X created it, Y created it, Z created it, what does it matter? And whether anybody created it or did not create it, that too is immaterial. This question is nonsense and it is not going to affect my life. If God created it so what? Or if, as the Buddhists and Jainas say, nobody created it, so what? The Jainas and the Buddhists live in the same way as the Hindus and Mohammedans and Christians, in the same stupid way; it makes no difference to their lives."

Any question is unreal which does not make a difference to your life, but it is easy to ask such questions. In the first place it shows your knowledgeability, that you are a great student of metaphysics, philosophy, religion; it shows that you know the scriptures.

People go on writing to me, "Krishna has said this in the Gita — what does he mean?" Whatsoever he means it is not going to affect your life. And there are one thousand commentaries already available; if they are not making any difference — and the one thousand commentaries are useless — then my statement is going to be the same: it is not going to affect your life.

Once I was delivering a talk on Mahavira, the Jaina *teerthankara,* and a Jaina scholar, a very famous scholar whose books I had read and whose scholarship I had always appreciated, stood up. I was not aware that this was the man who had written so many books, whom I had always appreciated. And he asked, "I have only one question. Buddha and Mahavira were both contemporaries. Who was older in age? — because for almost fifty years I have been working on it, but no conclusive decision has been reached yet. There are reasons to suppose that Buddha was older and there are reasons to suppose that Mahavira was older."

I looked at the man for a few moments. There was absolute silence. The scholar started feeling a little embarrassed — why was I looking at him in such a way? "Have I asked something wrong?" And then he said, "Why are you looking at me in such a strange way? Have I asked something wrong?"

I said, "Not only wrong — you have wasted your whole life! Fifty years! What does it matter? If Buddha was older, so what? If Mahavira was older, so what? It does not affect their philosophy, it does not affect their approach to life. It is not going to affect *you* either. Why have you wasted your fifty years? You seem to be just a goddamned fool!"

Somebody, the man who was presiding, nudged me and said, "Do you know who he is? He is a very famous Jaina scholar!" And he told me his name.

I said, "Then I will hit him even more hard, because I have always appreciated his books, but this man is stupid! How did he manage to write such good books? He must be functioning like a biocomputer, because looking at him, seeing him, listening to his question . . . and he says fifty years and he is almost bragging that he has devoted so much time to such a great question." He was showing his scholarship.

It is easy to ask metaphysical, philosophical questions; it shows your knowledge, it shows your ego, your pride. But when you ask a real question it can hurt, it can expose you, it can show your ignorance. It is bound to show your ignorance — not only your ignorance, it is bound to show your insanity, it is bound to show your schizophrenia, it is bound to show your neurosis.

That's why, Avinash. And you are an Indian, and the Indians are super-egoists. They have nothing else to brag about. Money they don't have, power they don't have, technology they don't have, science they don't have; they don't have anything else. They have only one thing: that egoistic attitude of "holier than thou." So Indians are very afraid to ask real questions; they never ask real questions. I have never come across Indians who ask real questions — they will never expose themselves. Even if they are going insane they try to cover it up in some beautiful way.

Just the other day I received a letter saying that one woman has gone a little berserk. But the people who had written, they wrote not that she has gone mad or berserk, they wrote: "She is behaving like Ramakrishna, like Meera, so, Bhagwan, only you can help."

A few days ago they phoned. The message was given to them: "Take her to the psychiatrist there." Now a very angry letter has come: "When you are here, why should we take her to a psychiatrist? She is not mad, she is in a very high state! And going to the psychiatrist can be dangerous because he will give her shock treatment or tranquilizers. He may bring her down to earth, back to her ordinariness — and she is flying very high. Only *you* can understand it."

Now that woman is simply mad — I know that woman. Just a few days before she was here and when she was here, and she came to touch my feet, I felt that this woman could go mad any time. But in India if you go mad you become a mystic, not mad. It is just the reverse in the West: if you become a mystic they put you in a mental asylum immediately! Indians don't like this idea that she is mad.

Nobody likes to bring his real problems. No Indian will talk about his sexual fantasies. He will come and ask, "How to attain celibacy, *brahmacharya*?" Now really he is suffering from sexuality, but he will not talk about it. And then people have become afraid that others will laugh. And that's what happens in an ordinary world.

This is not an ordinary place, Avinash. Nobody is going to laugh at you. People will have every compassion for you if your problem is real; in fact they will be more compassionate towards you if your problem is real. But people are hiding their real problems. And it is true as far as the outside world is concerned: if you tell the outside world your real problems, people will start laughing at you. They will not feel compassion, they will make you a laughing-stock. But not here. Here we have so many other things to laugh about. I give you so many opportunities to laugh that nobody has any laughter left to spare for your real problems. That's why I go on telling so many jokes: so that when real problems arise people can have compassion for you. But in the outside world it happens so — but this is a very special kind of place.

A man entered the doctor's office wearing a robe. Surprised, the doctor asked, "Why do you wear a robe?"

"Ah, you saw the problem right away," said the patient. "I have one huge ball and I can't wear trousers."

"Okay," said the doctor, "let me examine it."

"No, doc, you'll laugh at me!"

"Show me," said the doctor.

"I know you'll laugh."

"No, I won't."

"Promise?"

"Promise!"

So the man lifts his robe, exposing his left leg. The doctor, seeing the oversized ball hanging down to the man's knee, forgets himself and roars with laughter.

"You sonofabitch!" yells the patient. "You promised you wouldn't laugh! Now I ain't gonna show you the big one!"

15

The first question

Bhagwan,
How does it happen that I feel so at home
and so lost in this Buddhafield?

Deva Kamma,

THERE IS NO CONTRADICTION IN IT; it is as it should be. To be lost, utterly lost, is to be at home. Man ordinarily lives as an ego, separate from the whole, like an island, with a definite identity — the name, the form; he is somebody. And our whole life we make every effort to go on defining ourselves, who we are, for the simple reason that we don't know who we are. So we create an artificial, arbitrary identity; that's what the ego is.

When you enter into a love relationship with a Master — that's what entering into a Buddhafield is — you start losing your old identity, your definition becomes blurred. It was arbitrary anyway — it starts melting; your limits start merging with the unlimited. You are no more somebody; you start becoming a nobody, a nothingness.

Hence the feeling of being lost, because you are missing your old games, trips; you are missing your old miseries, your so-called old pleasures; you are missing all that you had known before as part of your being. A new being is arising, a being which is not isolated from the whole, not encapsulated but one with the whole — a wave which is part of the ocean. It is still a wave, but now a deep understanding is happening that "I am not separate," that "I need not be worried about myself," that "I have been before I was born and I will be after I am gone. This being a wave is only a phase, a momentary phenomenon. It is only a question of form; deep down I am one with the formless ocean, I am oceanic."

This is the experience, Deva Kamma, that is happening to you; hence you will feel lost — lost if you compare it with your old identity. And the comparison comes naturally because the old is well known. Maybe for many lives you have been decorating it, maintaining it, nourishing it, nurturing it. It is an ancient habit, almost perennial; you have forgotten when it began. It is as old as the creation itself; it has gone very deep — its roots have gone very deep. Now all that is changing. The old is dying, and you are acquainted only with the old, hence you will feel like a death is happening.

But if you look to the new, which is very fresh, just like a breeze, just like a dewdrop, just like a newly opening bud of a rose, very fresh. . . . You are not yet fully aware of it; it is so new, you will need a little time to be introduced to it, to become acquainted with it. But it is happening because both these processes happen simultaneously. The death of the old and the birth of the new are two sides of the same coin.

If you start looking at the new then you will feel at home. That too is happening: in a very very vague way you are becoming aware of that too. Slowly slowly the new will become settled; the old will become just a memory, a fading memory, a dream that you had dreamt while you were asleep, something that had not happened to you, maybe you had seen it in a movie or read it in a novel; it was somebody else's story. And slowly slowly it will go so far away from you that it will become difficult even to recollect it. Then the discontinuity has happened totally. Your umbilical cord is cut; you are really out of the womb of the past. You have started breathing on your own, in a new way, as a nobody.

It feels strange to be impersonal, but to be impersonal is the only way to be universal. Not to be is the only way of being. Shakespeare's dilemma, "To be or not to be. . ." cannot be resolved by philosophy, it can be resolved only by meditation, because in meditation not to be prepares the way for you to be. There is no question of choosing — you need not choose between the two, there is no question of either/or — not to be is the way for you to be. If you choose not to be you have chosen the other too: if you choose to be you will have to pass through the process of non-being.

Meditation is a process of death, of non-being, of becoming nothing on your own accord, of disappearing into the whole, into the harmony of the whole. But it is a miracle, the greatest paradoxical experience of life. There is no contradiction in it, but there is a paradox. Seen from the intellectual standpoint, there *is* a paradox.

You ask: *How does it happen that I feel so at home and so lost in this Buddhafield?*

That's how it happens, that's the way it happens. That's the way of the ultimate law — *ais dhammo sanantano*. If you had asked Buddha he would have said: Suchness, *tathata*. This is how the universal law functions: you disappear and you appear for the first time. But you appear in such a new way — not as a person, not as a name, not as a form, not as a separate identity but just as a total oneness with the whole, in unison with the whole.

That's what is happening here. Slowly slowly the energies of the sannyasins are melting and merging and becoming one. Thousands of my sannyasins are functioning in a kind of deep orchestra; they are no longer solo players. They have drowned themselves in this Buddhafield.

It needs guts, it needs courage, it needs intelligence, it needs awareness to move from the known into the unknown, to go into the uncharted sea.

Deva Kamma, you have left this shore. Your small boat is moving towards the unknown. Never look back. The old shore will call you back, it will try to seduce you, it will give you many promises, but remember, it has never fulfilled any promise. And you have lived on this shore for so long; don't forget the misery, the pain, the anguish, the nightmare that it has been for you for years together. Now go on moving. Don't look back, look ahead. And always look for the new, the fragile, that which is just arriving on the scene. You will need alertness to recognize it.

The second question

Bhagwan,
I have been a sannyasin for only three days
and yet I have started to dislike the non-
sannyasins. What is happening?

Dhyanananda,

THAT'S HOW FANATICISM IS BORN. That's how Christians, Mohammedans and Hindus have lived for centuries. That's how the foolish mind functions — beware of it. Being a sannyasin does not mean that you have to dislike the non-sannyasins. Never look at anybody as a non-sannyasin, always look at the non-sannyasins as potential sannyasins. They are all potential sannyasins — three days ago you were a non-sannyasin! Love them more because by your love you can help their potential to be actualized. If you dislike them *you* will become a cause of preventing them from becoming sannyasins. Help them.

This is not the way, but this is how the mind functions. I can understand. Mind is so ugly that it immediately starts creating new trips for the ego; even sannyas can become a trip for the ego. "Now I am a sannyasin, I am special. And the non-sannyasins? They are stupid people!" And just three days ago you were a non-sannyasin — just three days ago! But it does not matter whether it is three days or three years, it is the same. Even after three minutes the mind starts spinning and weaving. It starts walking in a different way, looking at others with condemnation, with that ancient saintly look of "holier than thou."

Rastus was tired of being black. One day he came across an advertisement in the local paper which said: "Super Omo special skin-whitening cream — makes skin whiter than white!"

Very excited, he purchased a packet and went home. He took a bath and scrubbed himself with the product. When he was finished, he looked in the mirror and found that his skin looked like that of a white man's.

Ecstatic, he ran out to show his wife who wasted no time in jumping into the bath herself. She too was very happy when she emerged looking like a white lady.

They found their young son and told him, "Hey, boy — this is your chance to become a white boy!"

"But I don't want to be a white boy!" he exclaimed. "I'm happy the way I am — I'm happy to be black!"

Rastus turned to his wife and said, "You know, I have

been white for only one hour and already these blacks are giving me shit!"

Beware of this mind. These are the ways of the mind. A sannyasin has to drop the mind. You have to be alert about the ways the ego takes grip of you. You are not to become holier than others; on the contrary, sannyas simply means an initiation into being ordinary.

The Pope is addressed as Your Holiness, the Shankaracharya is addressed as Your Divinity, the founder of the Hare Krishna Movement was addressed as His Divine Grace. You have to remember that I address you as Your Holy Ordinariness! There is nothing more beautiful than just being ordinary. The moment you are ready to be ordinary you become divine; that's the only way to become divine.

God is very ordinary. If he were not ordinary he would not become the rocks, he would not become the trees, he would not become the animals, he would not become human beings; he would not descend to such lower states. But he is so ordinary . . . and he is so happy to be a fish or even to be a cockroach or a beetle.

I have heard:

George Harrison was walking in the garden and he came across a beetle and he said, "Hey, beetle, do you know? You must be happy that we have called our group The Beatles — we have called our group by your name!"

The beetle looked at Harrison and said, "Do you call your group Eric? My name is Eric! I am no ordinary beetle."

Nobody is ordinary except a very few people — a Buddha, a Jesus, a Zarathustra. These people are ordinary people; they have the courage to be ordinary. In that very courage they reach the ultimate depth of being and existence.

My sannyasins have to gather that courage to be no-bodies; that's what I mean by being ordinary. Our whole effort here is to transform the mundane into the sacred. We don't want to create a rift between the mundane and the sacred; that has been the way for centuries — the rift. That rift has created a schizophrenic humanity.

People are constantly in a tense state of affairs. The mundane pulls them to one side and the sacred to the very opposite. If they go with the mundane they feel guilty. If you enjoy eating and drinking and making merry then you feel guilty — you are doing something wrong. If you stop eating, drinking, making merry, and you become an ascetic, you start feeling very anxious, very troubled, because you are going against nature. You start feeling, "What am I doing to myself? Is it right?" And then you have to constantly repress. You have to avoid the world, you have to escape to a monastery or to the Himalayas. And each small thing creates a problem for you. Rather than solving your problems you have created a thousand and one problems.

Your so-called saints live only in problems; everything is a problem. Eating is such a problem, they make so much fuss about it. They will eat this and they will not eat that. The Jaina monk cannot eat the poor potatoes. Why? What is wrong with potatoes? They look so innocent; one has never heard anything wrong about them — they have never done any wrong to anybody. But a Jaina monk cannot eat potatoes. It is prohibited in his scriptures because they grow underground, they don't grow in the sunlight, so something is wrong with them. They grow in darkness; eating them will create darkness in you, you know? And you have to be a light unto yourself. So anything that grows underneath the earth is prohibited, carrots and all — anything that grows underneath the earth. They don't believe in underground things.

367

I am a firm believer in underground things because they are very revolutionary! If you eat them they will help you to go underground. And finally everybody has to go underground, so why not prepare?

Once I was traveling with a Hindu monk. He would not drink milk from buffaloes. Why? — because Hindu scriptures say that buffalo milk creates laziness. As if Indians can be more lazy! And that Hindu saint was not doing anything, so I said, "I don't see what trouble there will be — you don't do anything at all. The buffalo milk can't harm you — you are already lazy, so why be worried about it?"

Not only that, he only used to drink the milk from a white cow. I said, "What is the matter with black cows?"

"Black is an evil color."

I said to the saint. "Then we should part our ways; we cannot travel together, not even for a single moment. You are the most stupid person I have come across, because even from a black cow the milk is white, the milk does not become black! If the milk were becoming black maybe there would have been some point in your idea."

But he wouldn't listen.

And he will take only warm milk immediately from the cow, not heated on the stove or on a fire. The cow had to be milked just in front of him so that he could drink it warm from the cow itself. I said, "Why don't you just do what the kids do? Just drink from the tits! That will be even warmer. Even with milking it and then bringing it to you. . . . And it is not so hot that it remains really warm. You just drink directly from the cow's tits!"

He said, "What are you saying?"

I said, "Yes, that will make you a far greater saint!"

But these fools are worshipped by people.

He would only eat food prepared by a virgin girl, otherwise not. How is the food affected? Whether it is prepared by a virgin girl or by a non-virgin, how is the food affected? He said, "There are subtle vibrations."

I said, "I can trust you only. . . . I will bring two, three *thalis* prepared for you, one by a virgin girl, another by a woman who is married and has children, and the third by a prostitute, and you just show me which one belongs to whom just by their vibe. If you cannot judge then stop this nonsense. Don't talk nonsense. What vibes are you talking about?"

You should drop this idea that only hippies talk about vibes; Indian saints have been talking about them for at least five thousand years.

Now he was at a loss; he could not discriminate. So I said, "Then drop it — you don't know what vibes are. You are just talking any stupid jargon. It may impress foolish people, but what vibes are you talking about?"

Hindu saints, Jaina saints, Buddhist monks are not allowed to sit in a place where a woman has just been sitting. A certain time has to elapse; after that they can sit, because that place goes on radiating sexual vibes from the woman. These people are utterly mad!

But these are the ways of the ego in order to make the demarcation that they are special, spiritual; they are not ordinary, mundane, wordly. Otherwise how to make a discrimination? How to condemn ordinary people? You have to create something; anything will do.

Jaina monks pull out their hair; they can't shave, they can't use scissors. As if scissors were great technology! They avoid technology — as if a blade were great technology. They will pull out their hair. Utterly stupid! But thousands of people gather to see them pulling out their hair because they are performing a great austerity. Do anything stupid but do something which is unnatural and people will start worshipping you.

Christian monks used to beat themselves every morning. There were sects of Christian monks who would

whip themselves every morning. Their bodies were continuously bleeding, their bodies had wounds all over
them from foot to head. And the man who would whip
himself the most would be thought to be the greatest
saint. And people would gather to watch and count who
was whipping himself more, who was bleeding more.
Now these people who were whipping themselves were
masochists and the people who had gathered to see them
were sadists. They were both ill, pathological, but this
pathology has persisted.

My whole work here is to drop this division between the mundane and the sacred. I want you to live
a very ordinary life so that you don't have to go on
any ego trips.

Remember, Dhyanananda, three days or three years
or thirty years, it is all the same; time makes no difference. Be aware of the fact that the ego is very cunning
and it will try to find out ways to puff you up. This is a
very simple way: to dislike the non-sannyasins. Immediately you are special and they are ordinary people, they
don't understand and you understand.

They are all people with potential. Love them, help
them, respect them. That is their decision whether
to be a sannyasin or not to be a sannyasin; that is their
freedom, it is your freedom. And freedom should be
respected.

The third question

Bhagwan,
Can you give me a new Zen koan to meditate on
because for all the old ones I can find the
answers in the Zen scriptures?

Nartan,

O<small>KAY</small>. Just the other day a young German took sannyas. He was a man of deep feelings, a man of heart. He was sobbing with joy. I asked him, "How long are you going to stay?"

He said, "Bhagwan, forever."

I said to him, "When you come next time, stay a little longer."

Now, Nartan, meditate over it. This is a Zen koan! And you will not find the answer in any scriptures; even I don't know the answer!

The fourth question

Bhagwan,
Why are you talking about tits so much?

Prem Chinmaya,

I <small>KNOW THAT IT IS</small> a touchy subject, but you know me —and that explains everything!

The fifth question

Are children really so intelligent, Bhagwan,
as you always say they are?

Priya,

T<small>HEY ARE FAR MORE INTELLIGENT</small> than I say they are. Every child is born absolutely intelligent because there is nothing to distract his intelligence. He has no prejudices to make him unintelligent, he has no information to make him unintelligent — he has no knowledge yet. Even if he wants to he cannot function in a knowledgeable way. How can he be stupid?

Stupidity needs a few qualifications. You have to go to the school, to the college, to the university. Stupidity needs a few degrees: you have to have M.A.s, M.Sc.s, Ph.D.s, D.Litt.s. Stupidity depends on knowledgeability: the more knowledgeable you are the less intelligence is needed because knowledge starts functioning as a substitute. You can depend on knowledge. Why bother? — you can simply look into the memory and the answer is there.

But the child has no memory, he has no ready-made answer. Whenever there is a problem he has to face the problem, he has to encounter it. He has to respond, he cannot react. And to be responsive is to be intelligent. He functions from a state of not-knowing. That's why I say every child is born intelligent.

But almost everybody dies stupid because this whole life is structured in such a way that it is impossible to remain intelligent — almost impossible. The trap is such that only very few people have been able to escape from it. And the trap gives you all kinds of comforts, conveniences. It is supported by the government, by the religion, by the society; it has all the supports.

The day I resigned my post of professor in a university I burned all my certificates. A friend used to live with me; he said, "What are you doing? If you have resigned. . . . I don't agree that you have done the right thing, but burning your certificates is absolutely unnecessary. You may need them some day; keep them. What is wrong in keeping them? You have such a big library — they won't take up much space, just a small file will be enough. And if you cannot keep them, I will keep them; you just give them to me. Some day you may need them."

I said, "I am finished with all this stupidity. I want to burn all the bridges. And I will never need them because I never look back and I never go back. I am finished with it. It was all nonsense and I have been in it enough."

But I had not compromised with any vested interest; that's why I had to resign: because I was not teaching what I was supposed to teach. In fact I was doing just the opposite. So many complaints against me reached the Vice-Chancellor that finally he gathered courage to call me. He never used to call me because to call me was an encounter! Finally he called me and he said, "Just look — all these complaints are here."

I said, "There is no need to bother about the complaints — here is my resignation."

He said, "What are you saying? I am not saying that you should resign!"

I said, "You are not saying it, but I am resigning because I can only do the things that *I* want to do. If any imposition on me is there, if any kind of pressure is put on me, I am not going to be here even for a single moment. This is my resignation and I will never enter this building again."

He could not believe it! I left his office; he came running after me. When I was getting into my car he said, "Wait! What is the hurry? Ponder over it!"

I said, "I never ponder over anything. I was doing the right thing. And if there are complaints — and of course I know there are complaints — there must be, because I am not teaching what your stupid syllabus binds me to teach, I am teaching something else. I am not talking about philosophy, I am talking *against* philosophy, because to me the whole project of philosophy is a sheer stupid exercise in futility. It has not given a single conclusion to humanity. It has been a long, long unnecessary journey and wastage. It is time we should drop the very subject completely. Either a person should be a scientist or he should be a mystic; there is no other way. A scientist experiments with objects and the mystic experiments with his subjectivity. Both are scientists in a way: one is of the outer, the other is of the inner. And the philosopher is nowhere; he is in a limbo. He is neither man nor woman, he is neither here nor there. He is impotent, hence he has not been able to contribute anything. So I cannot teach philosophy — I will go on sabotaging it. I was just waiting — whenever you called me I had to resign immediately."

It was very difficult to get out of it because all my friends came to persuade me, the professors came to persuade me, all my relatives tried to persuade me: "What are you doing?" Even the Education Minister phoned me: "Don't do such a thing. I know that your ways are a little strange, but we will tolerate. You continue. Don't take any note of the complaints. Complaints have been coming to me too, but I am not taking any notice of them. We don't want to lose you."

I said, "That is not the point. Once I have finished with something I am finished with it. Now no pressure can bring me back."

It was very difficult for me to be at school because I could see the stupidity of the teachers. And they used to get angry; they used to think that I was trying to be mischievous. I was not trying to be mischievous, I was simply trying to show them that this was all nonsense that they were teaching! It had no concern with life.

My geography teacher used to talk about places. I told him, "I am never going to visit these places so why should I remember them? Now how can I be concerned with Constantinople or Timbuktu? Whether they are or are not is irrelevant! All that I want to know is where I am right now — you tell me this!"

He was almost dumb. He said, "Where you are right now. . . ? No student has ever asked me, and I have been teaching geography my whole life!"

I said, "Then you never had a single student. I want to

know where I am right now. My whole concern is now and here."

My history teacher used to teach me about stupid kings and their names and I said, "I am not going to memorize them. Why? Why, what have they done for me? They didn't even know my name so why should I remember their names? It should be a give-and-take. Now this Nadir Shah and this Tamburlaine and this Genghis Khan, what have they done?"

But this is how we go on imposing stupid, unnecessary information. And the load becomes heavier. The person who carries the biggest load earns the biggest rewards; naturally, when stupidity is rewarded you settle for it. Intelligence is punished.

I was punished so much — you cannot imagine how much I was punished. From my primary school up to the university I was continuously punished and nobody was ever able to tell me why they were punishing me. It was almost always the case that I would be standing outside the classroom; it was very rare for me to sit inside the classroom. But that exercise has helped me: I have done so much exercise walking outside a classroom that now I need not do anything. I have done enough!

Whenever my headmaster used to come on his rounds I was the only person who was always walking in the corridor. Whenever he would not see me he would come to my class and say, "What is the matter? What are you doing inside?"

I said, "I don't know. I myself am puzzled because a single question and the teacher will say, 'You go out! Unless you stop asking you cannot come in.' " And it was a good excuse for me to be outside in the air. And that was so beautiful to be outside with the birds and with the trees. So whenever I wanted to go out, just a question, any question would do — any question that was unanswerable!

I was turned out of one college, expelled from this university and that university. One university accepted me, but accepted with the condition that I would not ask any questions.

I said, "I can accept that, but then you have to do one thing: that I will not have to go to the classes, because if I am in class and if the professor says something stupid, I will not be able to resist myself — the temptation will be too great — and there will be an argument and I will forget all about the promise I have given that I will not ask questions. So you have to give me permission that I need not attend classes and also that I will be given permission to appear in the examination without fulfilling the absolutely necessary requirement of being in class for at least seventy-five percent of the time."

He said, "That is my promise."

And I was so happy! For two years I simply never turned up at the college, I came only when there was an examination.

And the principal said, "You are a strange man! I was thinking that you may not come once in a while, but for two years I have not seen you at all!"

I was even sending my fee by post because I said, "Even with the head clerk, giving the fee or saying hello, something may happen! He may ask, 'How are you?' and that's enough. You know me! You just ask, 'How are you?' and then I go on for ninety minutes. And that has been my usual practice."

So I avoided all contact just to fulfill my promise, but it has been a boon, a blessing.

Children are certainly intelligent, Priya, very intelligent.

One little boy was overheard saying to another, "If I could have known what trouble parents were, I would never have had any!"

"How did you like the new preacher, son?" asked the mother.

"Don't like him much. He preached so long I couldn't keep awake and he hollered so loud I couldn't go to sleep!"

A little boy loses his mother in a big department store. A young man who was working there sees the crying boy and asks him, "What is the matter?"

"I've lost my mother," the boy mumbles through his tears.

"What does she look like?" the man inquires.

"She looks like a woman without me."

One six-year-old boy was reprimanded by his Sunday School teacher: "You've been nothing but trouble — you're just a rotten kid!"

The little boy pulled himself up to his three-foot height and answered, "That's not true. I am so a good boy — God made me and he didn't make no junk!"

"I had a funny dream last night, Mum."

"Did you?"

"I dreamt I was awake, but when I woke up I found I was asleep!"

Two small boys were swinging on a gate together, passing the time of day. In the course of their conversation one asked the other, "How old are you?"

"I don't know," said the other.

"You mean you don't know how old you are?"

"No."

"Do women bother you?"

"No."

"You're four in that case," observed his companion.

A little boy comes home from school one day and says, "Hey, mommy, I just saw a flat cat!"

"Uh," says his mother. "How did you know it was flat?"

"Because there was another cat pumping it up!"

"Papa," said little Johnny, "how do babies come into the world?"

"The stork brings them, son."

"Hey, pa, don't tell me you did it with a stork!"

The sixth question

Bhagwan,
It took you seven hundred years to get here.
What happened?

Devaprem,

Don't you know the indian trains?

The seventh question

Bhagwan,
I'm going to tell the truth. I'm a British
lady: my great-grandfather was Governor of
Delhi and my great-uncle was Prime Minister
of Kashmir. I know there's very little hope
for me, but is it not possible to defy the
laws of nature and fall in tune with you in
spite of this unfortunate heritage?

Anand Anupam,

Don't be worried — truth liberates! You have con-fessed the sin. That's the beauty of confession; now there is no worry.

Heinrich Heine was dying and these were his last words: "God will forgive me — it is his trait."

So don't be worried. Even if you are British, God is going to forgive you. All that is needed on your part is to confess. And don't take my jokes seriously. The British are beautiful people — I love them.

The eighth question

Bhagwan,
I cannot control myself when insulted. What should I do?

Dheeresh,

T IT FOR TAT — till you become enlightened. And do it quickly, because once you become enlightened then it is very difficult to do anything. When somebody insults you, somebody insults you. You have simply to accept it: *Ais dhammo sanantano.* So whatsoever you want to do, do it right now, finish it, because here you will soon become enlightened; it is not very far away.

And it is natural that when somebody insults you you cannot control yourself. I have never been telling you to control yourself because control can't help. If you control you repress; control is another name for repression. If you can watch, watch; otherwise if there is a choice between repression and indulging, prefer indulgence to repression because indulgence will teach you a lesson. Repression won't teach you anything. And you are not a machine, you are a man.

Warning in the year 2000: due to robot shortage, some of our bartenders are human and will react unpredictably when insulted.

You are not a robot so it is natural. It is better to react truly. But remember one thing: you are free to do whatever you like; you need only face the consequences — because I am not saying that you won't receive blows back. So first see who the other guy is, be a little careful. And you are alive, you are not dead yet. Once you are enlightened you are almost dead — alive on the other shore, dead on this shore. So before that calamity happens enjoy doing whatsoever you can manage to do.

Mulla Nasruddin was studying electricity. To show the class its practical uses, the teacher commanded that each pupil bring some electric tool to class the next day.

The following morning the class held a small exhibition: electric bulbs, irons, a hair drier, an oven. . . .

When Mulla arrived he was sweating and carrying a big artificial lung on his back.

"Mulla," said the teacher, "where did you get that electric lung?"

"I took it from grandpa, teacher."

"And he didn't mind?" she cried.

"I don't think so, teacher. He just said, 'Hrrr. . . .' "

So before that happens don't try to control, do something — there is nothing to be worried about. Accept your humanity; it is part of you. If somebody insults you he is challenging you to a fight, so give him a good fight! If you see that he is too big then meditate — what else to do?

The ninth question

Bhagwan,
I am a mathematician. Can I also become a
sannyasin?

Dharmavir,

I DON'T SEE that there is any difficulty — you can be a sannyasin. Of course you will have to learn something more than mathematics — you will have to learn a little poetry, a little music, a little dance. You will have to go beyond the calculative mind. You will have to take a little jump into the illogical, into the paradoxical. And of course habits die hard so I can understand your problem.

Mathematics is pure logic, it is nothing but logic, and sannyas is very illogical — or if you like big words, then it is supralogical. But that is only a word; the fact is, it is illogical. So if you are ready to go a little beyond the boundaries of logic, then you are welcome. It is going to be a little difficult but not impossible.

There are mathematicians here, there are scientists here whose whole life was devoted to some logical methodology, but now they have moved — moved beyond it. And they can move only if they have a deep longing to know whether there is something more than arithmetic or if that is all. If you are really an explorer, if you have some adventure in your life, then there is no problem.

I can understand your question. You may be too addicted to your mathematics; then there will be difficulty. All addictions create difficulties, and these are deep addictions. If you are addicted to some drug it is not so difficult. Within six weeks you can be hospitalized, treated, and you can get out of it. But if you are addicted to logic it may take a very long time. And unless *you* decide with your total being to come out of it there may be no possibility of anybody else bringing you out of it.

A mathematician goes to the whorehouse. Very excited, he picks the prettiest girl and goes off into a room with her.

"They say you girls from the capital do very incredible things in bed!"

"Yes, we certainly do!" she replied.

"So, I want one of your specialties!"

"I have one that you are going to love—come here! Let's do a sixty-nine!"

That appealed to the mathematician—sixty-nine. Immediately he understood the language—sixty-nine, that comes within his world. So they jump into bed and the woman does it very well. He loves it!

When they finish, he falls over onto his side, takes a deep breath and says, "This is too much! I think I am going to quit the other sixty-eight!"

But a mathematician is a mathematician—he is still calculating.

If you remain calculative. . . . You can become a sannyasin and you may still remain calculative: "What is happening? What is not happening? How many days have I been meditating? How many hours have I medi-tated? And what is the result? What is the outcome? Is it worth it?" All these things will have to be dropped.

Meditation is the world of lovers; not the world of calculation but the world of love. If you have fallen in love with me then you are welcome.

You say: *I am a mathematician. Can I also become a sannyasin?*

Dharmavir, yes. But my feeling is that the trouble will come from somewhere else—you are also an Indian. To be an Indian and to be *my* sannyasin, that is far more difficult than to be a mathematician and to be my san-nyasin. The Indian has lived with an idea of sannyas for at least ten thousand years, and I am putting things completely into a chaos, I am putting things topsy-turvy.

My sannyas is not the sannyas that you have always

understood it to be; it is totally different. I call it sannyas only to confuse you! I could have given it a new name, but that is not my way; I thrive on your confusion, on your chaos! My whole effort is to sabotage all patterns, all patterned thinking. That's why I chose the orange color — I could have chosen any color. In fact, the best color that would have fitted *my* idea of sannyas would have been a rainbow dress — all seven colors — because my sannyas is a rainbow phenomenon, multidimensional. That would have been absolutely in tune with my idea of sannyas, but I sacrificed it. I have to destroy this Hindu idea of sannyas. I have to create so many orange people that the old saints and sannyasins get lost — nobody knows who is who!

Your being Indian may create a little trouble. Mathematics you have learned only in this life, but being Indian may be part of your collective heritage, may be part of your collective unconsciousness. So when Indians become sannyasins they come with *a priori* conclusions, expectations, and when they don't find those expectations here they feel very disturbed.

I would like you to be alert from the very beginning that this is a totally new vision of sannyas. The old sannyas was renunciation, my sannyas is rejoicing. The old sannyas was other-wordly, my sannyas contains both worlds; it is not one-dimensional. It does not condemn this world, it makes this world the foundation for the other. The old sannyas was spiritualistic, my sannyas is not spiritualistic and against materialism, my sannyas is materialistic-spiritualistic. My sannyas is not anti-scientific, it contains science in it — it is vast enough to contain it. It goes far beyond it, but it is not against it.

An Arab, lost with his camel in the desert, felt very horny. Finally he grabbed the camel and tried to make love to it. But every time he tried, the camel moved aside and the Arab missed.

After a month of wandering in the desert, he came across a road which led to a town on the edge of the desert. There, sobbing, sat a sexy young lady next to her broken chariot.

Seeing him, the young lady begged him to fix her chariot, promising that he wouldn't regret it if he helped her.

"Ah, my sweet savior," she said as he finished, "come to me and I will reward you!"

"Thank you, lady," replied the Arab. "Would you just hold this camel for me for a minute?"

The tenth question

Bhagwan,
Is there any such thing as a real marriage?

Sugata,

NEVER HEARD OF IT — *real* marriage? There are real mirages but no real marriage! If it is real there is no need for marriage. The very need for marriage arises because there is fear. If you love a person you love a person; you can be together with the person. But there is constantly a fear that the other person may leave you, and the other person is also afraid that you may leave him or her. To make the future guaranteed, so that you cannot leave, so that the other cannot leave — easily at least — marriage was invented.

Marriage was invented only because love was missing. And if love is missing, how can the marriage be real? There is no need for marriage; if love is there, marriage is an unnecessary phenomenon. In a better world, where people will be more mature, they will be together because they love and they will keep each other free because, one never knows, love may disappear.

And that does *not* mean that the love was unreal and that that was why it disappeared. That too is a very wrong idea that has prevailed for centuries. We have been obsessed by wrong ideas and they are creating such trouble in our lives, and still we can't see their wrongness because they are so old and we have become so conditioned to them. If love disappears then we start thinking it was not real.

In fact, a real flower is bound to disappear by the evening; only the plastic rose flower will not disappear. The real rose flower blooms, opens up, dances in the wind, in the rain, in the sun, and by the evening is gone. That does not mean that it was unreal; in fact it was so real, that's why it appeared and disappeared. The plastic flower is so unreal that it does not appear and does not disappear, it remains; it is far more permanent.

Marriage is like a plastic flower; love is a real rose. And people are such cowards that they don't want to live with real roses. They are hankering after security, safety, guarantees, permanency so much that they are not ready to risk the real roses and they purchase plastic flowers. Of course those plastic flowers cannot satisfy you — you will remain miserable.

Just one month ago Sagarpriya wrote to me: "Bhagwan, what has happened? I have been here for two and a half years — has something gone wrong because Bindu and I are still together?" I did not answer her question because I was afraid that if I answered it something would happen immediately. So I kept quiet — and it has happened. Now I can answer because now I will not be thought responsible for it. Now Bindu wants to escape, but Sagarpriya is not going to leave him so easily. Just to escape from Sagarpriya he wants to go for a few weeks to America. Now Sagarpriya is following him; she also wants to go with him.

We don't allow each other freedom; we cling to the very end. We try every possible way. Even when everything disappears we go on clinging, we go on hoping against all hope. And the more we cling the more we destroy the possibility of love renewing itself again.

Now if Sagarpriya can allow Bindu to go and be there alone for a few weeks. . . . He needs his own space — everybody needs it once in a while because love alone is not enough. Love is beautiful, but meditation is far more important. And meditation needs a deep aloneness; nobody should interfere. And only lovers can interfere in meditation because only lovers are so close. The marketplace does not interfere, the people who are not related to you cannot interfere, but the people who are very close, very intimate, can be a real disturbance. They don't allow you any space, and if you want to be alone they immediately start feeling that they are being rejected. You simply want your own space — and everybody has a need, a tremendous need to have his own space.

But now Sagarpriya will follow him; if there is any possibility she will destroy even that. The best thing is to let him go, to say goodbye to him in a nice, beautiful, human way, with no grudge, with no complaint, with no quarreling. If you quarrel too much, if you make such a fuss, then people will start compromising, but compromise cannot fulfill you.

And remember, men are so tortured in the outside world, in the office, in the factory, in the shop, everywhere, that at least at home they want peace. For their peace ·they compromise. Hence almost all husbands become henpecked. And the problem is, no wife can love a henpecked husband, and every wife tries to henpeck her husband! This is how we create misery.

In the first place marriage is wrong. Marriage means clinging, legal clinging; you have legal support. You can force the person to the court, you can create so much financial trouble for him that he will think, "It is better to tolerate whatsoever is. And howsoever it is going I have become accustomed to it. Tolerate it." It is only a question of a few hours at night and then he escapes in the morning and finds a thousand and one excuses — overtime at the office, a party somewhere, or something else. He becomes a Rotarian, he becomes a member of the Lions Club; he finds ways and means to avoid. He starts drinking, so when he comes home he is so drunk he can't hear what the wife is saying, he does not know what is being done to him. But how can you love such a person? You hate such a person, but this is how you create the person.

And the man also is a clinger. This is a very strange thing: in each couple one is always a clinger. This is my experience of thousands of couples. It seems that one has to be a clinger — either will do; either the wife or the husband, one has to be a clinger. Whosoever clings is miserable and the other is miserable because he has lost his freedom — and you cannot be happy with a person who has lost his freedom.

Love is a meeting of two free individuals; it is not a marriage. Love does not need marriage. And if love disappears — which is far more possible than it staying — that does not mean it was unreal. The more real it is, the quicker it will disappear. The more intense it is, the quicker it will disappear because it will give you such ecstasy. And those peaks cannot be reached every day; it is bound to disappear.

But man does not want peaks of joy; rather he wants a smooth, comfortable, convenient, bourgeois life, which is almost not life at all but just vegetating. So people are vegetating together — cabbages and cauliflowers vegetating together!

There is no real marriage, Sugata, there is only real love. All marriages are unreal. But to live a real love needs a really courageous heart. It needs that you should live moment to moment and you remain open for the tomorrow — whatsoever surprises it brings it brings and you accept them. Even if your lover departs you have to be courageous enough to give him a beautiful goodbye. As beautifully as you say hello you have to say goodbye too, because he has given you such moments of joy that you have to be grateful to him.

The eleventh question

Bhagwan,
What do you say about divorce?

Mahesh,

SOME GREAT PHILOSOPHER said about divorce—I forget the philosopher's name, in fact I forget what he said —but I say divorce is useless. You get married for lack of judgment, get divorced for lack of patience, then you remarry for lack of memory.

In fact marriage is wrong. Once marriage disappears from the world, divorce will disappear of its own accord! I am against divorce—I want divorce to disappear from the world absolutely; but the only way to do it is to destroy marriage completely.

The last question

Bhagwan,
Laughing this morning was so pleasurable. I
felt like a baby that is being played with
and tickled. Please tickle some more.

Deva Eva,

THE TRAVELING SALESMAN'S CAR broke down on a

lonely country road just before nightfall, and being unable to repair it the salesman trudged to the nearest farmhouse to beg shelter for the night.

The farmer said okay but as there was only one bed, the salesman would have to share it with the farmer and his pretty young wife.

In the middle of the night the salesman, feeling horny, began making love to the wife. She said, "Okay, but please see if my husband is asleep — pull a hair from his chest to check."

The salesman did and the farmer slept on.

Some time later, feeling horny again, the same thing happened: another hair, more lovemaking. And then again a third time.

But this time the farmer exploded.

"Look," he shouted, "it's okay to fuck my wife, but quit keeping score on my chest!"

An Italian arriving in Australia for the first time gets a job on a farm. The first day the farmer's wife complains that the new worker has been chasing her chickens around the yard. The farmer says he is new and to give him a chance.

But later she is even more outraged when she sees him drinking his own piss. The farmer tries to console her by saying he is a good worker and that this is probably normal in Italy.

But later on the farmer sees the Italian with his head right next to his prize bull's arse while it's having a shit. This is too much for the farmer. Racing up to the Italian he shouts, "What the hell are you doing? First you chase my chickens, then you drink your own piss and now what are you doing with my bull?"

The Italian says, "But my friends-a tell me that-a when I get-a to Australia I'm-a supposed to chase-a the chicks, drink-a plenty of piss, and-a listen to all-a the bullshit!"

16

The first question

Bhagwan,
I cannot understand the philosophy of Zen.
What should I do to understand it?

Baula,

ZEN IS NOT A PHILOSOPHY AT ALL. To approach Zen as if it were a philosophy is to start in a wrong way from the very beginning. A philosophy is something of the mind; Zen is totally beyond the mind. Zen is the process of going above the mind, far away from the mind; it is the process of transcendence, of surpassing the mind. You cannot understand it by the mind; mind has no function in it.

Zen is a state of no-mind; that has to be remembered. It is not Vedanta. Vedanta is a philosophy; you can understand it perfectly well. Zen is not even Buddhism; Buddhism is also a philosophy.

Zen is a very rare flowering — it is one of the strangest things that has happened in the history of consciousness — it is the meeting of Buddha's experience and Lao Tzu's experience. Buddha, after all, was part of the Indian heritage: he spoke the language of philosophy; he is perfectly clear, you can understand him. In fact, he avoided all metaphysical questions; he was very simple, clear, logical. But his experience was not of the mind. He was trying to destroy your philosophy by providing you with a negative philosophy. Just as you can take out a thorn from your foot with another thorn, Buddha's effort was to take out the philosophy from your mind with another philosophy. Once the first thorn has been taken out both thorns can be thrown away and you will be beyond mind.

But when Buddha's teachings reached China a tremendously beautiful thing happened: a cross-breeding happened. In China, Lao Tzu has given his experience of Tao in a totally non-philosophical way, in a very absurd way, in a very illogical way. But when the Buddhist meditators, Buddhist mystics, met the Taoist mystics they immediately could understand each other heart to heart, not mind to mind. They could feel the same vibe, they could see that the same inner world had opened, they could smell the same fragrance. And they came closer, and by their coming closer, by their meetings and mergings with each other, something new started growing up; that is Zen. It has both the beauty of Buddha and the beauty of Lao Tzu; it is the child of both. Such a meeting has never happened before or since.

Zen is neither Taoist nor Buddhist; it is both and neither. Hence the traditional Buddhists reject Zen and the traditional Taoists also reject Zen. For the traditional Buddhist it is absurd, for the traditional Taoist it is too philosophical, but to those who are really interested in meditation, Zen is an experience. It is neither absurd nor philosophical because both are terms of the mind; it is something transcendental.

The word "zen" comes from *dhyan*. Buddha used a certain language, a local language of his times, Pali. In

Pali *dhyan* is pronounced "jhan"; it is from *jhan* that "zen" has arisen. The word comes from *jhan*; *jhan* comes from the Sanskrit *dhyan*.

To understand Zen you need not make a philosophical effort; you have to go deep into meditation. And what is meditation all about? Meditation is a jump from the mind into no-mind, from thoughts to no-thought. Mind means thinking, no-mind means pure awareness. One simply is aware. Only then, Baula, will you be able to understand Zen – through experience, not through any intellectual effort.

Yoka says:

> *There is one nature, perfect and penetrative,*
> *present in all natures;*
> *One reality which includes all, comprising all*
> *realities in itself.*
> *The one moon is reflected wherever there is*
> *water.*
> *And all moons in water are comprised in the*
> *one moon.*

The moment you move beyond the mind, suddenly you have moved from the many to the one. Minds are many, consciousness is one. On the circumference we are different, at the center we are one. That one can be called Brahma, can be called God, the absolute, the truth, *nirvana*.

Zen calls it no-mind for a particular reason. If you call it God, then people start thinking in terms of a person, they start imagining a person – of course the suprememost person, but their idea of personality is derived from human personality; it is a projection, it is not truth.

The Bible says God created man in his own image; that is not true. Man has created God in his own image; that is far more true. The God that we have created is *our* idea, it is anthropocentric. If horses were philosophers then God could not be a man, then God would be a supreme horse. If donkeys were philosophers — and who knows? — they may be; they look very serious, always brooding, as if in deep contemplation, thinking of great things. . . . Watch a donkey and you will be certainly aware of this simple fact that donkeys are great thinkers. They are constantly somewhere else far away, involved in great esoteric things; that's why people think they are fools. They are not fools, they are philosophers. If donkeys think, if they are theologians, theosophists, philosophers, then God will be a supreme donkey. God cannot be a man, that's impossible. They cannot imagine God to be a man.

Hence Zen avoids any anthropocentric terminologies, any words that can become associated with our circumference. It does not call God Brahma because that is a philosophical term; maybe the best philosophical term, but even the best philosophical term is still philosophy, and philosophy is something of the mind — you can *think* about Brahma.

In India we have been thinking about Brahma for centuries and there are as many interpretations of Brahma as there have been philosophers. Shankara interprets it in one way, Nimbarka in another, Ramanuja still in a different way, and so on and so forth. Not even two philosophers agree and the dispute still continues. Philosophers go on quarreling. They never come to any conclusions, they cannot, because mind has no capacity to conclude about the One.

Even Shankara, the greatest non-dualist, remains a dualist deep down. He talks about Brahma, the One, but to talk about the One he has to bring in *maya*, illusion; then One becomes two. If you want to talk about the real you will have to talk about the unreal; that is a necessity, an absolute necessity. Without talking about the unreal you cannot talk about the real; without the unreal the real loses all meaning. Human languages are dualistic, hence Shankara got into trouble, great trouble. He tried to sort it out but he could not, and for one thousand years many philosophers who have followed Shankara have tried to find a way out, but they have not been able to. Even if you say that *maya* means illusion, *maya* means that which does not exist, you have to talk about it. To define Brahma you have to use illusion as a support, otherwise who will define it? How will you define it? The One remains indefinable; the One needs something else to define it. So although the philosophy of Shankara is thought to be non-dualist, it is not. No philosophy can be non-dualist.

Zen is neither dualist nor non-dualist; it is not a philosophy at all. It simply says, "Move from the mind into the no-mind and see." It believes in seeing.

Yoka says:

> *The spirit operates naturally through the organs of sense.*
> *Thus the objective world is perceived.*
> *This dualism mists the mirror.*
> *But when the haze is removed, the light shines forth.*
> *Thus when each individual spirit and the objective world are forgotten and emptied suchness affirms truth.*

When all words are gone, your mirror has no more dust on it, no more mist on it. When you look at things you collect impressions; that is the dust — that's what you call thinking. When you see a rose flower, the rose flower is outside you but it makes a reflection inside you. The rose flower will fade away by the evening, the petals will fall and disappear, but the inner rose flower, the rose that has become imprinted in your memory will continue. It will remain forever with you, you can always remember it. And if you are a sensitive, aesthetic, artistic person you can visualize it again and again; you can imagine it as if it is true. In fact, if you try you will be surprised: you can even experience the fragrance of the rose again. If you create the whole situation in your imagination: the garden, the green grass, the dew on the grass, and you are walking with naked feet on the grass . . . and the sweet smell of the earth and the cool air and the birds singing; you just create the whole atmosphere . . . and then suddenly you discover a beautiful rose flower hidden behind a bush . . . and the fragrance! And then suddenly you will see: the fragrance has come back to you; the imprint is there. The outer rose is gone, but the inner rose is alive.

Now scientists, particularly brain experts, have discovered that if certain spots in the brain are touched by electrodes, certain memories become immediately active. Those memories are lying there deep frozen; touched by the electrode they start becoming alive. A very strange experience. If your brain is touched by an electrode at the point where the rose memory is lying deep, suddenly you will forget the present; you will be again in the same garden. Maybe twenty years have passed, but it will be again as real as if you were in the garden again: the same smell, the same wind, the same coolness, the same flower. And if the electrode is taken out, the memory disappears. Put the electrode back again in the same spot and again the memory starts revealing itself.

And one thing more has been discovered: you can do it thousands of times. Again and again the same memory comes, and again and again the memory repeats itself from the very beginning. The moment you remove the electrode it seems that there is an automatic rewinding; the memory coils back into the same original state. Touch it again with the electrode and as the electricity starts flowing the memory begins from the beginning: you are entering the garden again . . . and the same sequence of events. And this can be done thousands of times. In fact, scientists say there is no limit to it; it can be done millions of times.

The outer reality goes on changing, but the mind goes on collecting dust. Your consciousness is a mirror, and you are carrying so much dust from this life and from other lives — such a thick layer of dust! That's why you cannot understand Zen: because you cannot understand *yourself*, because you cannot understand life, because you cannot understand existence. Zen is not philosophy; it is existential, not philosophical.

> . . . *when the haze is removed*, says Yoka,
> *the light shines forth.*
> *Thus when each individual spirit and the objective world are forgotten and emptied suchness affirms truth.*

When all is emptied — you have forgotten all the memories, you have forgotten even your individual existence, your separate existence; you are no more an island, you have melted into the whole; you are not like an ice cube floating in the water, you have become water itself — this is what Zen is. Then suddenly truth is revealed.

> *Vision is clear*, says Yoka.

These four lines are of tremendous importance.

> *Vision is clear.*
> *But there are no objects to see.*
> *There is no person.*
> *There is no Buddha.*

This is the ultimate declaration of Zen. This is the lion's roar!

> *Vision is clear.*

This is a strange phenomenon. When there are objects to see, your vision is not clear because those objects are making impressions on you. Your vision cannot be clear; it is full of mist. When vision is clear, there are no objects at all, just clarity, just pure consciousness with no content, just seeing and nothing to see, just watchfulness and nothing to watch. A pure observer, a pure witness and nothing to witness.

There is no person.

And when there is nothing to witness, nothing to see, you cannot exist as a separate entity. The "I" can exist only with the "thou"; if the "thou" disappears, the "I" disappears. They are part of each other, they are always together like two sides of a coin; you cannot say "one." This is what many stupid religious people go on doing: they go on saying to God, "I am not. Thou art." That is sheer stupidity. In the very saying you are, otherwise who is saying "Thou art"?

There is a famous poem of Jalaluddin Rumi; I agree with him up to a point and then my disagreement starts. On the really essential point I cannot agree with him. My feeling is he must have written that poem before he became enlightened. He *was* an enlightened man, but the poem is decisive — it must have been written before he became enlightened. The poem is beautiful, because sometimes poets say things almost like seers, but remember they are *almost* like seers. There is bound to be some flaw, it can't be flawless. You may not be able to find the flaw.

Listen to the story of the poem.

Jalaluddin says:
A lover comes to his beloved's home, knocks on the door.
The beloved asks, "Who is there?"
And the lover says, "I am — your lover."
The beloved says, "The house of love is so small, it cannot contain two, so please go back. When you are no

more, then come again. The house of love cannot contain two, it can only contain one."

So far so good!

The lover goes to the forest, he becomes an ascetic. He meditates, he prays to God. His prayer is only one: "Dissolve me!" Many moons come and go, months pass, years pass, and one day he comes back. He knocks again on the door, and the beloved asks the same question: "Who is there?"

And he says, "Now I am no more, only you are."

And Rumi says:

The doors open and the lover is received in the home of love.

There I don't agree — it is too early! Then who is the person who is saying "I am no more"? Even to say that "I am no more," you are needed. It is as foolish as if you went and knocked at somebody's house and he leaned out of the window and said, "I am not at home." That is self-contradictory; you cannot say that. To say it is to prove that you are.

Jalaluddin must have written this poem before he became enlightened. He should have corrected it. But these enlightened people are crazy people. He may have forgotten all about the poem, but it needs correction. *I* can do the correction. I would like to say that the beloved says, "Go back again because you *are* still there. First you were positively there, now you are negatively there, but it makes no difference."

The lover goes back. Now there is no point in praying because prayer has not helped. In fact, prayer cannot help: in prayer the duality persists. You are praying to somebody; God becomes your "thou." God cannot help. Now he becomes a Zen monk — not a devotee but a *real* meditator. He simply goes deep within himself, searching and seeking. "Where is this 'I'?" He tries to find out where it is. And anybody who goes in is bound not to find it because it is not there; it is non-existential, it is only a belief. So he searches and searches and finds it nowhere.

So he comes back, knocks on the door. The beloved asks the same question: "Who is there?" And there is no answer because there is nobody to answer. Just silence. She asks again, "Who is there?" but the silence deepens. She asks again, "Who is there?" but the silence is absolute. She opens the door. Now the lover has come, but he is no more; there is nobody to answer. He has to be taken inside the home, taken by the hand. He is completely, utterly empty.

This is what Zen people call "emptied suchness."

> *Vision is clear.*
> *But there are no objects to see.*
> *There is no person.*
> *There is no Buddha.*

Everything has disappeared. Zen has achieved the ultimate peak of enlightenment; hence it can say that there is no enlightenment either because if the enlightened person goes on thinking, "I am enlightened," he is not enlightened. If he *claims* enlightenment then he is not enlightened, because every claim is an ego claim. Enlightenment is not a claim, it is a silent presence.

Baula, don't try to understand Zen. Go within yourself to find out who you are, where you are. You will not find anybody there, just pure emptiness. And then vision is clear. No person, no Buddha. All is silent, utterly silent. There is nothing to say. In that silence one becomes truth. Not only that one knows truth, one becomes truth. That is the only way to know it.

The second question

Bhagwan,
I find all questions to be false because they
imply answers. In my experience there are no
answers, only discovery. If this is so, why do
you insist on questions and answers? Are you
not misleading people into believing their
questions have answers?

Prem Dharmo,

Now what should i do about your question? If I answer you I will be misleading you; if I don't answer you I will not be showing respect towards you. And if you think that all questions are false, why do you bother to ask? If you think any question that implies answers is false, then do you think your question does not imply any answer? Either it is false if it implies an answer, or it is true, but then it cannot be answered.

You say: *In my experience there are no answers, only discovery.*

And what are answers? They are the discoveries of somebody else. I have discovered something; it is a discovery for me. When you ask a question and I answer you, it is an answer to you, not a discovery. The answer can be misleading if you start believing in it as if it were *your* discovery, but if you don't believe in the answer as your discovery but you keep remembering that it is somebody else's discovery, "I have to discover it too," then the answer is not misleading you, then the answer is a great encouragement. It is an encouragement to go on the great journey, the great pilgrimage of discovering. Discovery also needs encouragement.

Have you seen how when birds are born, when new birds come out of the eggs, their mother, their father teach them to fly? Watch it — it is one of the most beautiful processes to watch because it is the same process that transpires between a Master and a disciple. The older birds fly around the nest. The younger ones become intrigued by the idea of flying; they start fluttering their wings. They have small wings, but they start fluttering their wings; they become aware of their wings. Just by seeing their mother, their father and other birds flying around the nest a great curiosity arises in them. They would also like to fly; they are intrigued by the very idea, they start wondering whether they can manage it. Fear grips them. They come to the very edge of the nest — watch — they look around. It seems difficult, it seems impossible — they are so small and they have never done such a thing before. Who knows? — they may not be able to manage, they may fall, they may die; this may prove suicidal. Then the mother goes and sits on a nearby tree and starts calling them, wooing them, persuading them: "Come on!"

That is the function of the answers of the Master: it is just to woo you, to call you: "Come on! Don't be worried, don't be afraid."

And they try, they flutter, but the fear is there — the fear of the unknown. They do both things: they try in their small way to take the jump, but they also cling to the nest. It is so safe and so warm and so comfortable, so secure, and the insecurity of the sky and the winds . . . and who knows what else may be there in the unknown?

Finally the mother has to push them. But once pushed of course they have to make all the effort that they can — and suddenly they discover that they can fly. They immediately come back to the nest; but they are radically changed — you can see their joy. Now they know they have wings and their wings can function; they need not be so afraid. Now when the mother goes to the other tree, they follow. Soon they would like not to follow the mother because that looks so childish. They would like the mother to sit in the nest and watch and see that they can do the miracle themselves. And they fly around the nest and they go to the other tree and they start calling the mother, "Come on! See, we have managed it. We have done it!"

That's the way of discovery.

It all depends on you, Prem Dharmo. If you believe in my answers as *your* answers you are misguiding yourself. *I* am not misguiding you, I am constantly making you aware that my answers are my answers, not yours. So I am not telling you to believe in my answers, I am simply telling you that answers *are* possible. If they are possible for me they are possible for you. What *I* can do *you* can do because I am an ordinary man just like you.

That's why I am against the whole traditional idea of God's reincarnations or incarnations — *avataras.* I am against the idea that Jesus is a son of God; I would rather that he be the son of the carpenter Joseph, not the son of God, because if he is the only-begotten son of God, then of course he is a totally different kind of person; what he can do you cannot do. He can walk on water; you cannot walk on water. He can bring the dead from their graves and make them alive; you cannot do that. All these stories have been invented to emphasize the fact that he is special and you are ordinary. All those stories are false, irreligious, dangerous. They have not helped humanity, they have degraded humanity. They have insulted you, they have humiliated you.

The Hindus say that Krishna and Rama and Buddha, they are God's incarnations. God himself comes from above, from beyond. They are special people; what they can do you cannot do. Krishna can take the whole mountain in his hand; you cannot do that. He can do miracles; that is not possible for you.

These stories are the cunning inventions of the priests to create a distance between you and Krishna, between you and Buddha, between you and Mahavira, to make a special category so that you know your limits perfectly well.

I emphasize the fact that Krishna is as much a man as you are; there is nothing special about him. He needs food the way you need it, he needs water the way you need it, he sleeps the way you sleep, he dies the way you die. The only difference is that he has become aware of his infinite potential and you are not aware of your infinite potential. There is no difference in the potential, but you are unaware and he is aware; that's the only difference. Of course it is a difference that *makes* a difference, but it is not a difference that can make him a separate category. Nobody belongs to a separate category. Nobody comes from above, everybody grows from below. Life is a growth: you are growing from your humanity towards your divinity. If I can discover who I am, *you* can discover it.

All these answers are not to be made into dogmas, not to be made into beliefs. I am not preaching any theology to you — I am utterly against all creeds. What am I doing then? I am simply trying to persuade you that this is humanly possible. You are as divine as Krishna, as Buddha, as Christ, as anybody else. You have just fallen asleep and you are dreaming nightmares. Just wake up! All that is needed is an awakening.

But, Prem Dharmo, you seem to be a philosophical type. The philosophical type goes on brooding about pros and cons; he goes on thinking about everything. And this is not the place where you are supposed to think too much. This is a place to take a jump into a silent state of non-thinking, because thinking is parrot-like. Can you see that you have asked the question, yet you are asking a question *against* questions? You are asking for an answer, yet you think that all answers are misleading, misguiding — and yet you are asking! You see the philosophical complexity of the mind? You see the game?

A wandering Jew visiting Paris passes by a pet shop. He notices a sign on the window proclaiming that inside the shop there's a parrot that speaks many languages. The "yeedil," considering himself a linguist, enters. Slowly slowly he approaches the wonder-bird, stands by the side of the cage and gives the bird a look-over.

Clearing his throat, he starts testing the parrot:

"Parlez-vous francais?"

"Parlez-vous francais?" comes the reply.

"Speak English?"

"Speak English?" is the reply.

"Govarish po rusku?" he then asks.

"Govarish po rusku?" the parrot replies.

Then the Jew moves closer to the bird, clears his throat, looks at it again and asks confidentially, "Ahem. . . ! Tell me, little bird, if you are so smart, do you speak Yiddish, mm?"

The bird gives a look at the Jew, clears its throat, points to its beak with its wing and says, "Nu . . . with such a nose, you think I should not speak Yiddish?"

Even parrots are far better than philosophers! They have more understanding, they have more insight. Man becomes so burdened with ideas that he forgets completely what he is doing.

Be a little more aware, Prem Dharmo. See what is happening here. I certainly insist on questions from you because I know there are questions. You are full of questions — it is natural — and it is better to bring them out. My answers will not be your answers, but my answers will help you to see the point that answers are possible, that one need not live in questions. One can come to a point where all questions disappear and life is no longer a problem. When all problems disappear, life is no longer a problem but a mystery to be lived, to be loved, to be sung, to be danced.

The third question

Bhagwan,
Just two small questions.
First: how many psychiatrists does it take
to screw in a light bulb?

Anand Narayan,

Only one, but that bulb has got to want to change!

And the second:
And how many enlightened ones does it take to screw
in a light bulb?

Anand Narayan,

None, because they are already a light unto themselves!

The fourth question

Bhagwan,
How do you decide which questions to answer?

Anand Apurvo,

It is a secret! I will just give you a clue. I will not tell you the full secret, you have to find it out.

A priest, a minister and a rabbi have a talk together. They tell each other how God provides them with their daily bread.

"Every Sunday after the plate has been passed around in church, I empty it in a box with a hole in the bottom," explains the priest. "Whatever falls through it is for me; the rest is for God."

The minister has a different way of withdrawing his

weekly pocket money. "I draw a line on the floor," he tells, "and then I drop Sunday's collection from one meter above — the money that lands on the left side is mine, the right side is for God."

"Well," says the rabbi, "my system is much easier. I simply throw the money in the air and whatever God needs he can grab. . . ."

The fifth question

Bhagwan,
I was born a New York Jew and for seventeen
years in California I have been a promising tourist
in four different learned professions, numerous
avocations and an unsuccessful marriage. Joy and
satisfaction have not been my experience, except
for momentary glimpses. I am quietly desperate.
Please comment or tell some appropriate jokes.

Apurvo,

HEINRICH HEINE SAYS: "Sleep is good, death is better; but of course the best thing would be never to have been born at all."

Life certainly is a problem, and particularly in New York and for a Jew. For the Jews, life has always been a bigger problem than for anybody else and for the simple reason that they got this crazy idea that they are the chosen people of God; that has made their life impossible. Such crazy ideas have to be dropped. There is no chosen people of God. Jews have suffered from this nonsense because then everybody hates them. If you are the chosen people of God then everybody hates you, then everybody tries to find fault with you and to prove to you that you are not the chosen people of God.

For three thousand years Jews have insisted on this egoistic standpoint. And they are not alone in it; there are other peoples also. There are the Hindus; they also think that their country is the most sacred land, and they have suffered also. You can see their sacred land and their suffering.

It is time you dropped the idea of being a Jew. Once you are a sannyasin you are neither a Hindu nor a Mohammedan nor a Christian nor a Jew, you are simply a human being. And dropping that idea you will feel unburdened; otherwise there is a three-thousand-year burden. The Jews are carrying a long long burden, a traditional burden, an inherited burden, and they have become so attached to the burden that it becomes impossible to live.

You say that your marriage was unsuccessful. Have you ever heard of any marriage which was successful? I have not heard! If marriages were successful there would have been no sannyas in the world, in fact no religion at all. God has made it absolutely certain from the very beginning that marriage has not to succeed; if marriage succeeds, God fails! The whole of religion depends on the unsuccess of marriage. If you are happy, blissful, who cares about the other world? This world has to be such a misery that whether you want to believe in the other world or not you *have* to believe; that is the only consolation, the only solace.

Bertrand Russell is right when he says, "If people really become happy, religion will disappear from the world." I agree with him ninety-nine percent; only about one percent I will not agree with him. He was an atheist, but he is ninety-nine percent true. Ninety-nine percent of people who are religious are religious for wrong reasons — because their marriage fails, their ambition brings frustration, they waste their whole life in earning money, power and prestige and then the same emptiness, the same meaninglessness remains, the same hollowness; nothing changes at all. The life is gone, death is knocking on the doors, and nothing is fulfilled. That's why people become religious.

People become religious out of misery; hence the priests have a vested interest in your misery, remember it. They would not like your life to be happy, joyous. If you are joyous, blissful, all of their religions will disappear. Their religion depends on your dis-ease, on your pathology, on your restlessness, on your anguish, anxiety.

All the priests in the world are in favor of marriage. Why? — for the simple reason that marriage fails, and when marriage fails where do you have to go? — to the priest! All priests support, in a subtle way, educational systems which create in you a desire to succeed. All the educational systems prevalent in the world are nothing but strategies to create ego trips, to create ambitious minds. Priests and politicians both support them because if ambition is not inflamed in you there will be no politics, and if ambition is not inflamed in you, you will never feel frustrated. A non-ambitious man never feels frustrated. Why should he feel frustrated? He never expected anything in the first place; you can't frustrate him.

Lao Tzu says: You cannot defeat me because I don't want to be victorious at all. Jesus says: Blessed are those who are the last. Now such people are dangerous; they have to be crucified because they will destroy the whole structure of this society. They will destroy the priesthood and the power of the politicians. If this idea, "Blessed are those who are the last," spreads, then who would like to become the president of a country? — only fools, only stupid people! Even now only stupid people want to be presidents and prime ministers, but you don't think them stupid because you are also contaminated and poisoned in the same ways. You respect them; you think they have succeeded, they have attained the goals. Their names will remain in history. So what? They will just torture small children who will have to remember their stupid names, that's all. Their whole effort will succeed only in torturing small children and nothing else!

Priests are against me, politicians are against me, for the simple reason that I am teaching you a life of non-ambition, a life of egolessness — and I am teaching you that marriage is bound to fail; hence if you want to be happy and blissful, love is enough, marriage is too much.

Love is enough. So while the love lasts, good, be together; and when the love disappears say good-bye in deep gratitude, but don't cling to each other. Marriage means clinging.

And you never see the illogicality of your priests. On the one hand they say "detachment" and on the other hand they teach marriage. Marriage is attachment — it is legal attachment! Not only attachment: there is legal support for it — the court and the police and the magistrate are behind you. If you want to leave your wife you will be in trouble, and to live with the wife you are in trouble. If you want to leave the wife you will be in trouble, so one decides that when there is trouble anyway, why not remain in the conformist, traditional trouble, the conventional trouble? Why find out individual and private troubles? They can be more dangerous because everybody else will be against you.

You say: *Joy and satisfaction have not been my experience, except for momentary glimpses.*

Yes, in this life, the way we have managed this life, they can only be momentary glimpses. Even that is a miracle — how even for moments those glimpses can happen is unbelievable because the way you are made and conditioned will not allow even moments. You are supposed to be miserable. Ambition, ego, marriage, money, power — all these ideas are bound to make you miserable; you can't be blissful here. And the only thing that can make you blissful is never taught anywhere. That is meditation, that is Zen; that is not taught anywhere. People are really afraid of meditation — afraid because it will transform your whole way of life.

Now, Apurvo, meditate. Go deeper into yourself. You have tried all kinds of professions and you have tried marriage and you have tried everything that the West can make available to you. Try meditation. Go deeper into yourself, into your own aloneness, into your own solitude. Find out your center of being; it is there that eternal bliss prevails. Right now it prevails there. It is always there, we have just lost contact with it. It has to be discovered, or *re*discovered.

You say: *I am quietly desperate.*

That is not good for a Jew! Jews always find a way to get out of any kind of problem. For three thousand years that's what they have been doing.

Mr Goldberg was trying to sell a suit to Mrs Rubinstein for her young son. "Take it, madam," he said. "First quality. I can give you a nice price for it."

She tried the suit on her son and it fit perfectly so she bought it.

The first time the suit was cleaned, Mrs Rubinstein noticed that it looked quite a bit smaller, so she tried it on her son again. The sleeves only came to his elbows and the trouser legs came only to his knees.

Of course she was furious, so grabbing her son's hand she stomped over to the tailor's shop. As she entered the shop, Mr Goldberg looked up and said, "My God! Isn't it amazing how the boy has grown!"

It is not good for a Jew to be desperate.

Two men were discussing optimism and pessimism.

The one turned to the other and said, "Well, have you ever met a real optimist yourself?"

"Yes," said the other. "I was standing on the balcony of my fourth floor apartment when I saw a Jewish window cleaner high up on the twentieth floor slip and fall."

"How does that make him an optimist?" asked the friend.

"Well, because as he went by my balcony I heard him say, 'Alright so far!' "

An American and an Englishman and a Jew were in a small German airplane when a terrible hurricane hit them. The pilot screamed from his cockpit, "One of you has to jump out of the plane because it is too heavy!"

They tried to decide who had to sacrifice his life, but none of the three were willing. The pilot came in between and said, "Okay, I'll ask each of you a question. The one who doesn't know the answer has to jump out of the plane."

He turned to the American and asked, "At what date was the atom bomb thrown on Hiroshima?"

The American answered, "August 6th, 1945."

Next the pilot asked the Englishman, "How many people were killed at that time?"

"About two hundred and fifty thousand" was the answer.

He finally turned to the Jew and asked, "Can you give me the names and the addresses of the victims?"

But wait!

And the Jew started to give the names and addresses of the two hundred and fifty thousand victims! The American and the Englishman — both jumped out of the plane to save themselves from the Jew. And finally the pilot had to threaten him to shut up. If he did not stop, the pilot said he would also jump out of the plane!

A Jew and desperate? Never! A Jew always finds a way.

And you say: *Please comment or tell some appropriate jokes.*

Appropriate jokes? That I have never done in my life and that I am not going to do — I always tell *in*appropriate jokes! And I will tell a few inappropriate jokes to you.

Tarzan goes into town for a vacation. When he comes back to the jungle, his chimpanzee friend, Cheeta, meets him and says, "Tarzan, Tarzan! All the animals are rebelling! They have forgotten you. Everywhere there is chaos!"

Angry, Tarzan rushes into the deep of the jungle, where he meets a lion. He grabs the lion, lifts it up, and looking into its eyes he asks, "Do you know who I am?"

"Of course I know," says the lion. "You are the boss of the jungle!"

Still Tarzan is not satisfied, so when he meets a giraffe he grabs the animal by the neck and again asks, "Speak up — who am I?"

Trembling, the giraffe answers, "You are Tarzan, the king of the jungle!"

Then he meets an elephant. Grabbing the balls of the elephant, he throws it on the ground shouting, "Who am I? Answer!"

As the elephant doesn't answer he becomes even more furious and smashes the elephant's balls together shouting, "Now speak! Tell me, who am I?"

The elephant, very calmly, with a compassionate look, says, "Just look at this son of a bitch . . . he doesn't know who he is and he comes and breaks *my* balls!"

Now try to find out, if you can, whether it is appropriate or not!

An English army officer retired to the country and lost no time in enrolling at the local golf club. On his first appearance he was disappointed to find that the only prospective partner was a rather scruffy young man who sat picking his teeth at the bar, but as he was anxious for a game he went up to the man and after making polite conversation for a few minutes offered to partner him in a round.

They met on the first green. The officer was surprised to see the man appear with a sack on his shoulder from which he selected a garden spade, and even more surprised when he used it instead of a golfclub and drove the ball straight down the center of the fairway — a magnificent shot — almost to the green. This was followed by a second using an axe, and finally the putt was sunk with an old walking stick.

And so he continued in this manner, completing the course with all kinds of implements and eventually winning hands down. The officer, however, did not like to make any comment on this surprising behavior until they were back in the bar. Even then he continued to make polite conversation, but when the man began drinking his beer through a straw up his nose, balancing his glass on his shoulder, his curiosity was uncontainable.

"Excuse me asking," he said, "but I couldn't help noticing your strange conduct just now."

"Yes," replied the man, "it is a little odd, but it is the only way I am able to make life interesting. You see, I was born with this amazing dexterity which I need to exercise now and then."

The officer was thoughtful for a minute and then said, "Tell me, are you married?"

"Yes," said the other.

"And do you have any children?"

"Yes, three," said the man with a sigh, "and the answer to your next question is 'standing up, in a hammock'!"

The sixth question

Bhagwan,
Why do you tell so many jokes? Are you not
interested at all in higher things?

Pratima,

Is THERE ANYTHING HIGHER than a joke? Then you have not understood my jokes at all! These jokes are not just jokes, it is serious matter!

Paul Reps was invited to give a lecture at the University of B.C. He was advertised as a well-known mystic and philosopher and author of the famous *Zen Flesh, Zen Bones.*

The occasion attracted a number of noted intellectuals. Paul Reps sat very relaxed in a simple wooden chair telling his little Zen stories. Many people in the audience enjoyed the stories, but some of the great intellects got bored. Finally one of the more knowing ones stood up and said, "Sir, could you please speak on a somewhat higher level?"

Without pausing, Paul Reps placed his chair on the table and continued with his beautiful Zen stories.

Do you want me to do that? I can speak on as high a level as possible. I can sit on the roof. You will not be able to see me. That will be very esoteric! Just the way God used to speak in the past, from high above! You will only hear the voice . . . but I will still tell the jokes!

The seventh question

Bhagwan,
I am going madder and madder, but this seems

nothing compared to you. Each day you appear
madderer and madderer. Where will it all end?

Somendra,

I HAVE TO BE ALWAYS AHEAD OF MY DISCIPLES — you can't beat me! If you want me to be sane you have to be saner; if you go a little mad, I will be madder; if you go madder I will go madderer. This has been decided once and for all. And there is no end to it — even after I am gone from my body I will haunt you!

The eighth question

Bhagwan,
Have you got a really good joke I can bring
to a non-orange lover in the West who is a
scientist and has been reading and underlining
you for four years?

Patipada,

TELL HIM NOT TO DESTROY MY BOOKS, because the real thing is between the lines and that's what he is crossing out with his underlining! But it may be just old habit. Otherwise, a man who has been reading me for four years, can he still remain there and non-orange? It is impossible — just old habit. He can go on doing it for four lives or forty lives. Tell him it is time. Tell him enough is enough!

Maria was a student of sociology. For her research paper she decided to make a trip into the interior of Brazil. Caught in a tropical downpour she lost her way in the jungle. Finally two men found her, drenched to the skin.

"You'll never find your way out in this storm," said one. "The river is flooded. You're welcome to spend the night at our place."

Maria felt relieved and happy to have an opportunity to experience the authentic lives of some people of the interior. Once at the house, the men prepared a meal for her and afterwards played the guitar and sang folk-songs. When they grew tired, the Brazilian informed her that there was only one bed.

"That's okay," she said, "I can sleep in bed with the two of you!"

The men were reluctant, but finally agreed. After the three tossed and turned for a while, they decided to give in and make love. Maria gave each man a condom and then the three of them had a wonderful time for the rest of the night.

The next morning Maria thanked the two men for their hospitality and went on her way back home to write up her report.

Several days passed and the two guys were turning yellow and feeling quite uncomfortable. Finally one says to the other, "Hey, brother! I really don't care if that girl has a baby or not!"

The other says, "I can't stand it anymore! Let's take these plastic bags off our cocks . . . enough is enough!"

So you tell him, Patipada, enough is enough! It is time for him to come here and go orange — that means go mad! That is a new way of saying going mad: "Go orange." But he is a scientist and he must be calculating, measuring, thinking about the pros and cons, hesitating, observing, watching. He will miss the opportunity. That's how people go on postponing. Tell him there are a few things which have to be done immediately if you ever want to do them — now or never. His old habit of being a scientist must be there; he will have to put it aside.

Dave was going to marry Mabel, so Dad thought it best to tell him about the birds and the bees. "Now, Dave, see that knot-hole in the tree over there? I want you to go and practice in that hole so that on your wedding night you will know what to do!"

A few days later Dave got married. That night frantic screams were heard coming from Dave and Mabel's room. Dad burst in to find Dave ramming a broomstick up between Mabel's legs.

"What are you doing, Dave?" Dad shouted.

"I'm making quite sure that there are no bees in this one!"

The ninth question

Bhagwan,
Please tell me — enough what for today?

Anand Omkar,

Enough of the nonsense — in other words, enough of Zen!

And the last question

Bhagwan,
What is "Walking in Zen, sitting in Zen"?

Shraddan,

There is no need to say anything about it. I will walk to my car and sit in the car: *that* is walking in Zen, sitting in Zen.

BOOKS PUBLISHED BY RAJNEESH FOUNDATION INTERNATIONAL

THE DISCOURSES OF BHAGWAN SHREE RAJNEESH

Early Discourses
A CUP OF TEA
letters to disciples
FROM SEX TO SUPERCONSCIOUSNESS

The Bauls
THE BELOVED (2 volumes)

Buddha
THE BOOK OF THE BOOKS (volume 1)
the Dhammapada
THE DIAMOND SUTRA
the Vajrachchedika Prajnaparamita Sutra
THE DISCIPLINE OF TRANSCENDENCE (4 volumes)
the Sutra of 42 Chapters
THE HEART SUTRA
the Prajnaparamita Hridayam Sutra

Buddhist Masters
THE WHITE LOTUS
the sayings of Bodhidharma

Hasidism
THE ART OF DYING
THE TRUE SAGE

Jesus
COME FOLLOW ME (4 volumes)
the sayings of Jesus
I SAY UNTO YOU (2 volumes)
the sayings of Jesus

Kabir
THE DIVINE MELODY
ECSTASY: THE FORGOTTEN LANGUAGE
THE FISH IN THE SEA IS NOT THIRSTY
THE GUEST
THE PATH OF LOVE
THE REVOLUTION

Response to Questions
BE STILL AND KNOW
THE GOOSE IS OUT

MY WAY: THE WAY OF THE WHITE CLOUDS
WALKING IN ZEN, SITTING IN ZEN
WALK WITHOUT FEET, FLY WITHOUT WINGS
     AND THINK WITHOUT MIND
ZEN: ZEST, ZIP, ZAP AND ZING

Sufism

JUST LIKE THAT
THE PERFECT MASTER (2 volumes)
THE SECRET
SUFIS: THE PEOPLE OF THE PATH (2 volumes)
UNIO MYSTICA (2 volumes)
the Hadiqa of Hakim Sanai
UNTIL YOU DIE
THE WISDOM OF THE SANDS (2 volumes)

Tantra

THE BOOK OF THE SECRETS (volumes 4 and 5)
Vigyana Bhairava Tantra
THE TANTRA VISION (2 volumes)
the Royal Song of Saraha
THE BOOKS OF WISDOM (volume 1)
Atisha's Seven Points of Mind Training

Tao

THE EMPTY BOAT
the stories of Chuang Tzu
THE SECRET OF SECRETS (volume 1)
the Secret of the Golden Flower
TAO: THE PATHLESS PATH (2 volumes)
the stories of Lieh Tzu
TAO: THE THREE TREASURES (4 volumes)
the Tao Te Ching of Lao Tzu
WHEN THE SHOE FITS
the stories of Chuang Tzu

The Upanishads

THE ULTIMATE ALCHEMY (2 volumes)
Atma Pooja Upanishad
VEDANTA: SEVEN STEPS TO SAMADHI
Akshya Upanishad

Western Mystics

THE HIDDEN HARMONY
the fragments of Heraclitus
THE NEW ALCHEMY: TO TURN YOU ON
Mabel Collins' Light on the Path
PHILOSOPHIA PERENNIS (2 volumes)
the Golden Verses of Pythagoras

Yoga

YOGA: THE ALPHA AND THE OMEGA (10 volumes)
the Yoga Sutras of Patanjali

Zen

AH, THIS!
ANCIENT MUSIC IN THE PINES
AND THE FLOWERS SHOWERED
DANG DANG DOKO DANG
THE FIRST PRINCIPLE
THE GRASS GROWS BY ITSELF
NIRVANA: THE LAST NIGHTMARE
NO WATER NO MOON
RETURNING TO THE SOURCE
A SUDDEN CLASH OF THUNDER
THE SUN RISES IN THE EVENING
ZEN: THE PATH OF PARADOX (3 volumes)

Zen Masters

NEITHER THIS NOR THAT
Sosan's Hsin Hsin Ming
THE SEARCH
the Ten Bulls of Zen
TAKE IT EASY (2 volumes)
poems of Ikkyu
THIS VERY BODY THE BUDDHA
Hakuin's Song of Meditation

INTIMATE DIALOGUES between the Master and His disciples

HAMMER ON THE ROCK —*(December 10, 1975-January 15, 1976)*
ABOVE ALL DON'T WOBBLE —*(January 16-February 12, 1976)*
NOTHING TO LOSE BUT YOUR HEAD —*(February 13-March 12, 1976)*
BE REALISTIC: PLAN FOR A MIRACLE —*(March 13-April 6, 1976)*
GET OUT OF YOUR OWN WAY —*(April 7-May 2, 1976)*
BELOVED OF MY HEART —*(May 3-May 28, 1976)*
THE CYPRESS IN THE COURTYARD —*(May 29-June 27, 1976)*
A ROSE IS A ROSE IS A ROSE —*(June 28-July 27, 1976)*
DANCE YOUR WAY TO GOD —*(July 28-August 20, 1976)*
THE PASSION FOR THE IMPOSSIBLE —*(August 21-September 18, 1976)*
THE GREAT NOTHING —*(September 19-October 11, 1976)*
GOD IS NOT FOR SALE —*(October 12-November 7, 1976)*
THE SHADOW OF THE WHIP —*(November 8-December 3, 1976)*
BLESSED ARE THE IGNORANT —*(December 4-December 31, 1976)*

OTHER TITLES

BOOKS FROM OTHER PUBLISHERS

EDITIONS IN ENGLISH

UNITED KINGDOM

THE ART OF DYING —*(Sheldon Press)*
THE BOOK OF THE SECRETS (volume 1) —*(Thames & Hudson)*
DIMENSIONS BEYOND THE KNOWN —*(Sheldon Press)*
THE HIDDEN HARMONY —*(Sheldon Press)*
MEDITATION: THE ART OF ECSTASY —*(Sheldon Press)*
THE MUSTARD SEED —*(Sheldon Press)*
NEITHER THIS NOR THAT —*(Sheldon Press)*
NO WATER NO MOON —*(Sheldon Press)*
ROOTS AND WINGS —*(Routledge & Kegan Paul)*
STRAIGHT TO FREEDOM (Original title: UNTIL YOU DIE) —*(Sheldon Press)*
THE SUPREME DOCTRINE —*(Routledge & Kegan Paul)*
THE SUPREME UNDERSTANDING (Original title: TANTRA: THE SUPREME UNDERSTANDING) —*(Sheldon Press)*
TAO: THE THREE TREASURES (volume 1) —*(Wildwood House)*

Books on Bhagwan

DEATH COMES DANCING: CELEBRATING LIFE WITH BHAGWAN SHREE RAJNEESH
by Ma Satya Bharti —(Routledge & Kegan Paul)
THE ULTIMATE RISK
by Ma Satya Bharti —(Wildwood House)

UNITED STATES OF AMERICA

THE BOOK OF THE SECRETS (volumes 1, 2 & 3) —*(Harper & Row)*
THE GREAT CHALLENGE —*(Grove Press)*
HAMMER ON THE ROCK —*(Grove Press)*
I AM THE GATE —*(Harper & Row)*
JOURNEY TOWARD THE HEART (Original title: UNTIL YOU DIE) —*(Harper & Row)*
MEDITATION: THE ART OF ECSTASY —*(Harper & Row)*
THE MUSTARD SEED —*(Harper & Row)*
MY WAY: THE WAY OF THE WHITE CLOUDS —*(Grove Press)*
ONLY ONE SKY (Original title: TANTRA: THE SUPREME UNDERSTANDING) —*(Dutton)*
THE PSYCHOLOGY OF THE ESOTERIC —*(Harper & Row)*
ROOTS AND WINGS —*(Routledge & Kegan Paul)*
THE SUPREME DOCTRINE —*(Routledge & Kegan Paul)*
WORDS LIKE FIRE (Original title: COME FOLLOW ME, volume 1) —*(Harper & Row)*

Books on Bhagwan

THE AWAKENED ONE: THE LIFE AND WORK OF
    BHAGWAN SHREE RAJNEESH
by Vasant Joshi – (Harper & Row)
DEATH COMES DANCING: CELEBRATING LIFE WITH BHAGWAN
SHREE RAJNEESH
by Ma Satya Bharti – (Routledge & Kegan Paul)
DRUNK ON THE DIVINE
by Ma Satya Bharti – (Grove Press)
DYING FOR ENLIGHTENMENT
by Bernard Gunther (Swami Deva Amitprem) – (Harper & Row)
NEO-TANTRA
by Bernard Gunther (Swami Deva Amitprem) – (Harper & Row)

FOREIGN LANGUAGE EDITIONS

DANISH

Translations
HEMMELIGHEDERNES BOG (volume 1) — (Borgens Forlag)
HU-MEDITATION OG KOSMISK ORGASME — (Borgens Forlag)

Books on Bhagwan
SJAELENS OPRØR
by Swami Deva Satyarthi – (Borgens Forlag)

DUTCH

Translations
HET BOEK DER GEHEIMEN (volumes 1, 2 & 3) — (Mirananda)
GEEN WATER, GEEN MAAN — (Mirananda)
GEZAAID IN GOEDE AARDE — (Ankh-Hermes)
IK BEN DE POORT — (Ankh-Hermes)
MEDITATIE: DE KUNST VAN INNERLIJKE EXTASE — (Mirananda)
MIJN WEG, DE WEG VAN DE WITTE WOLK — (Arcanum)
HET MOSTERDZAAD (volumes 1 & 2) — (Mirananda)
HET ORANJE MEDITATIEBOEK — (Ankh-Hermes)
PSYCHOLOGIE EN EVOLUTIE — (Ankh-Hermes)
TANTRA: HET ALLERHOOGSTE INZICHT — (Ankh-Hermes)
TANTRA, SPIRITUALITEIT EN SEKS — (Ankh-Hermes)
DE TANTRA VISIE (volume 1) — (Arcanum)
TAU — (Ankh-Hermes)
TOTDAT JE STERFT — (Ankh-Hermes)
DE VERBORGEN HARMONIE — (Mirananda)
VOLG MIJ — (Ankh-Hermes)
ZOEKEN NAAR DE STIER — (Ankh-Hermes)
DRINK MIJ — (Ankh-Hermes)

Books on Bhagwan

BHAGWAN: NOTITIES VAN EEN DISCIPEL
by Swami Deva Amrito (Jan Foudraine)–(Ankh-Hermes)

BHAGWAN SHREE RAJNEESH: DE LAATSTE GOK
by Ma Satya Bharti–(Mirananda)

OORSPRONGELIJK GEZICHT, EIN GANG NAAR HUIS
by Swami Deva Amrito (Jan Foudraine)–(Ambo)

FRENCH

L'EVEIL A LA CONSCIENCE COSMIQUE—*(Dangles)*

JE SUIS LA PORTE—*(EPI)*

LE LIVRE DES SECRETS (volume 1)—*(Soleil Orange)*

LA MEDITATION DYNAMIQUE—*(Dangles)*

GERMAN

Translations

AUF DER SUCHE—*(Sambuddha Verlag)*

DAS BUCH DER GEHEIMNISSE (volume 1)—*(Heyne Verlag)*

DAS ORANGENE BUCH—*(Sambuddha Verlag)*

EKSTASE: DIE VERGESSENE SPRACHE—*(Herzschlag Verlag, formerly Ki-Buch)*

ESOTERISCHE PSYCHOLOGIE—*(Rajneesh Verlag)*

ICH BIN DER WEG—*(Rajneesh Verlag)*

INTELLIGENZ DES HERZENS—*(Herzschlag Verlag, formerly Ki-Buch)*

KEIN WASSER KEIN MOND—*(Herzschlag Verlag, formerly Ki-Buch)*

KOMM UND FOLGE MIR—*(Sannyas Verlag)*

MEDITATION: DIE KUNST ZU SICH SELBST ZU FINDEN—*(Heyne Verlag)*

MEIN WEG: DER WEG DER WEISSEN WOLKE—*(Herzschlag Verlag, formerly Ki-Buch)*

MIT WURZELN UND MIT FLÜGELN—*(Lotos Verlag)*

DAS HIMMELREICH GLEICHT EINEM SENFKORN—*(Fischer)*

NICHT BEVOR DU STIRBST—*(Edition Gyandip, Switzerland)*

DIE SCHUHE AUF DEM KOPF—*(Lotos Verlag)*

SPIRITUELLE ENTWICKLUNG—*(Fischer)*

SPRENGT DEN FELS DER UNBEWUSSTHEIT—*(Fischer)*

TANTRA: DIE HÖCHSTE EINSICHT—*(Sambuddha Verlag)*

TANTRISCHE LIEBESKUNST—*(Sannyas Verlag)*

DIE VERBORGENE HARMONIE—*(Sannyas Verlag)*

WAS IST MEDITATION?—*(Sannyas Verlag)*

Books on Bhagwan

BEGEGNUNG MIT NIEMAND
by Mascha Rabben (Ma Hari Chetana)–(Herzschlag Verlag)

GANZ ENTSPANNT IM HIER UND JETZT
by Swami Satyananda–(Rowohlt)

IM GRUNDE IST ALLES GANZ EINFACH
by Swami Satyananda—(Ullstein)
WAGNIS ORANGE
by Ma Satya Bharti—(Fachbuchhandlung fur Psychologie)

GREEK
I KRIFI ARMONIA —(Emmanual Rassoulis) THE HIDDEN HARMONY

HEBREW
TANTRA: THE SUPREME UNDERSTANDING —*(Massada)*

ITALIAN
Translations
L'ARMONIA NASCOSTA (volumes 1 & 2)—*(Re Nudo)*
DIECI STORIE ZEN DI BHAGWAN SHREE RAJNEESH (NÉ ACQUA, NÉ LUNA)
—*(Il Fiore d'Oro)*
IO SONO LA SOGLIA —*(Mediterranee)*
IL LIBRO DEI SEGRETI—*(Bompiani)*
MEDITAZIONE DINAMICA: L'ARTE DELL'ESTASI INTERIORE —*(Mediterranee)*
LA RIVOLUZIONE INTERIORE —*(Armenia)*
LA RICERCA —*(La Salamandra)*
IL SEME DELLA RIBELLIONE (volumes 1, 2 & 3)—*(Re Nudo)*
TANTRA: LA COMPRENSIONE SUPREMA —*(Bompiani)*
TAO: I TRE TESORI (volumes 1, 2 & 3)—*(Re Nudo)*
TECNICHE DI LIBERAZIONE —*(La Salamandra)*
SEMI DI SAGGEZZA —*(SugarCo)*

Books on Bhagwan
ALLA RICERCA DEL DIO PERDUTO
by Swami Deva Majid—(SurgarCo)
IL GRANDE ESPERIMENTO: MEDITAZIONI E TERAPIE NELL'ASHRAM DI
BHAGWAN SHREE RAJNEESH
by Ma Satya Bharti—(Armenia)
L'INCANTO D'ARANCIO
by Swami Swatantra Sarjano—(Savelli)

JAPANESE
THE MUSTARD SEED —*(Merkmal)*
UNTIL YOU DIE —*(Fumikura)*
THE EMPTY BOAT —*(Rajneesh Publications)*
THE HEART SUTRA —*(Merkmal)*
THE GRASS GROWS BY ITSELF —*(Fumikura)*
THE SEARCH —*(Merkmal)*
MY WAY: THE WAY OF THE WHITE CLOUDS —*(Rajneesh Publications)*
THE SECRET —*(Merkmal)*

DANCE YOUR WAY TO GOD—*(Rajneesh Publications)*
FROM SEX TO SUPERCONSCIOUSNESS—*(Rajneesh Publications)*
MEDITATION: THE ART OF ECSTASY—*(Merkmal)*
TANTRA THE SUPREME UNDERSTANDING—*(Merkmal)*
TAO: THE THREE TREASURES (volumes 1-4)—*(Merkmal)*

PORTUGUESE (BRAZIL)
O CIPRESTE NO JARDIM—*(Soma)*
EU SOU A PORTA—*(Pensamento)*
MEDITACÃO: A ARTE DO ÊXTASE—*(Cultrix)*
MEU CAMINHO: O COMAINHO DAS NUVENS BRANCAS—
(Tao Livraria & Editora)
NEM AGUA, NEM LUA—*(Pensamento)*
O LIVRO ORANGE—*(Soma)*
PALAVRAS DE FOGO—*(Global/Ground)*
A PSICOLOGIA DO ESOTÉRICO—*(Tao Livraria & Editora)*
A SEMENTE DE MOSTARDA (volumes 1 & 2)— *(Tao Livraria & Editora)*
TANTRA: SEXO E ESPIRITUALIDADE—*(Agora)*
TANTRA: A SUPREMA COMPREENSÃO—*(Cultrix)*
ANTES QUE VOCE MORRA—*(Maha Lakshmi Editora)*

SPANISH
Translations
INTRODUCCIÓN AL MUNDO DEL TANTRA—*(Colección Tantra)*
MEDITACIÓN: EL ARTE DEL EXTASIS—*(Colección Tantra)*
PSICOLOGÍA DE LO ESOTÉRICO: LA NUEVA EVOLUCIÓN DEL HOMBRE—
(Cuatro Vientos Editorial)
¿QUE ES MEDITACIÓN?—*(Koan/Roselló Impresions)*
YO SOY LA PUERTA—*(Editorial Diana)*
SOLO UN CIELO, 1 and 2—*(Colección Tantra)*

Books on Bhagwan
IL RIESGO SUPREMO
by Ma Satya Bharti—*(Martinez Roca)*

SWEDISH
DEN VÄLDIGA UTMANINGEN—*(Livskraft)*

RAJNEESH MEDITATION CENTERS, ASHRAMS AND COMMUNES

There are hundreds of Rajneesh meditation centers throughout the world. These are some of the main ones, which can be contacted for the name and address of the center nearest you. They can also tell you about the availability of the books of Bhagwan Shree Rajneesh—in English or in foreign language editions. General information is available from Rajneesh Foundation International.

USA

RAJNEESH FOUNDATION INTERNATIONAL
Rajneeshpuram, OR 97741. Tel: (503) 489-3301
DEEPTA RAJNEESH MEDITATION CENTER
3024 Ashby Avenue, Berkeley, CA 94705. Tel: (415) 845-2515
GEETAM RAJNEESH SANNYAS ASHRAM
Box 576, Lucerne Valley, CA 92356. Tel: (714) 248-7301
SAMBODHI RAJNEESH SANNYAS ASHRAM
Conomo Point Road, Essex, MA 01929. Tel: (617) 768-7640

CANADA

ARVIND RAJNEESH SANNYAS ASHRAM
2807 W. 16th Ave., Vancouver, B.C. V5Z 1R9. Tel: 604-734-4681
SATDHARM RAJNEESH MEDITATION CENTER
184 Madison Avenue, Toronto, Ontario M5R 2S5. Tel: (416) 968-2194
SHANTI SADAN RAJNEESH MEDITATION CENTER
1817 Rosemont, Montreal,
Quebec H2G 1S5. Tel: (514) 272-4566

AUSTRIA

PRADEEP RAJNEESH MEDITATION CENTER
Siebenbrunnenfeldgasse 4, 1050 Vienna. Tel: 524-860

AUSTRALIA

PREMDWEEP RAJNEESH MEDITATION CENTER
64 Fullerton Rd., Norwood, S.A. 5067. Tel: 08-423388
SAHAJAM RAJNEESH SANNYAS ASHRAM
8 Collie Street, Fremantle 6160, W.A. Tel: (09) 336-2422
SATPRAKASH RAJNEESH MEDITATION CENTER
108 Oxford Street, Darlinghurst 2010, N.S.W. Tel: (02) 336570
SVARUP RAJNEESH MEDITATION CENTER
9 Canning St., 169 Elgin St., Carlton, Victoria. Tel: 347-6274

BELGIUM

VADAN RAJNEESH MEDITATION CENTER
Platte-Lo-Straat, 3200 Leuven (Kessel-Lo). Tel: 016/25-1487

BRAZIL
SOMA RAJNEESH MEDITATION CENTER
Rua Roque Petrella 542, Brooklyn CEP 04581, Sao Paulo SP. Tel: 240-2928

CHILE
SAGARO RAJNEESH MEDITATION CENTER
Paula Jaraquemada 297, La Reina, Santiago. Tel: 227-1751

DENMARK
ANAND NIKETAN RAJNEESH MEDITATION CENTER
Strøget, Frederiksberggade 15, 1459 Copenhagen K. Tel: (01) 117909

EAST AFRICA
ANAND NEED RAJNEESH MEDITATION CENTER
Kitisuru Estate, P.O. Box 72424, Nairobi, Kenya. Tel: 582600

FRANCE
PRADIP RAJNEESH MEDITATION CENTER
13 Rue Bichat, 75010 Paris. Tel: 607-9559

GREAT BRITAIN
KALPTARU RAJNEESH MEDITATION CENTER
28 Oak Village, London NW5 4QN. Tel: (01) 267-8304
MEDINA RAJNEESH NEO-SANNYAS COMMUNE
Herringswell, Bury St. Edmunds, Suffolk IP28 6SW. Tel: (0638) 750234
GOURISHANKAR RAJNEESH MEDITATION CENTER
43 Iverleitch Row, Edinburgh, Scotland. Tel: 031-552-3993

HOLLAND
DE STAD RAJNEESH NEO-SANNYAS COMMUNE
Kamperweg 80-86 8191 KC Heerde. Tel: 05207-1261
GRADA RAJNEESH NEO-SANNYAS COMMUNE
Prins Hendrikstraat 64, 1931 BK Egmond aan Zee. Tel: 02206-4114

INDIA
RAJNEESHDHAM
17 Koregaon Park, Poona 411 001. Tel: 28127
RAJ YOGA RAJNEESH MEDITATION CENTER
C 5/44 Safdarjang Development Area, New Delhi 100 016. Tel: 654533

ITALY

CITTA DI RAJNEESH NEO-SANNYAS COMMUNE
15036 Villabella di Valenza Po, (AL). Tel: (0131) 953993
MIASTO RAJNEESH NEO-SANNYAS COMMUNE
Podere S. Giorgio, Cotorniano 53010, Frosini (Siena) Tel: 0577-960124
VIVEK RAJNEESH MEDITATION CENTER
Via Castelfidardo 7, 20121 Milan. Tel: 659-5632

JAPAN

SHANTIYUGA RAJNEESH MEDITATION CENTER
Sky Mansion 2F, 1-34-1 Ookayama, Meguro-ku, Tokyo 152. Tel: (03) 724-9631
UTSAVA RAJNEESH MEDITATION CENTER
7-19-34 Morikita Cho, Higashinada-KU, Kobe 658. Tel: 078-411-8319

NEW ZEALAND

SHANTI NIKETAN RAJNEESH MEDITATION CENTER
115 Symonds Street. Auckland. Tel: 770-326

PHILIPPINES

PREM SADAN RAJNEESH MEDITATION CENTER
39 Captain Guido Street, Heroes Hill, Quezon City 3010. Tel: 965 410

SWEDEN

DEEVA RAJNEESH MEDITATION CENTER
Surbrunnsgatan 60, 11327 Stockholm. Tel: (08) 327788

SWITZERLAND

GYANDIP RAJNEESH MEDITATION CENTER
Baumackerstr. 42, 8050 Zurich. Tel: (01) 312 1600

WEST GERMANY

ANAND SAGAR RAJNEESH SANNYAS ASHRAM
Lutticherstr. 33/35, 5 Koln 1. Tel: 0221-517199
DHARMADEEP RAJNEESH SANNYAS ASHRAM
Karolinenstr. 7-9, c/o Lorien, 2000 Hamburg 6. Tel: (040) 432140
RAJNEESHSTADT NEO-SANNYAS COMMUNE
Schloss Wolfsbrunnen, 3466 Meinhard. Tel: (05651) 70217
SATDHARMA RAJNEESH MEDITATION CENTER
Klensestr. 41, 8000 Munich 2. Tel: 089-282-113
VIHAN RAJNEESH SANNYAS COMMUNE
Urbanstr. 64, 1000 Berlin 61. Tel: (030) 691-2051